HANDS AROUND THE WORLD

For Angus
and children everywhere

This book could not have been written without the generous support and help of many people. I include all their names here, but am especially grateful to those who took the time to tell me what it is like growing up in other countries and cultures. I am also indebted to the individuals who confirmed what I had read or heard about elsewhere (resulting in the rejection of a lot of erroneous material), and to those who patiently repeated foreign words and names so that I could include the proper pronunciations in this book.

Many thanks to Mohamed Said Ahad, Inmaculada Aldmiz, Osama Altayi, Rumyana Apostolova, Jennifer Adkisson, Mahmut Aygen, Sally Baris, Edna Balzer, Galina Bubnovskaya, Kris Burnett, Linda Bulter, Wairimū Chege, Jun Chen, Charlie Clarke, Ineke Constantine, Carlos Croes, Ulrich Crüwell, Barbara Cuprys, Roman Demissie, Jody Diamond, Nguyen Ngoc Dinh, Cedric Dupont, Lai Heng Foong, Yukiko Fujimoto, Augustín García, Fay Georgousis, Miriam Goldburger, Ananda Glover-Akpey, Polly Gould, Nellie Grant, Maryann Guaraldi, Pete Guerue, Pushpa Gupta, Virginia Haaland, Birgitte Haedersdal, Lou Hance, Mary Hardy, Laura Hewitt, Kai Hirvonen, Cynthia Howe, Jennifer Ingersoll, Aqeel Ismail, Yoko Kato, Hyun-joon Kim, Roseanne Kramer, Wayne Kramer, Yan-jie Lee, Barbara Leibbrandt, Ted Levin, Luting Li, Betsy Lindfors, Kamila Louvenska, Kun-hong Lu, Revital Lubinsky, Rodolfo Luzio, Bosco Martí, Seyi Martins, Melissa Masnik, Michael McAteer, Judy McKenzie, Judy McKeown, Kathy Miller, Haris Mohamed, Lorette Moureau, Yasushige Nagahata, José Carlos Neves, Betty Ngoe, Birgitte Obtz, Larry Polansky, Inge Pompen, Kyle Power, Jean Ris, Andrew Scace, Judy Segal, Beth Shedd, Jacqueline Sices, Gretar Sigurdsson, Phoukhao Soulivong, Marketta Steck, Aki Suzuki, Alex Swift, Toshiko Takahara, Bidjere Tchotch, Xuefeng Tian, Denise Vargas, José Villanueva, Christoph von Andreae, Lily Wang, Qing Wang, Dewi Williams, Jack Williamson, Susan Williamson, Erick Yarboi, and Daphna Zuker. I would also like to thank those people whose names I was unable to get at the consulates general of Italy, Japan, Kuwait, the Philippines, and Switzerland; the Norwegian Information Service; the Embassy of the United Arab Emirates; and the Royal Saudi Arabian Embassy.

Lastly, I would like to thank my husband, Skip Gorman, and our son, Angus, for all their inspiration, and for the love and helping hands they extend to me.

6 CONTENTS

CONTENTS

AS THE WORLD TURNS

At this very moment somewhere on earth, children are waking up and starting their day, learning something new at school, sharing secrets with their friends, and sitting down with their families to enjoy a meal. If you've ever wondered what it's like to grow up in other countries with different cultural traditions, you're in for a treat!

Hands Around the World invites you to experience some of the traditions that shape people's lives everywhere. Within these pages, you'll find an entire year's worth of ideas for getting to know and appreciate how children around the world live — through the different foods they eat, the stories they listen to when they're growing up, and the art that they make with their own hands. You'll be celebrating some of their favorite holidays — there are 50 to choose from! — and playing some of the best games kids everywhere enjoy.

Of course, some of the cultural traditions described in this book may be your very own! You, or people you know in your neighborhood, may celebrate some of the holidays included here; you may speak some of the languages mentioned. Your grandparents, your parents, or even you and your brothers and sisters may have been born in another country, bringing with you many traditions from your homeland.

Above all else, *Hands Around the World* is about sharing — sharing with your family the rich traditions that have been handed down one generation after another, and sharing your experiences with others from different backgrounds. You'll discover that for all our little differences, there is a lot we all have in common!

COMMON GROUND

While this book touches on traditions found in many different countries, some of what you read may seem very familiar. Even if you don't share a particular culture's heritage, you may find yourself saying, "We do that in our family, too!"

By the same token, not all children in the countries mentioned in this book necessarily share the customs ascribed to those countries. Just as in North America, children everywhere living in cities, for example, lead very different sorts of lives than children living in rural areas. Poor children have fewer opportunities than wealthier ones; some families are more religious than others.

You can be sure of one thing, however. Children all over the world have many of the same joys and frustrations you do. Their families are their "anchors," just as your family is yours. And children everywhere look on the bright side. They truly believe many of the world's problems can be solved, and they're ready to do what they can to see that this happens!

DAY BY DAY

You'll notice that this book is organized like a calendar — one that can be used year after year. You can use it as a calendar, following the suggested activities day by day, or you can flip through the book and see what catches your eye — and jump right in wherever you want to!

The daily suggestions themselves are grouped by theme, many tied in with the 50 holidays and festivals described in this book. The first section (January 1 through 6), for example, covers not only the beginning of a brand new year (something you'll learn doesn't happen on January 1 everywhere!), but also your beginning an appreciation of different cultures and countries by hanging a world map in your room and starting an international collection.

Other sections are similarly organized. Take *Sky High*, on pages 60 and 61, as another example. The carp-shaped windsocks tied to bamboo poles on *Tango no sekku* (a day on which Japanese boys are honored) are a natural lead-in to other high-risers, such as kites and a delicious yeast bread! Want to know more about alphabets, how people in cold climates keep warm, or how other nations are working to save the environment? Turn to those sections for some thought-provoking activities and hands-on fun!

Use the index, too, to help you find what you're looking for. You'll find the separate entries labeled *Art & Crafts*, *Cooking*, and *Games* especially helpful. Under those headings, are all the art projects, recipes, and games with rules found in this book. When you're looking for something to make with your own hands or a fun way to spend some time with your friends, you'll be able to locate an activity as quick as a wink!

LET'S CELEBRATE!

The holidays and festivals included in this book underline the importance of celebrations all over the world. Family and community festivals not only keep traditions alive, they also bring excitement to people's lives!

You'll find many festivals celebrated in different countries here, as well as holidays observed by different religious groups. There are also five special days set aside by various branches of the United Nations, which are observed worldwide.

VERY ADAPTABLE

Some of the projects included in this book yield wearable art and delicious dishes identical to those made in other countries. The instructions for the knotted friendship bracelet on page 95, for example, outline the same steps Guatemalan children follow. The Thai recipe on February 25 calls for authentic ingredients, and if made with these, is just like the dish enjoyed in Thailand.

Many of the projects and activities, however, are clever adaptations. Readily available materials are substituted for hard-to-find items. When practicing wrapping a turban around your head, you can just as easily use a torn sheet; when folding an origami frog, you can use origami paper (one art material that is found most everywhere), or cut your own squares from gift wrap or old telephone books.

The same goes for enjoying the world holidays highlighted in this book. Families in Iran eat specific foods beginning with the Arabic letter "s" when they sit down to their *Noruz* dinner (March 21), and you can select foods that begin with the English letter "s" to still get a feeling for the festive occasion. Children in Denmark may not color world flags on *Valdemars dag* (June 15), but it's the perfect activity for honoring these important national symbols.

SAFETY CHECK

Most of the materials and procedures in this book are perfectly safe. There are a few potentially dangerous tools, however, that you must handle with extra care.

Have an adult help you if you are unsure how to use a tool, such as a kitchen knife, hand saw, an X-acto knife, or if you are not allowed to use one by yourself yet. The same goes for working at the stove. Be sure to use a potholder whenever you're handling hot pots and pans. Be especially careful when melting paraffin (it's flammable) and working with hot wax (making candles is a project that should be done ONLY under adult supervision).

Take care when blowing up balloons (and keep them away from younger children) and when using a sewing needle and pins.

Throughout the book, there are reminders to get an adult's help before starting certain projects. Please do this. Remember, it's far better to be safe than sorry.

TIME TRACKER

Hands Around the World naturally follows the Gregorian calendar, the one you're familiar with and the one that is used throughout the world.

The Gregorian calendar takes its name from Pope Gregory XIII who instituted it in 1582, making a few changes in the existing Julian calendar that Europeans had been using since 46 B.C.

The Gregorian calendar has 365 days and is a solar calendar, based on the time it takes the earth to make one complete revolution around the sun — 365 days, 5 hours, 48 minutes, and a tad over 45 seconds. Because these extra minutes eventually add up to another day, an extra day is added to February once every four years (Leap Year) and whenever a centenary year (such as 1600 or 2000) can be evenly divided by 400.

But the Gregorian calendar isn't the only calendar in use around the world today. While most countries conduct business and governmental affairs according to the Gregorian calendar, other calendars of special regional or religious importance are also used.

YEAR OF THE KID!

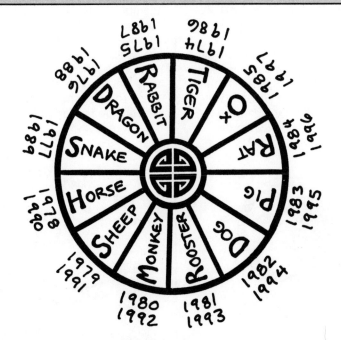

The Chinese calendar is the oldest continuously used calendar in the world. As of 1992, it is 4,690 years old!

This venerable calendar is made up of cycles of 12 years, each year named after an animal. The design at left shows these animals and current years (according to the Gregorian calendar) to which these animals "belong."

It is said that people possess some of the characteristics of the animal of the year of their birth. Those born during the Year of the Dog are faithful companions; those born during the Year of the Monkey are sure to be mischief makers! Do you share any of the characteristics of the animal of your year?

Muslim countries use the Islamic calendar, which is a lunar (moon) calendar. It has only 354 days, which means each year the Islamic calendar "moves back" 11 days. Holidays and other celebrations observed each year (such as birthdays) eventually fall in every month of the Gregorian calendar. An Iraqi child born on Safar 17 might celebrate his or her birthday in June one year, May the next, and so on.

The Jewish calendar is a lunisolar calendar, which is — you guessed it! — a combination of a lunar and solar calendar. The years are calculated according to the sun, but the months are tracked by the moon's phases. The Jewish calendar has 12 months, with a thirteenth month added every 3rd, 6th, 8th, 11th, 14th, 17th, and 19th years in a 19-year cycle. This helps to keep the lunar months somewhat aligned with the solar yearly cycle. A holiday such as Hanukkah, which starts on the 25th day of the Jewish month of Kislev, always falls in December, but on different December dates each year.

Christians also use their own calendar for religious holidays. Some holidays, such as Christmas, fall on the same date each year (December 25). Others, such as Easter, are movable, or variable holidays. Easter is observed on the Sunday following the first full moon after the vernal equinox (first day of spring). This means Easter may be as early as March 22 or as late as April 25. Different branches of the Christian church observe some holidays on different dates according to their particular traditions.

Other calendars include the Chinese calendar, with 12 months based on the lunar cycle, and several Hindu calendars, the majority of which also have 12 months. Hindu months are measured from full moon to full moon, and each of these months is divided into a dark half (when the moon is waning, or decreasing in size once it's full) and a light half (when the moon is waxing, or increasing in size).

ONE WORLD, ONE CALENDAR

With so many countries and cultures using so many different calendars, you might wonder why there isn't just one calendar that the whole world could follow — perhaps even one that would simplify when world holidays took place. This has been proposed a number of times, but has met with little success.

The best-known of these world calendars is called just that — the World Calendar. It was proposed by Elizabeth Achelis, an American member of the World Calendar Association, in 1930. The World Calendar is a repeating calendar, one that is exactly the same year after year. Each new year starts on Sunday, January 1, and is 364 days long. To bring the calendar in line with the 365¼-day solar year, a non-numbered day known as Worldsday is added each year after December 30 (there would also be a Leap Day inserted between June 30 and July 1 once every four years). It has even been proposed that Worldsday be a worldwide holiday!

So why hasn't this world calendar caught on? Existing calendars are deeply rooted in tradition, and many annual holidays and celebrations are closely linked to natural cycles, such as the moon's phases. As logical as the World Calendar may seem, it ignores the ancient traditions that are near and dear to people's hearts. So, until there is a pressing need for a world calendar such as this one, the closest thing to a world calendar is the Gregorian calendar.

MAPMAKER, MAPMAKER

You'll have a much better appreciation of the cultural customs and traditions mentioned in this book if you brush up on your world geography. Time to get out the atlas! Here are a few suggestions for using various maps to their best advantage.

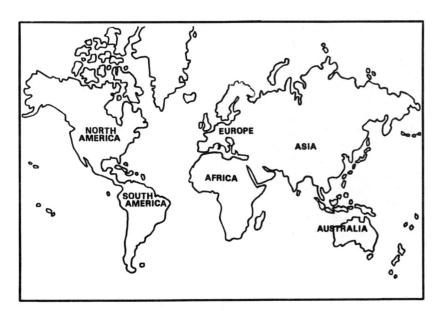

A political map, one that shows national boundaries, is the type of map to study to learn the location of the 170 or so recognized nations. You'll note that six continents — Europe, Asia, Africa, Australia, North America, and South America — are inhabited and divided into nations. (A seventh continent, Antarctica, has no permanent settlements and does not "belong" to any nation.)

Can you find a country that takes up an entire continent? That's right — it's Australia! How about the smallest independent country? That would be Vatican City, the seat of government of the Roman Catholic Church. It is located in the heart of Rome, Italy, and has an area of only .17 square miles (.44 sq km)! See if you can name (and locate) countries that start with every letter of the alphabet. With the exception of "x," you should be able to do this!

On many maps you'll notice that some countries have two names, the second usually a smaller name in parentheses. When countries change their names (as Burma did in 1989, officially adopting the new name Myanmar), the former national names continue to be included on maps for several years, until it is no longer necessary. Despite the fact that maps are periodically updated, changes can occur so quickly that maps can become obsolete overnight!

Some atlases also include foreign geographical terms. These are very helpful when you're studying more detailed maps of countries and want to imagine what the terrain is like.

Algeria, for example, is crisscrossed with large areas labeled *erg*, which is the Arabic word for "desert." A German or Austrian town with *wald* (vahlt) in its name is probably located in or near a forest, as *wald* means "forest." The word *serra* written on a map of Portugal indicates a mountain range.

NAME GAME

Here are the former names of a few countries found around the world. Do you know what these same countries are called today? (The answers are shown below.)

1. **Gold Coast**
2. **Celebes**
3. **Rhodesia**
4. **Belgian Congo**
5. **Ceylon**

1. Ghana 2. Sulawesi 3. Zimbabwe 4. Zaïre 5. Sri Lanka

As important as it is to know where different countries are located, it's even more valuable to have an idea of what a region's climate is like. Climate, after all, affects the clothes people wear, the foods they eat, the types of homes they live in, and the very customs of everyday life.

Some larger countries, such as China, have several different climates, which means certain customs may differ from one part of the country to the next. In some parts of the world, such as in northern Africa, many different countries share the same climate (in this case, a desert climate). Lifestyles are similar for many people living in Chad, Niger, and Libya.

The map on the following page shows five distinct climates (more detailed maps can be found in some atlases). The legend or key will help you distinguish between these climate types:

Tropical

Temperate, with mild and rainy winters

Temperate, with cold and snowy winters

Dry

Polar

Generally speaking, climates are hotter closer to the equator, and colder as you travel north and south. But land surface has an enormous influence on climate, too. Higher elevations are colder. Although the equator cuts across the Andes Mountains, which run down the western side of South America, the climate high up on this range is much different from the climate in Borneo, for example, which is also on the equator.

Large bodies of water also affect climate. Much of Southeast Asia receives months of rain when the monsoon winds bring moisture from the Indian Ocean each summer. Surrounded by water, the British Isles have a much milder climate than the interior of Russia at the same latitude, due to the warmth from the ocean current known as the Gulf Stream.

Many atlases also include maps that show other useful information, such as where the major world religions are practiced. Others show where languages such as English, Spanish, French, and Arabic are taught in schools and spoken as second languages in commerce. Some atlases even include a map that shows all 24 time zones around the world, so you can guess what children in Cambodia, Cameroon, and Czechoslovakia are doing when you're starting your day!

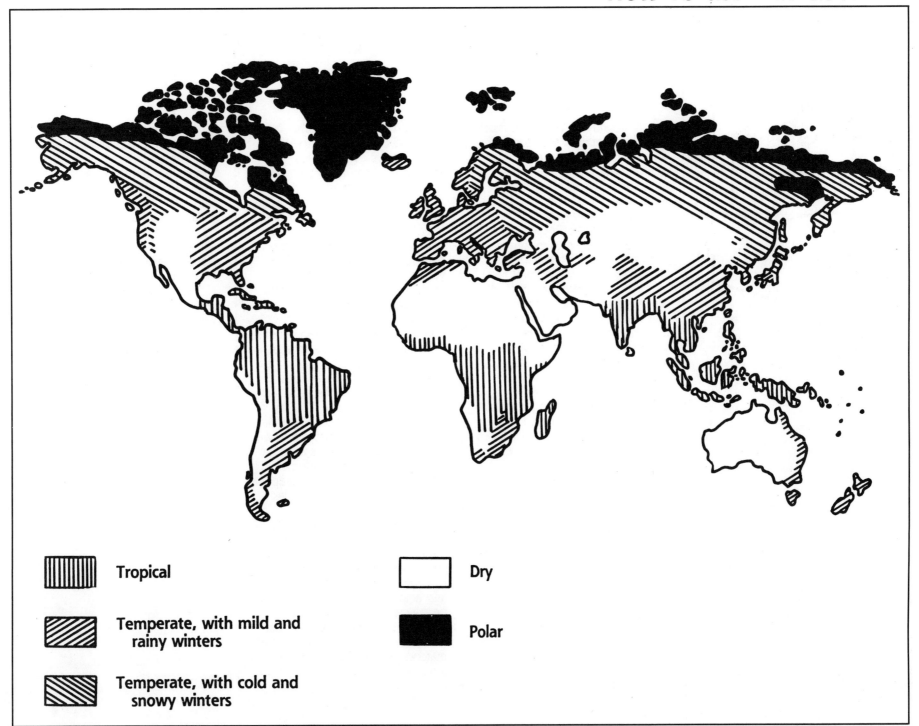

Tropical

Dry

Temperate, with mild and
rainy winters

Polar

Temperate, with cold and
snowy winters

Hands Around the World is as much a book for families as it is a children's book. What better way to demonstrate strong family ties found in every country of the world than by enjoying this book as a family yourselves!

As parents, you have a lot to offer your children to make this book a truly special one. First of all, there's your own cultural heritage. You may have only recently moved from another country or, as a Native American, your ancestors may be considered the true settlers of this continent. More likely, you're of mixed ancestry, with branches of your family going off in all directions! You may have a wealth of different cultures in your background to be proud of and to share with your children.

The same goes for other cultures and countries of interest to you. If you've ever traveled abroad, you may know something about the crafts, music, and food of various regions. You may be familiar with certain aspects of different cultures through some of your hobbies, such as knitting or playing a folk instrument. Share your enthusiasm with your children, for it's this rather than your knowledge that will really impress them!

Your children will also benefit from your practical assistance. A knowledge of gardening or craft techniques makes you an ideal partner for many of the activities suggested in this book. You can also help by rounding up materials needed to complete projects and by bringing home books from the library for more information on topics of interest (the bibliography in this book lists dozens of titles you'll find helpful).

Younger children will need a helping hand with many projects, but even older children will appreciate your joining in. They are encouraged to seek your permission and help throughout the book, especially when cooking at the stove, or handling potentially dangerous tools and materials, such as matches and hot wax used in making candles.

You can also be available to explain and discuss certain issues, such as racial and religious discrimination. It's no secret that children learn many of their attitudes from their own parents, so it's especially important to stress accepting others as they are, and work with your children to establish peace at home and throughout the world.

Let us join hands and work together to make our world a better place for our children, and for our children's children and all those that come after.

THE YEAR BEGINS

Begin at the Beginning

January 1 signals the beginning of a new year, and with it comes the promise of a fresh start. It's time to put those New Year's resolutions to the test!

This is also a good time to hang up a world map and set aside an area in your room to display things from around the world that you find and make. Appreciating the world beyond our own backyards begins at home!

1

Welcome in the New Year.

How do you and your family spend the first day of the year? Get the year off to a good start — make this day an extra special one!

This is a good day to invite some friends over. Many cultures believe in beginning the New Year in the company of good friends and food, to insure there will be plenty of both in the days to come. In Belgium, children share traditional stamped cookies with their friends on New Year's Day. (You'll find the instructions for making your own stamped cookies on January 3.)

Children look forward to a number of other special New Year's treats in various countries around the world. Some of these are described below.

FIRST DAYS

In Russia, the New Year's celebration has largely taken the place of Christmas. On this day, children receive gifts which are brought by *D'yed Moroz* (dih-YEHD more-ohs), or "Grandfather Frost," a white-bearded man dressed in splendid robes and a cap. He is often accompanied by the Snow Maiden, a popular Russian folk figure.

Gifts are also exchanged in Greece on the first day of the year, which happens to be the feast day of St. Basil. Children eagerly bite into slices of *Vassilopita* (vahs-eel-OH-pee-tah), or "St. Basil's cake," which contains a hidden coin. The lucky person who finds the coin in his or her slice is said to be blessed with extra good fortune for the next twelve months.

Austrian children are given good luck toy pigs on New Year's Day. The little pink pigs usually have either a coin or four-leaf clover in their mouths, and may be made from wood, clay, or something edible, such as marzipan. Mmmm!

2

Check dates of New Year celebrations.

The first day of the year is celebrated with fanfare all over the world, but in some places it falls on a date other than January 1. That's because certain cultures and religions use different calendars. (For more on calendars, see pages 11 and 12.)

The Vietnamese New Year, *Tet Nguyen Dan* (teht noo-WIN dahn), for example, falls sometime in January or February. The Jewish New Year celebration, *Rosh Hashanah*, begins sometime in September (and is actually one of four New Year celebrations in the Jewish calendar!).

The following are just some of the months in which a new year begins in other countries and cultures. Are any of these observed in your family or community?

Nigeria (*Ibo people*) — March

Iran — March

Burma — April

Bangladesh — April

Ghana (*Ewe people*) — September

Ethiopia — September

3

Stamp New Year's cookies.

Start the year out sweet! Bake stamped New Year's cookies to share with family and friends.

Belgian cookies exchanged on New Year's Day are traditionally stamped with a cross. Make yours in any designs you like, such as six-pointed stars (a common Scandinavian motif) or simple animal designs (popular in Germany). It's easy to make your own stamps using air-hardening clay.

Roll the clay out about ½" (1 cm) thick and cut into 1½" (4 cm) circles. Carefully draw designs in the clay (remember what you carve into the stamp will show up raised on the cookies). Turn the stamps over and attach a sturdy handle to each. Let dry completely, then seal with varnish or a coat of acrylic paint.

Use your stamps to place designs in just about any soft cookie dough. Form the dough into walnut-sized balls, place on baking sheets, and flatten with the stamps. Bake according to recipe instructions, let cool, and then share!

4

Tack up a world map.

Learning about people and customs around the world is a lot easier if you know where different countries and regions are located. A political map, one that shows national boundaries, is especially helpful.

Maps can be found in atlases and other books, but a large wall map is one reference tool you'll use over and over again. At a glance, you can see which countries are located below the equator (where they experience summer when it's winter in North America), or why fish is an important food in Japan (that country is a series of islands). A world map also illustrates how environmental problems in one part of the world can affect the entire globe.

Hang your map where you can get right up close to it. You may wish to mark certain places you learn about with map tacks—tiny, round-headed pins designed especially for maps. See *Mapmaker, Mapmaker* on page 13 for more on maps and how they can help you make sense of the world.

5

Start an international collection.

Start collecting some items that pertain to different cultures around the world. You'll find a lot is available at little or no cost.

Check magazines for pictures of people dressed in regional styles of clothing, for example. Cut the pictures out and save them. Add any actual items of traditional clothing from other countries that you may have in your wardrobe.

Ask your friends who speak other languages at home for a copy of a newspaper written in a different language or alphabet. An international pen pal can send you empty food packages and labels to add to a collection of food from around the world. Don't forget to save the stamps on the letters these friends send you!

Page through gift catalogues for pictures of world art and crafts. Save examples of traditional designs to inspire you when you make a prayer rug (see June 27) or folding fan (August 4). You never know when some item might come in handy for broadening your understanding of the world!

6

Create a mini-museum.

As your collection of cultural items from around the world grows, you'll be able to create displays to show off your discoveries. Set up a mini-museum, one with changing exhibits. This is something you can do at home and at school.

Turn a wall or corner of a room into an exhibit space, taking advantage of features such as windowsills and backs of doors. Come up with creative display/storage solutions, such as using oversized cardboard boxes as freestanding dividers (give the outsides a coat of paint). Lightweight items can be hung from string stretched between two points.

Use this book to help you come up with ideas for exhibits. Many of the themes lend themselves to displays, such as *Alphabet Soup* (May 22–26) and *One Nation . . .* (June 12–17). Create other displays to tie in with holidays. Use your mini-museum to show how much we all have in common!

Climate Control

If you had to name one thing that is responsible for many of the differences in lifestyle around the world, it would have to be climate. As climates vary, so do the foods people eat, the clothes they wear, and even the color of their skin.

Yet, for all these little differences, people around the world have much in common. Ahead are ways to celebrate our "oneness," too!

What's the difference between climate and weather? Climate describes the usual weather patterns of a particular region. Rain, for instance, is a type of weather, but how much it rains (or snows or is sunny) year in and year out determines a region's climate.

7

Study a climate map.

Our earth's climate varies tremendously from place to place. Amazingly, people are able to live in just about every climate, with the exception of the extreme polar regions. Brrrr!

Check an atlas for a map that clearly shows the different climates of the world. There you will be able to see which tropical regions are hot and rainy year-round, and which have distinct rainy and dry seasons. Europe and North America both lie in the so-called temperate (moderate) zone, but there's a big difference between, say, the climate of France and that of Canada. While France enjoys mild, rainy weather all year (except in higher elevations where it snows), much of Canada has short, cool summers followed by cold and snowy winters.

The illustration below shows how Australia has six distinct climate zones! The same is true for other continents. What climate do you think would be easiest to live in? Why?

8

List ways climate affects lifestyle.

More than anything else, climate has a strong influence on people's lifestyles. How many things can you think of that might be affected by climate?

How about the foods people eat? People generally eat what can be gathered or grown in their particular climate, but some foods may be popular for other reasons. Spicy foods, for instance, are enjoyed in hot climates because of the cooling effect they have on the body.

Climate affects what people wear, what kinds of houses they live in, even the games children play (vigorous outdoor games are more common in cold regions)! As you learn about people around the world, try to imagine how climate affects what they do day to day. You'll have a keener appreciation of the different ways of the world when you keep this in mind.

9

Compare seasons around the world.

If you were asked to name the seasons, you would probably say "spring, summer, autumn, and winter." While these four distinct seasons (and they aren't always so clear-cut!) are found in much of North America and Europe, local climate determines different types of seasons, in other parts of the world.

Take a country like India, for example, which experiences two seasons—a dry season and a rainy one. El Salvador also has two seasons. Children there learn that winter lasts from May to October, which is followed by summer (from November to April). Further south along the equator, especially in areas that are hot and rainy year-round, there really are no seasons as such. Day length is about the same all year long, and it's hot and rainy just about every day, too!

What is your favorite season, and why? What do you think it must be like where there are only one or two seasons?

10

Learn how skin color evolved.

Climate has also had a role in determining the color of our skin. Let's travel back in time to see how variations in skin color may have come about.

The first human beings are believed to have evolved in sunny Africa. Knowing as we do today how skin darkens (tans) as self-protection against the harmful rays of sunlight, it seems likely that those with darker skin were better protected in that climate. Over the course of tens of thousands of years, the natural protection of dark skin was handed down from one generation to the next.

The opposite happened in northern Europe where there is much less sun. When early humans settled there, many were stricken by rickets, a disease which weakens and twists the bones. Rickets can be prevented if the body gets enough vitamin D, which the skin absorbs from the sun's ultraviolet rays. Lighter skins absorb these more readily, so once again, over time, a certain skin color was favored because of a particular climate.

So what does this say to us? Skin color is our way of adapting to our climate and it truly is only skin deep.

11

Paint a mural of the world's peoples.

Celebrate the differences — and the "oneness" — of the world's peoples with a painted mural.

This is something you can do on paper (use a continuous length of paper such as newsprint or photographer's seamless background paper), or directly on a wall or other flat surface, with your parents' permission. This would also make a good group project at your school. Liven up those hallways!

Sketch your figures lightly in pencil so that their whole bodies show, from head to toe. "Dress"

them in different styles of clothing. Traditional costumes vary considerably around the world, as do some everyday outfits (see August 22–26 and November 15–19 for more on clothing).

You can use paints to complete your mural, or markers, colored pencils, or crayons. Have fun coloring in the intricate designs found on much of the world's clothing. Be sure to complement the clothing styles with appropriate hair styles, eye color, and skin tones.

ALL OF A KIND

12

Cut paper figure chains.

Represent some of the world's people, this time linked hand in hand, with a cut paper chain. Here's how to make one.

Carefully fold a long, narrow length of paper zigzag fashion. Sketch the outline of two figures on the top layer. The illustration below shows how just half a figure is drawn on either side, their hands meeting in the middle. You can make your figures boys or girls, or both as shown.

Cut along the outline of the figures with scissors and unfold the paper. Color each figure, taking care to represent different styles and color of hair, facial features, and skin.

A Name I Call Myself

Our names are an important part of our identity. In fact, in many cultures, children are given names that will hopefully *shape* their identities.

The following offers ways to learn about first and last names around the world. But let's start with you and the names you were given!

13

Learn the meaning of your first name.

Your first name, or given name, is one you hear a lot! But do you know what your name actually means?

Your parents may be able to answer that question for you, although they may have chosen your name simply because they liked the sound of it. You may have better luck looking in a book of baby names. Check your library for a copy. Baby name books list thousands of common (although mostly European) boys' and girls' names, giving the meaning and origin of each.

There you'll learn that Linda is "pretty" in Spanish; Sarah is Hebrew for "princess." Jennifer is derived from the Welsh for "white spirit." Charles means "man" in Old German; Jerome is Greek for "holy name." The Scottish name Donald means "world ruler."

Now that you know what your name means, do you think it was a good choice for you?

14

Compare naming traditions.

In many cultures, a child's name reflects what his parents expect or hope for him or her.

A Vietnamese boy named *Tuan Ahn*, which means "famous person," hopefully will be one someday. The Arabic boy's name *Sa'id* (*Saideh* for a girl) might bring that child good fortune, as the name means "lucky." A Chinese boy or girl named *Qi* (chee) is expected to grow tall, as that is what the word means.

In some branches of the Jewish religion it is taboo to name children after living relatives. The opposite is true among some Kenyan peoples, where a firstborn daughter is always given the name of her father's mother. A second daughter would be named after her mother's mother.

In Ghana, a child is given several names, including one that tells of the time of day, day of the week, or special event that was taking place when the child was born. A boy born on Thursday has *Kwao* as part of his name.

Some of your friends from other cultures may have been named for certain reasons. Ask what their names mean, and share the meaning of your name!

15

Make up a name for yourself.

Here's a tough one! If you could call yourself by any name, what would it be?

You might give yourself a name based on your interests or abilities. Many Native American names are descriptive in this way. Tames Wild Horses might be the tribal name given to a boy who has a way with horses. This would not be the name given to the child at birth but when he was older, perhaps after winning some blue ribbons at a rodeo riding a horse the boy had trained himself. Many Native Americans and Australian Aborigines are given several different names during the course of their lives.

Think about your physical characteristics (your height or the color of your hair or eyes) or your manner (quiet or giggly!), and see if you can come up with a name that suits you. It can be a "real" name or one you invent.

Give yourself a name from a culture you admire, or borrow a name from a character in a book. The possibilities are endless!

FLORA

16

MY NAME IS CHRIS

Uncover the origins of your last name.

There was a time when everyone had only one name, a first name. Eventually, there was a need to distinguish people who shared the same name. Last names, or family names, were born!

Your own last name has probably been in your family for generations, and says something about your ancestors. But do you know what? The box below offers some clues!

TRADES & TRAITS

Surnames (another name for last names) were first used in Europe in the 13th century. Many were formed from a father's first name. If Jack's father was named William, Jack was called Jack Williamson. This was true in Russian (*Ivanovich* means "son of Ivan") and Spanish (*Martinez* is "son of Martin") as well as in other languages.

People were also named for physical traits (Short, Brown), after places (Mr. Hill probably lived at the top of one), and for occupations (Baker, Taylor, and the most common surname of all, Smith, as in blacksmith). Similar last names are found in many languages.

Eventually, surnames didn't change from one generation to the next but were handed down. Iceland is a modern day exception. There Karl Jósefsson's sons will have the last name Karlsson, while his daughters will go by Karlsdóttir. Their children, in turn, will take their own father's first name as part of their last names.

In China, surnames were first required about 2,000 years ago. Some historians believe people at that time were asked to choose names from the words of a short poem, explaining why there are relatively few Chinese last names. *Wing* ("warm") and *Lee* ("pear tree") are two examples.

Japanese surnames date from the 1800s, and these invented names reflect the Japanese reverence for nature. *Hana* ("flower") and *Togukawa* ("virtuous river") are typical.

17

Illustrate your name.

Draw a picture to illustrate the meaning of your name. If you don't know what your name means yet, make something up, according to how it sounds to you. For instance, is it gentle, strong, or dramatic?

Girls named after flowers, such as Rosa and Daphne (Greek for "laurel") can draw these flowers. Margaret might draw a self-portrait within a sun, as the name is Persian for "child of light."

A boy named Leon could draw a picture of a lion. At one time, a baby boy would be given this name in the hopes that he would grow up to have some of the characteristics of a lion. Boys with Japanese names indicating their position in the family, such as *Jiro* ("younger boy") can show that in their drawings. Stephen might draw a picture of a crown, as that is the meaning of the name in Greek.

Make your drawing realistic, if you like, or experiment with stylized representations, such as the illustration for Melissa (Greek for "honeybee") shown here.

18

Carve a chop.

In Southeast Asian countries, a person's signature is stamped instead of written, using a personal seal known as a chop. The custom-made chops are small, only about ⅜" (1 cm) square, and are usually carved from soapstone. The chop is inked and an impression made wherever a signature is required.

You can make a simple chop from an art eraser. An X-acto knife works well for carving a design, but have an adult help you as this is a sharp tool. You can also make a chop by drawing a design onto a small square of recycled styrofoam using a pencil or other blunt instrument. Ink your chop with printmaking ink or paint. Use it to stamp your "mark" on drawings, letters to your friends, even homework!

Family Tree

Family ties form strong bonds in cultures all over the world. In some places, several generations of the same family traditionally live together. Grandparents are a vital part of the family, and the wisdom of these elders is greatly respected.

Here are some ways to honor the members of your family and to preserve your own precious family memories for future generations.

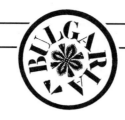

19

Count the members of your family.

How many people are in your family? Are there fewer children in your family than were in your mother's and father's families?

In many countries, family size has shrunk in recent years. As fewer people work the land to grow their own food, fewer children are needed as helpers. With improved health care, however, the world's population is growing at an alarming rate, and in places like China, parents are encouraged to have only one child to help avoid overpopulation.

In some places, family members living under one roof might include grandparents, aunts, uncles, and cousins. This is called an extended family, and it, too, is on the wane. In many African countries, extended families are traditional, but as more people move from rural areas to cities in search of jobs, extended families are broken up. Housing for everyone together is just too difficult to come by.

It saddens many people that the family unit has had to change with the times. How do you think extended families can remain close, even if they don't all live together?

20

Remember your grandparents on *Babin Den.*

Babin Den (bah-bean den), or "Grandmother's Day," is a day Bulgarians traditionally honor grandmothers, mothers, and sometimes doctors and nurses. At one time, all babies were born at home, and the midwives, or women who assisted with the births, were affectionately called *baba,* or "grandmother." It was thought that each *baba* imparted some of her wisdom to the babies she helped deliver. Parents and children would bring flowers to the midwife each year in January, as a show of thanks.

Honor your grandparents on this day! Send cards to both sets of grandparents, or spend the day with them if they live nearby. Did any of your grandparents move here from another country? There's a lot you can learn from them about language, customs, and what it was like moving to a strange land. And don't forget great-grandparents! They can tell you what it was like for them 20 or 30 years earlier. They may even remember things their parents told them about yet another era!

21

Start a family history scrapbook.

No history is quite as exciting as the history of which you are a part. Learning about the people in your past helps put historical events in perspective, but also explains a lot about you. Why do you have red hair and freckles? Why, if you are black, is your last name White?

You may have some old photographs, newspaper clippings, letters, and even diaries that have been carefully preserved. Use these to start a scrapbook that chronicles the families on both your mother's and father's side. Your parents can tell you what it was like for them when they were growing up. Your grandparents (and great-grandparents) can fill in any missing details.

Make your own scrapbook or photo album (see January 22), or use a purchased one. Now is a good time for you to save some things you can share with your own children and grandchildren. They'll be just as curious about you someday!

22

Make a scrapbook.

Keep family memories safe in a Japanese-style accordian scrapbook, perfect for bulky items.

Make your scrapbook any size you like. You need two pieces of sturdy cardboard for the covers, and heavy drawing paper that comes in large sheets. You'll also need white glue and narrow cloth ribbon.

Cut the drawing paper in strips and fold them zigzag fashion. Join sections to make one continuous folded length of paper.

Cut the cardboard ½" (1 cm) larger than the folded pages on four sides. Cut two sheets of paper 1" (2.5 cm) larger than the covers; decorate and glue to the cardboard with slightly watered down glue. Glue a length of ribbon to the inside of each cover.

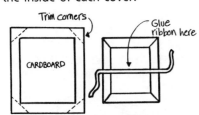
Trim corners
Glue ribbon here
CARDBOARD

Glue one cover to the first page of the book, and one to the last page. Items can be taped or glued to both sides of pages.

23

Chart your family tree.

Keep all the members of your extended family straight with a family tree! This is a visual device that shows everyone's relationship to each other as far back as is known. Use your family tree to chart not only when different family members lived, but also to show which, if any, countries they may have moved from.

The diagram below shows the most basic family tree. You may choose to include any brothers and sisters you have, as well as any your parents and grandparents have. Don't forget cousins and second cousins (those are your parents' cousins). How far back can you go? How many cultures or countries are represented in your tree?

THE TREE OF LIFE

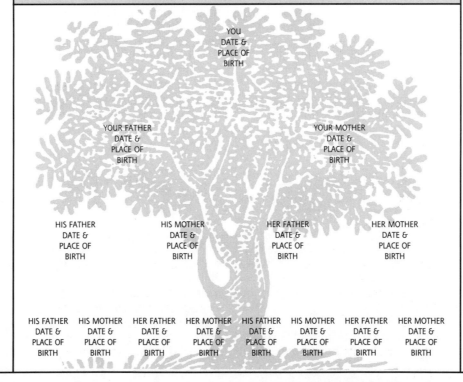

YOU
DATE &
PLACE OF
BIRTH

YOUR FATHER
DATE &
PLACE OF
BIRTH

YOUR MOTHER
DATE &
PLACE OF
BIRTH

HIS FATHER
DATE &
PLACE OF
BIRTH

HIS MOTHER
DATE &
PLACE OF
BIRTH

HER FATHER
DATE &
PLACE OF
BIRTH

HER MOTHER
DATE &
PLACE OF
BIRTH

HIS FATHER
DATE &
PLACE OF
BIRTH

HIS MOTHER
DATE &
PLACE OF
BIRTH

HER FATHER
DATE &
PLACE OF
BIRTH

HER MOTHER
DATE &
PLACE OF
BIRTH

HIS FATHER
DATE &
PLACE OF
BIRTH

HIS MOTHER
DATE &
PLACE OF
BIRTH

HER FATHER
DATE &
PLACE OF
BIRTH

HER MOTHER
DATE &
PLACE OF
BIRTH

24

Design a family crest.

Throughout history, families have been unified by readily recognizable designs worn on clothing or made into flags.

The Highland clans of Scotland, for example, go back to the 5th century, but in the 1700s distinctive plaid patterns were used to identify the different families. Every clan from Abercromby to Wemyss had its own tartan, as the fabric designs are called today.

Important families in Japan once had their own crests, which were pictured on clothing. In the 1860s, many ordinary Japanese families and businessmen copied this idea. Seldom used today, the crests were simple but striking designs like the ones shown below.

Design a crest or emblem for your family! Think about the meaning of your last name, or illustrate a line of work many in your family have entered, such as science or the arts. Picture a country a grandparent came from, or something from a culture that's important to you.

Home, Sweet Home

Most of us spend many hours each day away from our homes, at school and at play. Perhaps that is why we value the familiar surroundings of our own homes.

Ahead, you'll see how varied homes around the world can be. There are also suggestions for making yours a truly welcome place!

25

Compare housing around the world.

People build homes that not only suit their climate but also take advantage of natural building materials. You would no more see an adobe, or sun-baked mud, home in the tropics (it would be washed away in no time with all that rain!) than you would see a bamboo structure on stilts up near the Arctic Circle.

Look for pictures of different types of houses found around the world. Design a house you think would work well in another part of the world. Would you like to live in one of these, or in any of the houses described below?

HUMAN HABITATS

In parts of rural Ghana, people live in round mud huts. Each family owns a group of huts that are joined to one another with thick, freestanding walls. The huts have no windows, and the doors are small and low, which helps keep the heat out and the coolness in. As in many warm places throughout the world, cooking is done outdoors.

In hot, rainy Malaysia, houses are elevated on stilts. The continual flow of air all around them helps keep the homes both dry and cool.

High in the Himalayas in Nepal, it can get quite cold. Two-story homes house animals on the ground floor; rising heat from their bodies helps to heat the upper floor where the family lives.

The Bedouin in the Middle East herd camels, goats, and sheep. They live in tents made from woven goats' hair. These movable homes make it easy to pack up and go in search of better grazing.

Many people around the world live on water in boats, including the Bajau Laut in the Philippines. The living quarters on their boats are made from a framework of bamboo covered with woven rush mats. Even cooking is done on board, atop a small fire contained in an earthenware pot.

26

Construct a model of a dwelling.

Choose a type of house that is of interest to you and build a model of it.

Although you'll be working on a smaller scale, you can use many of the same materials that are used to make the real houses to construct your model. Make an adobe dwelling, such as an African hut or New Mexican pueblo structure out of clay. Use felt to cover the frame of a yurt, a dome-shaped tent found in central Asia. (Real yurts have wooden frames, but you'll find it easier to make a wire one.) Weave some straw for the walls and roof of a Marsh Arab's house.

For wooden, brick, and stone buildings, you can paint cardboard to resemble these materials. Do any painting before you erect your model. Windows and doors can be cut out with an X-acto knife (have an adult help you with this sharp tool).

Add some landscaping, a few people, animals, and other tiny objects made from bread "clay" (see March 4), and your dwelling will look just like the real thing!

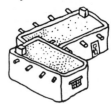

27

Build a playhouse.

Children all over the world turn everyday materials into special hideaways and playhouses.

In India, children sometimes borrow one of their mother's *saris* (SAHR-ees), a long piece of fabric that is folded and draped to make an ankle-length dress. The children create simple tents held together with pins and rope.

You can do the same with blankets and sheets. Make a tee-pee using long poles lashed together at the top. Or arrange some chairs in a circle, drape the blankets over them, and you have a yurt!

Outdoors, you can build a permanent structure. In England, these are known as Wendy houses, named for Wendy in *Peter Pan*, who lived in a tiny house the Lost Boys built for her. Turn some scrap lumber into a freestanding playhouse or a tree house. Have an adult help you so that you're sure your house is perfectly safe. Tree houses are not used as permanent homes anywhere, but not long ago unmarried girls in New Guinea spent time in tree houses as part of their coming of age.

28

Get ready for bed.

At the end of each day, tired children everywhere tumble into bed. Having a room all one's own in which to sleep is a luxury many children do not have, however. In many places, children also share their bed with other family members.

In lots of homes around the world, living spaces double as bedrooms, so getting ready for bed means actually making up the beds. This is true in traditional Japanese homes where *futon* (FOO-tawn), cotton-stuffed mattresses, are brought out of cupboards and placed on the floor each evening. In the morning, the bedding is stashed away to make room for the day's activities.

Do you prefer a soft mattress or a hard one? It depends on what you're used to. In Germany, some children sleep on feather mattresses that are so soft they literally sink into them! Chinese children are accustomed to the firmer surface of straw mats. The Yanomamo Indians living in the Amazonian jungle sleep in hammocks, which are comfortably cool in that sticky climate.

29

Mix up a simmering scent.

Homes all over the world are freshened with sweet scents. A pot of basil is found in many Italian homes, where its odor perfumes the air and keeps flies away! Indian homes often smell of *patchouli* (paht-CHEW-lee), a strongly-scented plant native to that country. It is used to make incense, a popular way of spreading pleasant odors throughout Asian homes.

In France, homes are sometimes perfumed in a similar way. Cloves or mixed spices are heated in a heavy iron frying pan until they begin to smoke, then the pan is taken from room to room.

You can make up some herb and spice blends to simmer in water. The steam will carry the aroma throughout the house. Have an adult help you when you're at the stove.

Experiment with herbs and spices you have in your pantry. A few cloves, some cinnamon, and anise seeds make a pleasant scent. A mixture of mint, camomile, and orange rind is nice. Other sweet-smelling herbs in your garden are possibilities, too.

30

Make a welcome sign.

Let your friends know they are welcome in your home with a sign that proclaims just that — Welcome!

The sign pictured below is an example of German folk art, and *Willkommen* (VEAL-koh-men) is — you guessed it — German for "welcome." You can design your sign any way you like. Choose another language, one that you speak at home, or that has special meaning for you. Here are a few ways to write "Welcome" from around the world:

HÌN HẠNH DÓN TIẾP — Vietnamese
WELKOM — Africaans
KARIBU — Swahili
BIENVENIDOS — Spanish
HOS GELDINIZ — Turkish

Wood makes a sturdy base for a sign, but you can use thick cardboard or plywood. Acrylic paints are a good choice because they are waterproof when dry. If you plan on hanging your sign outdoors, however, be sure to weather-proof it with several coats of varnish.

The Farmer in the Dell

Farming is a way of life for many people in the less industrialized countries of the world. There's plenty for children to do, too, from looking after the family flock to helping with the harvest.

Farmers jokingly say they are in partnership with the devil — the weather! You can be sure they keep a close eye on that changeable partner at all times.

31

Compare farming around the world.

People grow food just about everywhere, even in some rather unlikely places. Icelanders enjoy fresh fruits and vegetables — even bananas! — that are grown in greenhouses. These are heated with geothermal heat (heat that comes from within the earth), which is in abundant supply on that island.

Much of the farmland in Southeast Asia is planted with rice, a main crop that feeds literally billions of people. Many farms are communal, where everyone works together on the land, sharing the harvest. Communes called *kibbutzim* (key-BOOTS-eem) are found in Israel. Children are a vital part of a *kibbutz*, but often live apart from their parents in children's housing.

A farm in Brazil likely produces that country's major crop, coffee beans used to make coffee. Everyone in the family helps with the harvest, as each bean must be picked when it's just ripe. Children are valuable helpers in other countries, including Jamaica (supplier of much of the world's allspice) and Zanzibar, a major producer of cloves.

1

Make a *crois Bride* for St. Brigid's Day.

February 1 is the feast day of St. Brigid, the patron saint of the dairy and its cows. There was a time when every barn and house in Ireland was decorated with a *crois Bride* (cris breedge), or "St. Brigid's cross," which was thought to protect buildings from fire and other harm. Today, Irish children learn to make these in school.

There are many different versions of the *crois*. Some are diamond-shaped, others look like pinwheels. The instructions here are for a simple woven cross. While a traditional *crois* is made from rush, you can use any tall, stiff grass or even six drinking straws.

Gather the rushes, or grass, into two bunches, and wind string or yarn around one end of each bunch. Divide each bunch into three parts, and weave the two bunches under and over one another as shown.

Tie the loose ends with more string. Hang above the front door of your house, or on a barn or shed, or doghouse!

2

Watch the weather.

Farmers all over the world are close observers of the weather. Some consider weather prediction to be a science now, but many folk beliefs still exist.

Historically, February 2 has been a day to predict upcoming weather in European countries. (The day is also known as Candlemas, a Christian holiday when candles are blessed.) You probably have heard about the groundhog and his shadow. Did you know this idea originated in Germany, where farmers used to keep an eye out for badgers? It's easier to understand why everyone hopes the day will be overcast if you think of this British rhyme:

**If Candlemas be fair and clear,
Two winters will you have this year.**

In other words, fair weather may result in an early thaw, which is often followed by a damaging frost or "second winter."

A few other weather sayings from around the world can be found in the box on the following page.

3

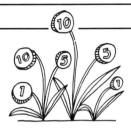

Learn some farming legends.

Many cultures have stories about farming. Here's one from the Caucasus Mountains region of central Asia:

Once there was a hard-working man whose sons were rather lazy. On his deathbed, the old man told his sons there was buried treasure on their property that would provide nicely for them. The sons dug up the ground in search of the treasure, but to no avail. When a wise person in the village suggested the sons take advantage of the newly turned soil and plant seeds, they did so. The bountiful harvest that autumn turned out to be the treasure their father had spoken of!

The Danes have a proverb about farming:

The foot of the farmer manures his fields.

What does this mean? It's a farmer's hard work that makes his fields productive!

WEATHER . . . OR NOT!

A protective layer of snow is desirable where winters are cold. In Russia, they say:

Corn is as comfortable under the snow as an old man under a fur coat.

Animals sometimes provide clues as to the changing weather.

**If bees stay at home,
Rain will soon come.
If they fly away,
Fine will be the day.**

The Plains Indians put it this way:

When buffalo herd together, the storm god is herding them.

And in India they say:

When the frog croaks in the meadow, there will be rain in three hours time.

British schoolchildren have the final world on weather:

**Whether the weather be fine,
Whether the weather be not;
Whether the weather
Whatever the weather,
Whether we like it or not!**

For more on rain, see pages 54 and 55.

4

Sample some cheese.

Not all farmers grow crops, of course. Dairy farmers herd cows, sheep, goats, even reindeer (in northern Scandinavia). These animals are valued for their milk and the products made from it, including butter, yogurt, and cheese.

Because many cheeses "travel" well, some countries export theirs. You'll find a dazzling array in your local markets. Have a cheese tasting party with selections from around the world.

Look for *gjetost* (YEH-toast), the national cheese of Norway, which is caramel-colored and, not surprisingly, slightly sweet. Try *Queso Sardo* (KAY-soh SAR-tho), a grating cheese from Argentina, and *Emmenthaler* (EM-en-tahl-uh), the original Swiss cheese with big holes or "eyes."

Sample some of the moldy cheeses from around the world (go on — they're good!). From England comes the blue-veined *Stilton;* from France *Roquefort* (rohk-FOR). For something a little milder, try *Gouda* (HOW-dah) from the Netherlands or *Danbo* from Denmark. No cheese board would be complete without French *Brie* (bree), a creamy cheese with a chalky white crust.

You can also make your own cheese at home with some help from a grown-up. Here's a recipe for cream cheese, a fresh cheese enjoyed in many countries.

Cream Cheese

4 cups (1 liter) light cream
1 cup (225 ml) heavy cream
1 tablespoon (15 ml) cultured buttermilk

Stir all ingredients together in a heat-proof bowl. Place the bowl in a pan of water and heat on the stove until the cream is 72°F (23°C). Remove from the stove, cover, and put in a warm spot for 18 hours.

Heat the cream again in the same way until it reaches 130°F (54°C). This will take 30–45 minutes. Be sure to stir the cream before inserting the kitchen thermometer for an accurate reading. Stir in 1 tablespoon (15 ml) salt. Put the bowl in the refrigerator and chill for 4 hours.

Drain the thickened cream into a dishtowel held like a sack. Squeeze out as much liquid as possible. Line a colander with ice cubes; put the clothful of cheese on the ice. Place a small plate on the cheese, topped with a quart jar of water as a weight. Place the colander in a pan (to catch the drips) and refrigerate for 24 hours. Unwrap the cheese and enjoy!

Cold Without, Warm Within

People who live in cold climates have to be good at one thing in particular — keeping warm!

There are plenty of fun ways to stay warm outdoors, especially if there's snow to play in. Dressing appropriately for the weather is a must, however. Then it's indoors for a nice cup of something to warm your insides!

5

Enjoy some cold weather sports.

Winter's cold and snow provide plenty of opportunities for outdoor fun all over the world.

The Dutch enjoy skating, no doubt because they have the perfect place to skate. In the province of Friesland, eleven towns are connected by canals which freeze over in the winter — 120 miles (192 km) of them! When the weather is cooperating, there's even an "Eleven Towns Race" along the whole length.

The Finns and Canadians are avid ice hockey players (the game got its start in Canada), but artificial ice enables even oil-rich nations in the hot Middle East to take advantage of the sport.

Skiing originated in Scandinavia at least 5,000 years ago (the remains of skis that old were preserved in Swedish bogs). The terrain there is ideal for what is known as cross-country skiing.

Downhill skiing, on the other hand, is only about 150 years old! Nordic skis were adapted to steeper inclines found in the mountainous regions of Europe. From there the sport spread, even to some places you might not expect to find skiing, such as Japan.

6

Make a snow snake.

If you have a steep, snow-covered hill nearby, you and your friends can have fun playing a traditional Iroquois game called Snow Snakes.

You'll need to make your own snow snake first. Look for a straight tree branch about four feet (1.25 m) long. (If you can't find a branch, use an old broom handle or quarter-round molding from a lumberyard.) Peel the bark off the branch, which is easy to do if the branch is dead. Smooth any rough spots with sandpaper, rounding off any sharp corners.

Attach a washer with a screw on each side of one end of the snake. These are the snake's eyes, positioned to add weight at the "head." Paint decorative designs on the snake with acrylic paints, if you like.

To play the game, prepare a track by dragging a log through the snow on a steep incline. Pack the snow down firmly. Make a lip along the sides of the track to keep the snakes from flying off it. One by one, send the snakes down the hill. The one that travels farthest is the winner!

7

Organize a snow festival.

You and your friends can organize an outdoor festival to honor the "white stuff." Here are some ideas to get you going.

Host a snow sculpting festival. These are popular wherever it snows. In Sapporo, Japan, hundreds of giant snow sculptures tower over spectators in one of the city's parks each February. Your sculptures needn't be on such a grand scale. Do as Japanese children do, and make snowmen in the shape of *daruma* dolls (see March 18)!

Make a snow dwelling, or igloo, large enough for your family or group of friends. Heat it with a camping stove, or even cook a meal inside it.

Once it gets dark, light the way to your igloo with snow candles. These are popular in Scandinavia. Form a pile of snowballs into tiny igloos; place a votive or other squat candle inside each one. Leave a small opening at the top of each, then light. You may need to poke a few extra holes at the base, if the candles need more oxygen to burn properly.

8

Decorate sticks for *Bolladagur.*

Sometimes the short cold days of winter can get to you. Icelandic children beat the winter blahs with some playful fun on *Bolladagur* (BOWL-eh-DAW-goor), or "Bun Day."

Bolladagur is a pre-Lenten holiday when children playfully spank their parents with decorated sticks in exchange for cream-filled buns, an Icelandic treat. Each strike is worth one *bolla* (BOWL-ah), or "bun," and because they are so tasty, a parent may be teasingly tapped many times! As you might expect, everybody likes to get in on the fun — long after the buns are all eaten.

Decorate your own sticks in recognition of the day. Glue several long ribbons to one end of a stick. Form each ribbon into four or five loops, as shown in the illustration, holding the loops in place with glue. These make lovely decorations any time of the year. Or start your own tradition, and beg for a special treat on this day! What will you ask for?

9

Put on something warm.

When the mercury drops, kids all over the world reach for something warm to wear. What do you put on when it's cold?

Since much of our body heat is lost through our heads, hats are important cold weather gear everywhere. In Peru, tight-fitting hats with long ear flaps called *chullos* (CHEW-yohs) are knitted from llama's and alpaca's wool. In parts of Russia, hats are often made from *astrakhan* (ass-trah-CAHN), the dark, curly fleece of young lambs also known as Persian lamb.

While some garments are made from fur, such as the outerwear made from reindeer hides in Lapland, woolen garments are more common all over the world. After all, wool is a renewable resource! Wool can be made even warmer by felting it, or matting it into a dense fabric. The ultimate cold weather garment is one worn by shepherds in Turkey. Called a *kepenek* (KEH-pehn-ehk), it's a huge, hooded cloak made from thick, felted wool. So stiff it practically stands on its own, a *kepenek* serves as a coat, a blanket, and even a tent!

10

Knit a scarf.

Wool is spun into yarn and then knitted into garments in many European countries as well as in the higher elevations of South America. There, children learn to knit at an early age.

Do you know how to knit? It's really quite simple. Have someone who knows how show you the basics, because it's easiest to learn by watching. Then you're ready for your first project!

A good beginner's project is a garter stitch scarf, which is made by knitting every stitch in every row. Make your scarf reflect knitting's international heritage by selecting special yarn.

Choose a yarn from another country, such as alpaca's wool from Peru or a bulky Icelandic yarn. Make a striped scarf in the colors of a favorite flag, such as the red, yellow, green, and black of many African flags. Choose a good luck color like Chinese red, or a muted heather tone reminiscent of the Scottish landscape.

Someone in the yarn shop can advise you on the size needles that are best for the yarn you've chosen, as well as how many stitches to cast on for the width you want.

11

Sip a hot drink.

There's nothing like a hot cup of something to warm you on a cold day!

A hot drink does more than warm the body, however. Did you know that offering someone a cup of tea or coffee is a gesture of welcome in many cultures? The Bedouin even have a saying to describe a generous person — "He makes coffee day and night!"

Tea is the national drink of Libya. It is poured over roasted hazelnuts and sugar, and is very sweet. It's greatly enjoyed by children as well as adults. The British are renowned tea drinkers, as are the Russians who use a *samovar* (SAH-moh-vahr), or special urn, to heat the water. Nowadays most *samovars* are electrified, but the traditional ones are brought out for picnics and special occasions.

Hot chocolate, or cocoa, is a favorite worldwide. Mexican children drink a frothy cup made with Mexican chocolate, which is a mixture of chocolate, sugar, cinnamon, and ground almonds. They also enjoy *atole* (ah-TOE-lay), a hot beverage thickened with corn meal.

Louder Than Words

People everywhere communicate not only with words but with gestures. There are ways to say "hello," "goodbye," and "I like you" without uttering a sound!

Here are a few of those ways, plus a special way to say "Be my friend!"—with a Valentine's card you make yourself!

St. Valentine's Day traces its origins to the ancient Roman lovers' festival called Lupercalia which was held each February. Only when an Italian priest named Valentino was martyred on February 14 in the 3rd century was the day dedicated to St. Valentine, and he became the patron saint of lovers. In Italy, the day is observed by adults only.

12

Compare greetings around the world.

How do you greet your friends when you see them? Do you say "hello" to adults in the same way? There are certain unwritten rules for greeting people, which differ around the world.

In France, for instance, children regularly shake hands with one another. A Korean child would be honored to shake the hand of an adult, but will more usually bow and nod his or her head. Instead of saying "Good morning," both Koreans and Somalis from Somalia ask, "Have you been in peace during the night?" or "Is it peace?"

Bowing is something many people around the world do as a form of greeting. In Japan, the bow is usually low, from the waist. In Malaysia, Malay children bow only slightly when greeting one another, as well as when passing on the street.

Most Hindus use the *namaste* (nah-MAHS-tay) gesture when they greet each other. They place their palms together as though in prayer, and nod their heads slightly. Most people also say "*Namaste*" while gesturing.

13

Show good manners.

Greeting people is considered good manners, a way of showing respect. There are other ways to show good manners, including these from around the world.

Children everywhere show respect to their elders in their speech. This is a "built-in" feature of many languages. For instance in Spanish, a child refers to a friend as *tu* (too), and addresses respected persons such as parents, teachers, and other adults as *Usted* (oo-STETH). Different verb forms are also used when speaking directly to friends versus adults.

In some African countries, it is considered bad manners to disappoint people. For this reason, questions that require a definite "yes" or "no" are avoided. A child might say to a friend, "Come to my house today if you like," rather than "Can you come to my house?" Parents are also more likely to say "not yet" instead of "no." Likewise, "perhaps" is more acceptable than "yes."

Your friends from other cultures may show good manners at home in these and other ways. How do they differ from what is considered polite in your family?

14

Make cards for St. Valentine's Day.

English children enjoy St. Valentine's Day in much the same way children in North America do. Families exchange cards, as do friends and classmates in school.

Have you ever made your own cards? Here's a simple card that's rather "surprising"! If you seal it shut with a small sticker, you can even do without an envelope.

Cut two pieces of paper, one 4″ x 8½″ (10 cm x 21.5 cm), the other 5½″ x 8½″ (14 cm x 21.5 cm). Fold both in half crosswise; set aside the smaller one. Cut a 1½″ x 2½″ (4 cm x 6 cm) piece from the top right-hand corner, as shown. Fold down along the dotted line, then snip this part into a heart shape.

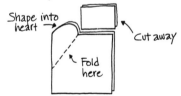

Push the heart so that it's folded up inside the card.

Glue the two cards together, carefully avoiding the heart. Decorate both inside and out. When the card is opened, the heart will pop up!

15

Give someone a hug.

How do people show they like you? Your mom might give you a great big hug, or a peck on the cheek. Your teacher might pat you on the back. Your best buddy might ruffle your hair affectionately.

Not if you live in Indonesia. There, and in other parts of the world, touching the head is considered bad luck. It is believed that the head is the home of the soul, and that it is easily harmed. A favorite aunt in Sumatra would be more likely to touch her niece's arm, or gently pinch her cheek.

In the Middle East and in Italy and Spain, boys and men outwardly show affection, embracing one another and kissing on both cheeks. Young children everywhere hold hands, but in many countries people enjoy this close contact well past childhood. It's a warm way of showing friendship.

How do you show people you like them? Are you and your family "huggers"? Then don't be shy . . . give someone a great big squeeze!

16

Compare gestures around the world.

People use gestures not only to show affection, but to communicate other things. You've seen how a bow can be used as a greeting. A shrug of the shoulders is a useful gesture to indicate "I don't know."

Gestures such as these are often used alone, or they are combined with words to emphasize a point. The Italians are said to "talk" with their hands, and it's true that they move their hands actively while they're speaking.

Body language, as communication with gestures is sometimes called, varies around the world. Some of these differences are described below. What other gestures can you think of, and what do they mean?

WIGGLES & SHAKES

In most places around the world, a horizontal shake of the head means "no." Not in Bulgaria and Sri Lanka, it doesn't! In those two countries it signifies "yes." To show you mean "no," you must nod your head up and down. In Greece, people jerk the head back, at the same time closing the eyes and raising the eyebrows, to indicate "no."

The Japanese use a special gesture to show they don't understand something, or don't know the answer to a question. They wave a hand back and forth in front of the face. Japanese children hook pinkies to show they intend to keep a promise. Italian kids trace an invisible cross on their chests to show the same.

In Korea and the Philippines, it's considered rude to beckon someone by moving the index finger back and forth. Instead, the hand is held palm-down, and the fingers wiggled.

17

Say "goodbye."

The English word "goodbye" is derived from the phrase "God be with you." Parting words in other languages are similar. In Spanish, it's *adios* (ah-dee-OHS), in French *adieu* (ah-DYUR). Both words literally mean "to God."

There are other ways to say "goodbye," however. English children shout "Cheerio!" when parting, and in Switzerland, Germany, and Italy they say *ciao* (chow) which is the informal way of saying "goodbye" in Italian.

A wave of the hand accompanies most goodbyes, at least in the West. In Japan, people bow when they part, and Hindus press their hands together and say, *"Namaste,"* just as they do when greeting one another.

In some households in India, it's considered a bad omen to say "goodbye." Instead people say, "Go and come back." If you are the one leaving, you announce, "I'm going and I will be back."

What other ways do you know of to indicate farewell?

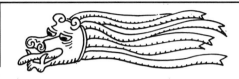

Benevolent Beasts

Not all beasts are fearsome creatures. Just think of beasts of burden, such as donkeys and camels. Or consider the dragons of Asia. The Chinese, for one, view dragons in a kindly light.

Meet some beasts beloved by children all over the world, including some animals that are kept as pets!

18

Make a dragon streamer for *Chun Jie*.

Chun Jie (choo-OON jee-EH), or "Spring Festival," falls at the beginning of the Chinese year.

Children help as homes are cleaned and painted, and other preparations made. On the eve of the new year, there's a fabulous feast in every home. Children are allowed to stay up late, in the belief this will bring long life to their parents.

The next day, everybody dresses in their best, complete with a new pair of shoes! Children are given money, presented in red envelopes. There will be plenty of treats for them in the next two weeks, including fireworks and parades.

The dragons that figure in Chinese folklore are everywhere, even wriggling through the streets (some dragon costumes are huge, with as many as 100 people supporting them!). Are children frightened by them? The younger ones may be speechless with awe, but the dragons are familiar creatures the children know of from stories.

You can make a dragon streamer for *Chun Jie*. Draw a dragon's head on a sheet of stiff paper. Color it, and cut it out. Staple or glue a strip of poster board to the underside of the head, as a handhold. Attach crepe paper streamers or ribbons to the back of the head. As you run, the streamers will dance behind you, in imitation of a dragon's writhing body.

SUPER SERPENTS

Chinese dragons are found everywhere! There are dragons thought to be supporting the mansions of the gods in the sky. Certain dragons live underground, guarding the jewels and metals found in the earth.

There are weather dragons, dragons that watch over rivers, and several different dragons in charge of protecting everyday objects, such as bells, bridges, even writing. The ancient Chinese also believed dragons could change form, and that they often assumed the shape of other animals as well as humans.

19

Play a beast game.

Many games around the world have something to do with beasts — both ferocious and tamer ones. In Kenya, kids play a game about hunting a leopard; in Iran, there's a game called "Wolf and Flock." Chinese children enjoy a game called "Catching the Dragon's Tail," honoring their beloved beasts.

This game is best played with a group of at least ten kids — the more, the merrier! It can be played either indoors or out. One person is chosen to be the head of the dragon; everybody else lines up behind him or her, each with his hands on the shoulders of the next person.

At a signal, the person at the head tries to catch the tail (the very last person in the line). With everybody squirming and trying to hold onto each other's shoulders, this isn't easy! If the head successfully catches the tail, he or she continues to be it. If the body breaks at any time, the head becomes the tail, and the next in line gets to be the head.

20

Read tales about good beasts.

Benevolent beasts crop up in folk tales all over the world. Have you heard of any of these?

The *Baku* (bah-koo) is a Japanese creature that supposedly lives on dreams. Children learn how it can be "willed" to eat a bad dream before it turns into a nightmare! The *Baku* is usually pictured as a stout creature with a long, trunk-like snout.

Greek mythology tells of benevolent beasts such as the winged horse Pegasus, and the Centaur (a creature that is half man and half horse). There are also tales about dolphins, real animals of course, but given extra powers in many of the stories.

In some tales, kind beasts are actually humans who have been turned into animals by an evil force. European folklore is full of these, including the Beast in *Beauty and the Beast* and the Frog in *The Frog Prince*.

What other tales about good beasts do you know?

BAKU

21

Draw some of the world's dinosaurs.

The fossilized remains of dinosaurs have been found all over the world. As you can imagine, kids everywhere are fascinated by these beasts that lived so long ago.

In all, over 350 different types of dinosaurs have been identified. Many are named for where they were discovered. The Edmontosaurus was found near Edmonton, Canada; the Saltasaurus in Salta, Argentina. Austrialia was home to some dinosaurs found nowhere else (just as its living animals are unique to that continent). Muttaburrasaurus is named for a town in Queensland, Australia.

Where did some of your favorite dinosaurs live? Choose a country and see if you can find out which dinosaurs lived there, and when. What did these beasts look like? Draw a picture of some dinosaurs in a likely setting. Who knows, maybe at some point 200 to 65 million years ago, there were dinosaurs making themselves at home right where you live now!

22

Visit a zoo.

Zoos are great places to look for some of the benevolent beasts from around the world. True, you won't find any dragons, but you'll discover lots of other amazing things!

Stand near an Asian elephant and you'll get a sense of the power of these animals that do the work of heavy machinery in Southeast Asia. You'll be amazed at the beauty of the national bird of India, the peafowl. Meet the stately, long-neck llama of Peru which is kept both as a beast of burden and for its fleece.

Today's zoos are research centers, educational institutions, and museums all rolled into one. You can witness the work being done to help save some the the world's endangered species. You can also learn something about the habitats animals and people share. Some walk-in exhibits at zoos are so realistic you can be fooled into thinking you're strolling through the Amazonian jungle, or diving underwater alongside penguins in Antarctica!

23

Care for a pet.

Caring for pets is one of the pleasures of growing up in many places throughout the world. Do you and your family keep any animals as pets? What kinds?

In some places, however, pets are a luxury many people cannot afford. Instead, children form bonds with farm and working animals. In Vietnam, the patient water buffalo that is used to plow rice fields and pull loads is treated like a member of the family. The Bedouin in the Middle East feel much the same way toward the cantankerous camels they herd and use as beasts of burden.

In parts of China, people capture wild birds and keep them caged as pets. As the Chinese become more prosperous, they are turning to other types of pets, including cats and dogs. In some places in China, however, dogs are eaten as food, and are treated like any other food animal.

A Little Extra

Because every four years the Gregorian calendar adds an extra day in February, this is a good time to look at some customs that have to do with little "extras."

That something "extra" might be a second helping at dinner, or extra time before going to bed. It may also mean using up extra foods before a religious fast.

For more on food, see October 15–21.

24

Have second helpings.

Having a second helping of food at mealtimes is something normal in many cultures. In fact, it's even expected in some.

In Japan, at least two bowls of rice are eaten at meals. Rice is called *gohan* (GOH-hahn), which is the same word for "meal," proof of its importance. Japanese children never finish off one dish at a time, rather they sip some soup or sample other dishes between bites of rice.

In homes around the world where the family gathers around a single, large communal dish of food, such as Ethiopia and Pakistan, each person in turn takes a mouthful, using just the right hand (considered the clean hand). Everyone continues eating until the food is gone. There are no "seconds" as such. In Bangladesh, it is customary for the men to eat first; the women and children share what is left.

In Malaysia, serving dishes are placed on the table and everyone helps himself onto a plate. The serving spoons, however, are never allowed to touch individual plates, which would make them "dirty."

25

Make a meal from leftovers.

Because refrigeration is relatively uncommon in many countries, ingredients for meals are usually purchased daily, and just enough food is made for each meal.

In some places, however, extra food is saved and turned into new meals. In Asia, left-over rice is reheated for lunch or a quick snack. Here's a recipe for such a dish from Thailand.

Fried Rice with Chicken and Curry Powder

2 tablespoons (30 ml) oil
2 garlic cloves, finely chopped
2 teaspoons (10 ml) curry powder
1 boneless chicken breast half, sliced
2½ cups (450 g) cooked rice
1 tablespoon (15 ml) soy sauce
1 tablespoon (15 ml) fish sauce
¼ teaspoon (1–2 ml) sugar

Heat the oil in a frying pan or wok; add the garlic and fry until golden brown. Stir in the curry powder; add the chicken, and cook until it turns white. Add the remaining ingredients, and cook until the rice is heated through.

Note: Fish sauce is an essential ingredient in Thai food. You may omit it if you are unable to find the bottled sauce at your market.

26

Compare fasting rituals.

Fasting, or going without food for a certain amount of time, is a part of many religions. Older children and adults, for instance, fast on *Yom Kippur*, the holiest day in the Jewish year. Fasting is a way to reflect on or atone for unkind deeds done during the year.

Christians "give up" certain foods for Lent, which is also a type of fasting. The French call the day before Lent *Mardi Gras* (MAR-dee grah), or "Fat Tuesday." They use up all the butter and fat in their homes by making *beignets* (bay-NYAY), delicious fried pastries. Some Christians also fast from Good Friday until Easter Sunday, celebrating at that time with a large meal.

Muslims, followers of Islam, fast each year during the month of *Ramadan* (RAH-mah-dahn), the ninth month of the Islamic year. They neither eat nor drink during the hours between sunrise and sunset. The meal each night, however, is often sumptuous! Children, elderly people, and those who are ill are not required to fast. In fact, in Bahrain, children encourage those who are fasting by singing songs. In return, they are given nuts and sweets.

27

Make *cascarones* for Carnival.

For Christians, the days before Lent (a 40-day period of penitence ending the day before Easter) are often very festive, filled with little "extras." In Switzerland, Brazil, and Trinidad, there are parades and street fairs, complete with revelers in costume. There's lots of rich food (last chance before Lent!), and good cheer.

In many countries, this time is known as Carnival (from the Latin *carnelevarium* which means "the removal of meat"). Pranksters, especially, have lots of fun. In Central and South America, everyone gets a laugh from cracking *cascarones* (cahs-car-OWN-ehs) over people's heads. These are decorated egg-shells filled with confetti. Crack! and the brightly colored bits of paper shower down.

You can make your own *cascarones* for this or any other festive occasion. The box below tells you how.

CRACKERS!

Cascarones can be filled with confetti or water (watch out!). Here's how to make the confetti-filled ones.

Cut a quarter-size opening in an egg by first making a hole at one end with a needle or nail, and then enlarging it with scissors. Remove the egg (be sure to save it for cooking); wash the shell carefully, and let dry.

Fill the eggshell with confetti. Use purchased confetti, or make your own with a paper punch, or by cutting thin strips of paper into tiny squares. Seal the opening in the egg with a small circle of tissue paper glued in place. Decorate the outside of the shell with paint or markers.

Cap with tissue paper circle

28

Ask to stay up late.

What time do you usually go to bed? It probably depends on whether it's a "school night," or if you get to sleep late the following morning. It's the same for kids everywhere.

You may find it easier getting to bed on time when it gets dark early, say in the winter. Come late spring, when the days are longer, it's hard to come in from outdoors to go to bed! It's hard, too, for kids living up near the Arctic Circle. That's because the sun is visible in the sky nearly every hour of the day during the middle part of June. (For more on this, see June 21.) Bedroom windows in northern Scandinavia and Canada have to be furnished with heavy shades and curtains to block out the light so that everyone can get some sleep!

29

Do something special on Leap Day.

This is a good day to do something you don't ordinarily do. After all, February 29 only comes once every 4 years! Some people call this Leap Day, others Leap Year Day.

Did you know that other calendars also have leap days, and in a few cases, leap months? The Buddhist and Jewish calendars both add an extra month every few years to bring their lunar calendars closer in agreement with the solar year. (For more on calendars, see pages 11 and 12.)

This is a good day to play Leap Frog or one of the jumping games played around the world (for more on these, see March 25–27). It's a good day to squeeze in an extra activity, or be extra nice to someone. Does today happen to be your birthday? Being born on the year's "extra" day is very special in itself!

Babes in Toyland

It should come as no surprise that kids everywhere enjoy playing with toys. But did you know many children make their own toys? Ready-made toys simply aren't as common in many countries as they are here.

Ahead are a few ideas for some homemade toys you can make yourself. Just think — you'll have twice the fun. You'll get the enjoyment of making the toys, plus the fun of playing with them!

1 Make toys from natural materials.

Did you know that outside your door is a giant toy shop? That's right — nature is a veritable warehouse filled with objects and materials just waiting to be turned into toys!

Different countries have different traditions for creating toys out of flowers, feathers, sticks, and stones. A lot depends on what resources are available in a particular region. Below are just a few of the clever ways children turn nature's plenty into playthings.

PETALS & PODS

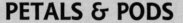

Girls in many countries turn flowers into petticoated dolls. Poppies are a popular choice in England. The flowers are cut from their stems and the petals are carefully turned inside out to form skirts. Extra pieces of stem are fashioned into arms and legs.

African children poke sticks into vegetables such as yams to make toy animals. In the jungle regions of that continent, children amuse themselves by making string figures using a length of bendable vine (for more on string figures, see October 8).

In Germany, older kids carve knobby bits of roots and branches into animals and human figures. Sticks are used to make pretend weapons all over the world, although Japanese boys find bamboo grass make especially fine swords.

Kids everywhere create miniature worlds from leaves, bark, lichen, and moss. Ukrainian children play with toys made from straw, while Peruvian and Czechoslovakian children often have dolls made from corn husks.

2 Launch a floating toy.

In the warmer regions of the world, children do most of their playing outdoors. If there's water nearby, you can be sure the kids will be playing with toys that float!

The simplest floating toy is a stick, of course, but what other things found in nature do kids turn into boats? Polish children have boat races with walnut shell halves. In Thailand, lotus blossoms make good floating craft.

Japanese children know how to make a short-lived boat from a square sheet of paper. Here's how:

Fold the paper in half; unfold. Fold the top and bottom edges so they meet at the center crease (1). Turn the paper over and fold the four corners down (2).

Fold the paper in half (3). Pull the layers apart at the longer edge (two layers to one side, and one to the other). At the same time, push up slightly at the bottom to form a boat (4).

Note: Place a tiny rock in the boat to keep it upright.

3

Line up your dolls for *Hina Matsuri.*

Japanese girls look forward to the third day of March when *Hina Matsuri* (HEE-nah maht-SOO-ree), or "Doll Festival," takes place. On this day, the family's collection of ceremonial dolls (handed down, in some cases, from one generation to the next) is put on display. A complete set of 15 dolls includes an emperor, empress, and members of the royal court, all in historically-correct costumes.

The girls themselves are also honored on this day. They may receive gifts and be taken out to dinner.

Have you ever seen some of the popular dolls from other countries? Russian *matryoshki* (mah-TROYSH-key) are nesting dolls that fit one inside the other. The Inuit of northern Canada make traditional dolls from caribou antler pieces held together with sinew strips. Scandinavian dolls are typically made from turned wood. Cloth dolls are made all over the world, and are often clothed in native costumes.

Do you have any dolls from other countries? Display them on March 3!

4

Make *migajón* miniatures.

Children all over the world love to play with miniatures.

You can make your own miniature playthings using an adaptation of a modeling material called *migajón* (mee-gah-HONE). Thought to have originated in Ecuador as a substitute for clay, *migajón* is used to make tiny toys and decorations throughout Central and South America today.

To make your own *migajón*, trim the crust from a piece of white bread; tear the bread into pieces. Using your hands, mix one tablespoon (15 ml) white glue into the bread. It will be *very* sticky at first, but will gradually become clay-like.

Use the *migajón* to mold miniatures of all sorts, from tiny tea sets and food for dolls to figures that can sit in toy cars. Let the bread "clay" air dry, or bake in a 200°F (100°C) oven for an hour or more until hard (turn the pieces periodically to speed the drying). Use acrylic paints to decorate your miniatures if you like.

Migajón can also be tinted with food coloring before it is modeled.

5

Make a tumbling toy.

Acrobatic toys are popular in many countries, including China where this tumbling man is thought to have originated.

You can make your own tumbler from poster board scraps, felt, glue, and a heavy ball. A steel ball works best so ask a local auto repair garage for a worn ½" (12 mm) wheel bearing.

Glue a 1" × 2½" (2.5 cm × 6 cm) piece of poster board into a cylinder, slightly larger than the ball. Cut two poster board circles. Glue one to one end of the cylinder; insert the ball, and cap off the other end with the other circle.

Cut a body from felt, following the pattern below. Fold the upper body in half, insert the cylinder, and glue securely. Draw a face on the cylinder.

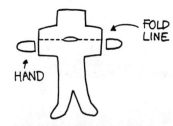

Place the tumbling man on a cloth-covered angled surface, and watch him turn over and over!

6

Try a toss-and-catch toy.

Some toys are trickier than they look! Have you ever played with a toss-and-catch toy, the kind where tethered rings are tossed into the air and caught on a stick?

Toys that require skill—and patience!—are common all over the world. Many are ancient toys, once used in developing hand-eye coordination (useful for hunting). The ring and stick version was common among many Native American peoples. In Colombia, children play with a similar toy where a ball is caught in a cup.

Make your own toss-and-catch toy. Tie a 16" (40 cm) length of string to one end of a short stick. Slip the string through five curtain rings or rubber canning jar rings; tie the end of the string to the very last ring. Toss the rings in the air . . . and try to catch them!

The Sound of Music

Most Africans, it is said, are born, live their lives, and die within earshot of drums. Music plays a very important part in their lives.

Children in other countries grow up listening to various types of instrumental music, often learning to play an instrument themselves when they are young.

Here are some of the types of instrumental music found around the world, as well as a few other kinds of sounds!

7

Listen to instrumental music from around the world.

Music is sometimes referred to as "food for the ears" — an apt description! Different cultures and countries have their own musical traditions, and the best way you can learn about these is to listen to some of the beautiful music from around the world.

Check your library for recordings of instrumental music from other countries, or ask a friend from another culture if he or she has tapes you may listen to. Better yet, check your area for concerts and festivals that feature international music. Watching how instruments are played adds greatly to the enjoyment of music.

Instrumental music is often played by a group of performers. Some of these groups are described below. Which are you familiar with?

NOTEWORTHY

All over the world, people enjoy making music in groups. The Western orchestra is a particularly large group. There are as many as 25 different instruments in a full-sized orchestra (with as many as 105 musicians playing them!).

The Javanese *gamelan* (GAH-may-lahn) is a percussion orchestra made up of various types of gongs, wooden and metal xylophones, and cymbals.

Japanese classical music called *gagaku* (gah-GAH-koo) is played on eight instruments, several of which lay flat on the floor. Classical music in India is played on only three instruments. The *sitar* (SIH-tar), a large lute-like instrument, provides the melody, and the other two instruments provide the accompaniment.

Other musical groups are made up of just one type of instrument. In New Guinea, side-blown flutes ranging in size from 10″ (25 cm) to almost six feet (1.8 m) are played together.

8

Make a drum.

Drums are the most important instruments in many African countries. They provide the rhythm for dances, although some drums such as the Nigerian *iya-ilu* (ee-YAH-ee-LOO) are known as "talking drums" because they are used to send messages.

You can make your own drum to beat to music or dance to (for more on dance, see August 15–21). You'll need a container such as a terracotta flowerpot or empty round oatmeal box, a paper grocery bag, and paper tape (the kind that is moistened with water to make it stick).

Cut a circle from the paper bag about 4″ (10 cm) larger than the container's open end. Dampen the circle and tape it in place, making pleats, or folds, to ease in fullness. Wrap tape all the way around for extra stability.

Wrap tape around

Once the paper dries, the drumhead will be nice and tight. You can use your hands to produce the sound, or use a short stick as a drumstick.

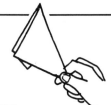

9

Learn to play an instrument.

Children all over the world are encouraged to learn to play instruments. Do you play or want to play an instrument? Which one?

In England and Germany, schoolchildren learn to play the recorder. Japanese children get an early start on the violin using the *Suzuki* (soo-ZOO-key) method. In Hungarian schools, music is taught using the *Kodály* (koh-DIE) method, inspired by the Hungarian music educator who believed music was a way for children to get in touch with all forms of art.

In African countries, such as Ghana, children play percussion instruments such as drums. A child who learns very quickly might study under a master drummer.

Chinese children have a choice: they may learn to play traditional instruments or Western instruments, such as the piano. Instruction is offered at Children's Palaces — centers where sports, music, and other arts are taught.

10

Trace an instrument's origins.

Many musical instruments have a very long history. Pick a favorite instrument and see what you can learn about its origins and its close relatives around the world.

Do you like the sound of the flute? Stone Age flutes made from bone are among the oldest surviving instruments. Today flutes come in all shapes and sizes; some are blown at one end, others side-blown. There are even nose flutes, that are sounded by breath from the nostrils, found in Polynesia, where nose breath is thought to have special powers.

There is a wide variety of stringed instruments, as well. They range in size from the single-stringed *rebab* played with a bow, found in the Middle East, to the Japanese *koto*, a long zither-like instrument which is laid on the floor. It has 13 strings made from silk.

You'll discover many different types of reed instruments, brass instruments, and members of the percussion group, too.

Iraqi rebab

11

Raise a ruckus on *Purim.*

Jewish children all over the world have a special fondness for *Purim,* one of the happiest of Jewish holidays.

The holiday commemorates an event in Jewish history when King Ahasuerus of Persia ruled. He had a wicked advisor named Haman who wished to have all the Jews in the area killed. The King was going to draw *purim* (purr-EEM), or "lots" (like drawing a name out of a hat), to determine the day of execution. Somehow, Ahasuerus's wife, Esther (who was herself Jewish but had carefully kept it a secret), was able to persuade her husband to hang Haman from the gallows instead. The people were saved!

Every year this story is told in Jewish homes and synagogues. Children often dress up and reenact the historic event. In some communities, schoolchildren get to wear funny clothes to school in celebration of the happy occasion. All over the world on this day, whenever wicked Haman's name is mentioned, people stamp their feet and make as much noise as possible. You can see why kids think this is a great holiday!

12

Make a banger.

Some noises are definitely not music, but they're fun to make anyway!

Kids living near coastal areas look for dried seaweed, such as rockweed or bladderwrack. The bladders, or hollow sacs that keep the seaweed afloat in the water, make a nice pop when they are pinched between the fingers.

Children everywhere know how to make another popper — or banger — from paper. You need a large rectangle of paper, such as 12" × 18" (30 cm x 45 cm) drawing paper. Fold it in half, first one way and then the other; unfold. Fold the four corners so they meet the horizontal line (1). Fold the paper in half (2).

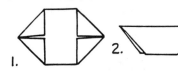

1.

2.

Bring the two points down so the edges meet (3). Fold in half so the squared-off section is to the inside.

3.

To produce the sound, hold the bottom point and thrust your arm down quickly. The inside portion will pop out with a bang!

Believe It or Not

Lots of people all over the world are superstitious — and who's to say, maybe they have cause to be. There are plenty of little things about life that simply cannot be explained.

On the pages ahead you can compare superstitions as well as tales of legendary monsters and unbelievable feats. And just in case, there are a couple of good luck charms that might come in handy someday!

13

Name some legendary monsters.

Werewolves, vampires, and ghosts . . . these send shivers down the spines of children everywhere!

The idea of werewolves (men who can change themselves into wolves) no doubt grew out of a fear of wolves. In some regions of the world, scary stories feature other animal beings. In India and Cambodia, for instance, children quake at the thought of were-tigers. In parts of Africa, tales are told of were-hyenas, were-lions, and were-leopards.

Vampires, or the "undead" as supposedly they prefer to be called, figure in dozens of tales from Ireland to Polynesia. Perhaps you've heard of ghouls. The original ghoul was said to be an Arabic demon who feasted on human blood.

Ghosts, of course, inhabit every country. It's often the unhappy ones who create mischief. We call a noisy ghost a *poltergeist,* which is a German word meaning just that. The ghosts of animals supposedly haunt people in various countries, too. There's an old Danish superstition that claims if you bury a live pig in a wall it will become a ghost. Who's to say?

14

Tell a ghost story.

Almost everyone loves scary stories, at least when they know there's nothing to fear. Do you know any good ghost stories?

Children in Costa Rica are told tales about *La Cegua* (lah SAY-gwah), an apparition that is said to seat itself behind anyone riding past a cemetery on horseback late at night. Irish children scare one another with tales of the Banshee, a female spirit whose screams can sometimes be heard.

One Japanese ghost story is about a shrine near a waterfall. The waterfall is believed to be made from the writhing figures of ghosts. In the shrine is a box for coins left as offerings for the dead. A young woman is dared to visit the shrine late at night, proving she has done so by bringing the money box back with her. Naturally, this displeases the ghosts who follow her home crying, "Greedy woman!" Only when she promises to fill the box to the top with her own money is she no longer plagued by the ghosts.

Ask your friends from other cultures to tell you some of the scary stories they know . . . if you dare!

15

Read some tall tales.

Some of the best stories told around the world are those we call tall tales. Also known as exaggerated tales, these stories certainly do stretch the truth!

Many tall tales — not surprisingly — are about giants. From Scandinavia to South Africa, these enormous beings left their imprint on the world (sometimes literally, if you believe the tales about lakes formed from giant footprints!). Some of these giants were fearsome creatures, but others were kind and helpful. Russian children are told about a friendly giant who lived on a tiny island far from land. He once saved a luckless sailor named Ivan, scooping him up from the sea and carrying him to safety.

Other tales tell of people with superhuman strength or powers. You may know the German legend of the Pied Piper of Hamelin. When the piper was not paid for leading the town's rats away with the sound of his flute, he led the town's children away in the same way. Some historians feel the story may be based on fact, and that it may be about the children who were victims of the plague in the 13th century. What do you think?

16

Learn some superstitions from other cultures.

Are you at all superstitious? Do you "knock on wood," for example, to bring good luck, or avoid walking under ladders (most people agree this is simply common sense!)?

Superstitions such as these are rooted in ancient beliefs — most so old no one remembers how they became a part of our lives. Other centuries-old superstitions gave us many of the activities and customs that enrich our lives today, from blowing out birthday candles to decorating our homes with evergreens each winter.

Below is a sampling of superstitions from around the world. Which of these have you heard of? What others can you think of?

JUST IN CASE!

Greek children ward off evil by making "horns" with their index and little finger held upright.

People in Thailand always step over thresholds in doorways. They do not want to harm a spirit that is thought to dwell in the thresholds of homes and other buildings.

In China, odd numbers (1, 3, 5) are considered unlucky.

Italian children "touch metal" for good luck.

Many Native Americans believe it is bad luck to kill a spider.

Malaysians believe stepping over anyone resting on the floor is unlucky.

The Japanese say if you sneeze once that means someone is saying something nice about you.

17

Make a good luck charm.

People have been putting their faith in good luck charms for thousands of years. What kinds of things do you wear or carry with you that bring you luck?

People in Tibet often wear a tiny silver box called a *gao* (rhymes with *cow*) around their necks. It's filled with prayers and items that have been blessed by a Buddhist monk. The Yoruba of Nigeria wear protective charms called *giri-giri* (GEAR-ee GEAR-ee), which might be a leather band worn on the arm or a goat horn filled with "spirit powder."

In the Middle East, a charm known as the "hand of Fatima" is thought to protect its wearers from harm. You can make your own to wear around your neck. You need 16-gauge wire, wire-cutters, and some thin ribbon.

Bend a piece of wire to form a hand shape, twisting the two ends to make a loop. Snip off any extra. Thread the ribbon through the loop, tie securely, and wear with assurance!

Fatima was the daughter of the prophet Muhammed.

18

Make a wishing *daruma*.

The *daruma* (dah-ROO-mah) doll is a Japanese folk toy, named for Bodhidharma (also known as Dharma), the 6th-century founder of Zen Buddhism.

Daruma dolls come in many styles, but all are squat figures without arms or legs. According to legend, Dharma spent nine years meditating, during which time he lost the use of his arms and legs. One type of *daruma* has no eyes either, and is used to bring good luck. One eye is painted at the beginning of a new venture (or new year), or when a wish is made. Only when the task is completed, or the wish comes true, is the doll given its other eye.

You can make a simple "wishing" *daruma* from papier mâché. Cover a small round balloon with paper strips and a paste made from equal parts of flour and water. Make a coiled base so the *daruma* can stand. When it's completely dry, paint the doll to resemble the one here. But don't paint the eyes — leave those until you're ready to start a big project or make a wish!

Spring Fling

The arrival of spring is eagerly awaited in many places around the world. Gardeners — and children — can't wait to get their hands in the dirt!

Ahead you'll discover ways to get a head start planning a garden, as well as how to make paper garlands and springing toys in celebration of the season.

19

Sow seeds indoors.

Now is a good time to start planning an international food and flower garden. It's too early to dig in the dirt in much of North America, but some vegetables, such as peppers and tomatoes, have a long growing season and benefit from being started indoors early.

Need some ideas for plants to grow? Check out the suggestions on pages 64 and 65. Purchase seeds and note which can be started indoors (the backs of the seed packets will tell you everything you need to know). You can also sow fast-growing plants such as lettuce indoors year-round. The box below tells you how!

HEAD START

Get a jump on nature! Start seeds indoors using purchased potting soil and paper milk cartons.

Split the cartons in half lengthwise and lay them on their sides. Punch some holes in the bottoms with a fat nail. Fill the cartons with thoroughly dampened potting soil, squeezing out the excess water with your hands first.

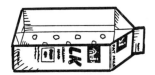

Plant seeds about 2″ (6 cm) apart, barely covering the tiny ones with soil; bury the larger ones ¼″ (.5 cm) to ½″ (1 cm) below the surface. Label the cartons and carefully slide them into plastic bags. Check daily for signs of sprouting.

As soon as the seeds sprout, remove the bags and place the plants in a sunny window or under fluorescent lights. Leave the lights on for 12–16 hours each day, positioning the bulbs about 3″ (8 cm) above the plants. You'll need to raise the light or lower the plants as they grow. Your parents can help you figure out the best way to do this.

Transplant the seedlings as they require more room, and "feed" them now and again (ask for organic fertilizer at your garden center). Now sit back and watch your plants grow!

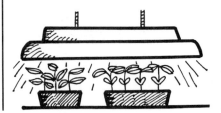

20

Smell the air on the first day of spring.

The first day of spring (or first day of autumn for those living in the Southern Hemisphere) falls on or about March 20. Do something special to welcome in the season!

Throw open your windows and breathe in the fresh air. That's what Egyptians do in celebration of spring. On the Monday following Coptic (Egyptian Christian) Easter, families go on picnics. They call this day *Shm al-Nessim* (shuhm ahl ness-EEM), which means "breathing in the breeze!"

People in Poland usher in the season with an ancient custom of their own. They dress a large straw doll in old clothes and lots of brightly colored ribbons. Once the ice has broken up in the rivers, townspeople parade down to the riverbank and toss the doll — which represents winter — right into the water.

Your friends from other cultures may know of other ways that spring is celebrated. Add or adapt some of those observances to your own way of welcoming in this first day of the season of awakenings!

21

Eat foods that begin with "s" for *Noruz.*

In Iran, the arrival of spring is heralded with great fanfare. *Noruz* (noh-ROOZ) means "the new day," and is also the first day of the Iranian year.

During the nearly two weeks of the *Noruz* celebration, families do many special things together. One of these is sitting down to a traditional *Noruz* dinner. Seven foods beginning with the letter "s" (that represent the seven archangels of God in the Zoroastrian religion) are placed on a white cloth spread on the floor. They include *serkeh* (vinegar) and *senjed* (olives). What foods beginning with "s" would you serve?

The family also gathers together a mirror, some brightly colored eggs, candles, and the *Quran,* the Islamic holy book. The children all watch to see if the eggs will move. According to legend, the earth trembles on the first day of the year. Nowadays, great cannons announce the arrival of spring, so almost certainly the earth *and* the eggs move!

22

Make paper garlands.

While it may *be* spring, it doesn't look like it yet in much of North America. Add a burst of color to your home with paper garlands.

Paper decorations are popular throughout Asia, and in countries such as Cambodia, children often make their own. Paper garlands such as these are sometimes made from tissue paper, but they are easier to assemble from a heavier paper, such as gift wrap.

Cut the paper into 6" (15 cm) circles. Fold each circle in half, then in half again, and in half once more. Cut a series of curved lines in each, as shown below.

Open the circles. Glue the first two circles together at the four points indicated (1). Glue the next circle at the middle (2).

Continue adding circles, alternately gluing them at the outer edges and at the middle. Let dry; then pull at the first and last circles to stretch out the garland, and hang in a doorway, window, or on a wall.

23

Fold a springing frog.

A square sheet of paper can be turned into a springing toy. Here's how!

Use origami paper or cut your own 6" (15 cm) square from thin paper. Place the paper colored-side down. Fold in half one way and then the other. Unfold completely (1). Now fold each corner to the center (2).

1.   2.

Fold two sides in to meet at the middle, as shown (3). Fold the bottom up (4).

3.   4.

Fold the sides in so that the points meet halfway (5). Then fold the bottom up along the creaseline visible at the back (6).

5.   6.

Fold the bottom section in half (7) and the top point down (8).

7.   8.

To make the frog jump, press your finger down on its back and then slide your finger off. Watch it fly!

24

Play on a springboard.

Children's playgrounds all over the world have swings and slides, climbing bars and see-saws. But in some places some of this playground equipment is used a little differently.

Take Korea, for example, where see-saws are constructed and used in a slightly different way. A long board is centered on a low support, and one child stands on one end of it. Another child jumps down onto the free end of the board, sending the first child up into the air!

You can make your own springboard set-up from a sturdy plank positioned on top of a thick log or large, flat stone. Set it on grass or sand so you have a soft place to land. Take turns with your friends jumping on the board and being sprung into the air.

Jump for Joy

Easter is a Christian holiday commemorating the time Jesus Christ is believed to have risen from the dead. According to legend, the sun jumped for joy on that day, so it's fitting that we look at ways of jumping.

Decorating eggs for Easter is popular in many countries. Ahead you'll find a nice way to display yours, as well as a delicious recipe that uses up all those leftover yolks and whites!

25

Jump rope.

Jumping rope is something children enjoy doing all over the world. Just as in North America, kids take turns jumping and turning the rope, usually chanting to the rhythm of the rope.

What are some of the jump rope rhymes you know? Ask your friends from other cultures to chant (and translate) some of their favorites.

Double Dutch is a version of jump rope that originated in — you guessed it! — the Netherlands. Two long ropes are swung at the same time in opposite directions. You have to be sure-footed to jump this way.

In China, children play *tiao pi jin* (tee-OW pee zjeen), or "rubber rope." You may know this as Chinese jump rope. Two people stretch a long circular elastic rope around their ankles. The jumping players jump in and out of the ropes, sometimes catching them with their feet and crossing them. The rope is raised little by little to make the game more challenging.

26

Invent a hopscotch game.

Hopscotch is another jumping game played wherever a bare patch of ground or pavement can be found. There are literally hundreds of variations, some of which you may know yourself.

Why not invent your own rules and course for hopscotch? Here are some diagrams from around the world to give you some ideas.

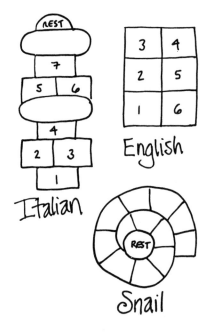

Burmese children play hopscotch in a squatting position, with their hands on hips.

27

Play *Alquerque.*

Alquerque (ahl-CARE-kay) is the Spanish name for an ancient board game that originated in the Middle East. For two players, it's one of many games where playing pieces capture one another by jumping. Can you think of other games played like this? If you said chess or checkers, you're right!

You can make your own *Alquerque* board by drawing the line design shown below on a 12" (30 cm) square of poster board (use a ruler for best results). Use checkers, buttons, or colored pieces of paper as playing pieces (12 per player), setting them up as indicated by the black and white circles.

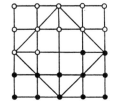

In Spain, the game is played like this: Pieces move along the lines one space at a time in any direction. You must jump and capture your opponent's pieces whenever there's an opportunity, otherwise your piece goes to your opponent. You may also make multiple jumps. The winner is the first to capture all of his or her opponent's pieces.

28

Make an egg tree for Easter.

This year decorate and display Easter eggs on an Easter tree.

The Easter tree is thought to have originated in the Netherlands, but its popularity has spread throughout Europe. A branch from a tree or bush not yet in bloom is cut and placed in a vase of water or anchored in a pot of moist soil. Willow branches are popular in Germany, while the Swedes favor birch branches. Choose one of these or a flowering specimen such as forsythia or apple.

Lightweight Easter eggs, such as those made from blown eggshells, are perfect for hanging on your tree. To blow eggs, poke a small hole at each end of an egg with a sharp pin. Holding the egg over a bowl, blow hard through one hole. The yolk and white will come out the other hole. Wash the shells out with water, and let dry. (See March 29 for one way to use up the yolks and whites.)

Decorate the shells in any number of ways. Dye them as you would any eggs; decorate them with markers; apply tissue paper cut-outs using a decoupage lacquer.

Make hangers for the decorated eggs by breaking wooden toothpicks in half and tying a length of thread to the middle of each. Push the stick all the way into the hole at the top of an egg. Pull the thread up carefully until you feel the stick is lodged in place horizontally. Tie the thread to a branch.

Be sure to keep your "tree" watered. Before long, the bare branches will be covered with the first blossoms or leaves of the year.

Ukrainian Easter eggs are among the most beautiful in the world. They are decorated using a wax-resist technique. Here are some of the traditional designs and what they symbolize.

Good health   Fertility   Life and Growth

29

Bake *flan*.

Turn all those leftover egg yolks and whites into a delicious dessert called *flan* (flahn). This is one of the most popular desserts in Spain and the Americas.

Flan

1½ cups (300 g) sugar
2 cups (500 ml) milk
4 eggs, beaten

Melt 1 cup (200 g) sugar in a heavy saucepan, stirring constantly. When it's at the runny, dark stage, pour it into a 1-quart (1-liter) casserole dish. Swirl to coat the dish; set aside.

Heat the milk in another pan until it is very hot, but not boiling. Pour slowly into a bowl containing the beaten eggs and ½ cup (100 g) sugar. Mix well; pour into the casserole dish.

Place the dish into a shallow pan of water and bake in a preheated 350°F (180°C) oven for about 1½ hours, or until a knife inserted into the *flan* comes out clean. Run a knife along the outside of the *flan*, place a plate over the dish, and turn upside down. Serve warm, or refrigerate until thoroughly chilled.

EASTER BEST

Eggs are for decorating and hanging on Easter trees, but don't forget the ones the Easter hare or rabbit leaves behind!

In some European countries, such as France, children hunt for eggs that the Easter bells (not bunny) have left. As the story is told, each year church bells travel to Rome to visit the Pope and pick up eggs (they say this is why the bells are silent following the mass on the Thursday before Easter).

When the bells ring on Easter morning, the children run outdoors to search for the eggs.

Children everywhere enjoy decorating eggs, but in Greece they also enjoy challenging one another to egg-knocking contests. Hardboiled eggs, which are usu-ally dyed red on "Red Thursday" before Easter, are used. Two players face one another, each holding an egg with the pointed end up. The eggs are knocked together, and the winner holds the egg that cracks last.

In Sweden, Easter isn't complete without fireworks. The noise is thought to frighten away witches! Swedish girls also dress up as hags and go from house to house asking for treats.

Laughter is the Best Medicine

There's nothing like a good laugh to make you feel better. No wonder they say laughter is the best medicine!

A lot of humor relies on the richness of language, as you'll see ahead. But come the first day of April you'll need something else — to be able to keep a straight face!

30

Make up some riddles.

Do you know any riddles? You know, like this old favorite:

What has four wheels and flies?

The answer, of course, is a garbage truck! Riddles like this are found all over the world. In fact, riddles are thought to be the oldest and most widespread type of word game.

British children enjoy riddles that are told in rhyming verse. Do you know the answer to this one?

**Little Nanny Netticoat
With a white petticoat
And a red nose.
The longer she stands,
The shorter she grows.**

Give up? It's a candle! In Hungary, children are asked to solve this: "A queen sits on her chair. She wears a white gown, and her tears fall into her lap." The answer is also a candle.

Here's a clever Chinese riddle:

Who wears a basket on his head, and has two pairs of scissors to cut his meat, and two pairs of chopsticks with which to eat?

The answer is a crab.

Bantu children of East Africa are fooled by this riddle — until they learn the answer!

What is the white hut that has no door?

The answer is an egg.

Some riddles use letters of the alphabet, either in the question or the answer.

Why is Paris like the letter F?

Because it's the capital of France.

Your friends from other cultures may know some riddles they can share with you. Do the same for them. Then make up some of your own!

31

Read some international comics.

Comic books may not be great literature, but kids everywhere love them! Some of the cartoon and funny paper characters you know, such as Superman and Snoopy, are familiar to kids all over the world. Most countries also publish their own comics, too.

Nigerian children eagerly read about the exploits of *Pa Ajasco* (pah ah-JAHS-coh), a clever boy who is a bit of a trickster. The adventures of *Samir* (sah-MEER) and *Meeky* (MEE-key), two boys who are friends, are well known in Egypt. Throughout South America, kids giggle over *Malfalda* (mahl-FAHL-dah), the spunky heroine of a comic strip from Argentina.

You and your international pen pal can exchange comic books in the mail. Even if you're unable to read the words in the comics you are sent, you may be able to figure out what's happening by looking at the pictures.

1

Fool a friend on *Premier Avril.*

Premier Avril (preh-me-YEAH ah-VREEL), or "April First," may sound just like any other day, but the French have a very special April Fools' Day tradition. Children try to pin a paper *poisson d'Avril* (pwah-SAW da-VREEL), or "April fish," on their friends' clothing without getting caught—not an easy thing to do when everyone is watching his or her back! Today is a day for fooling family and friends, and for a special seasonal treat—fish-shaped chocolates.

Mexican children fool one another in December on Holy Innocents Day. How this sad occasion meant to honor the children sentenced to death by Herod in Bethlehem became a day of tomfoolery is a bit of a mystery. The kids try to trick one another into handing over small possessions. If they're successful, the kids chant a verse that roughly translates as "Innocent little dove, you've let yourself be tricked. Now this item of yours belongs to me!"

2

Read a trickster tale.

Every culture has its share of trickster tales, stories usually about animals that trick others in order to accomplish some goal. Most of these tricksters are not bad; rather they triumph over hardships by being clever.

Anansi (ah-NAHN-see) the spider is one of these. The Ashanti of Ghana tell many Anansi stories, but he also pops up in other countries throughout West Africa. So admired is he that there is a proverb from Ghana that states:

The wisdom of Anansi is greater than that of all the world.

The raven is a trickster in many Native American stories. In one Inuit tale, he is outwitted by the marmot, another trickster! Raven is tired of being taunted by some sea birds who call him a "dirty thing" because he eats only carrion, or dead animals. To prove he's not dirty, Raven attempts to eat Marmot, who tricks Raven into dancing with his eyes closed, allowing Marmot to slip away to safety!

3

Dress up like a clown.

Clowns delight children with their silly antics in many cultures. In Asia, for instance, clowns are an important part of traditional theater. An Indian clown named *Vidusaka* (vee-doo-SAH-kah) helps explain the action during performances of the Hindu epics, the *Mahabharata* and the *Ramayana,* while at the same time making everyone laugh.

You can dress—and act—like the popular French clown, the mime. Mimes usually wear simple clothing and often just paint their faces white, with a touch of black, to make their facial expressions really stand out. Make up your face in this way with Halloween makeup.

Practice some of the ways mimes show emotions without words (how would you show surprise or puzzlement?). Use exaggerated movements to indicate invisible props (pretend you're moving something heavy or slippery). Work up a funny skit in mime and perform it for your friends!

4

Play Charades.

Put your miming talents to the test—with a game of Charades!

Charades is an old French game that is very popular in England and the United States. You and your friends can make the game even more international by acting out the names of different countries.

Divide yourselves into two teams. One team chooses a word and whispers it to the person on the other team chosen to act out that word for his or her teammates.

Let's say the word is Hungary. Using only gestures to mime the word, the actor might divide the word into syllables (indicating this with a chopping motion). He could convey the first syllable, "hung," by putting his hands around his throat. Or he could choose to act out the entire word, rubbing his belly and looking hungry!

If his teammates' guesses are along the right lines, the actor uses a beckoning motion; if wrong, he shows this with a brushing away movement. Once the word is guessed (and a time limit is sometimes put on this), the other team is given a chance to act out a word chosen for them by the first team.

To Your Health!

There's a lot each and every one of us can do to feel our very best. By eating the proper foods, getting enough exercise, and visiting a doctor and dentist regularly, we can make sure our bodies are in tip-top shape.

Ahead are some of the ways children around the world look after themselves, starting with a nutritious breakfast!

5

Start your day with breakfast.

Breakfast is one of the most important meals of the day. Your body can really use some fuel after going without for so many hours.

What do you like to eat for breakfast? Here are some international favorites kids around the world enjoy.

The Japanese start their day with *miso* (MEE-soh) soup, a soy paste broth, and rice. Rice is found in most Asian breakfast bowls, although in northern China, where wheat is eaten regularly, fried bread dipped in soy milk is typical breakfast fare.

Oats have an important place on the Scottish breakfast table. Porridge is very popular, a dish you probably call hot oatmeal.

While you may enjoy English muffins in the morning, in England these are most popular at tea time in the afternoon. There they are called scones (rhymes with lawns). Do the Danes eat Danish pastry? Yes they do, but in Denmark it is known as *Wienerbrot* (vee-nehr-BRURH), which means "Vienna bread!"

6

Do your exercises.

Regular exercise is one of the best ways to make our bodies healthy. Running around will help keep you fit, but you can also make your body stronger and more flexible with specific exercises.

The Chinese are great believers in *Tai Chi* (tie jee), graceful, dance-like exercises. Schoolchildren do these exercises as well as required eye exercises (they massage the forehead and alongside the eyes for five minutes while their eyes are closed) several times each day.

Hatha Yoga is an Indian method of stretching and toning the muscles that is also very relaxing. The specific exercises have such names as Tree, Cobra, and Candle. The picture below illustrates the two parts of the Candle exercise for you to try.

What other types of exercises do you know? Do your body a favor—do some exercises!

HOLDING POSITION   RELEASING POSITION

7

Try a cold remedy for World Health Day.

In honor of the World Health Organization, a branch of the United Nations founded on this day in 1948, try some cold remedies found around the world.

There is no cure for the common cold, of course, but there are many ways people try to make themselves feel better when they have a cold. From India to Italy, many people think eating garlic helps (it is said that eating lots of garlic and onions actually *prevents* colds). In China, ginger is thought to be effective against colds.

Herbal teas are drunk all over the world to help relieve cold symptoms. Mint tea is especially good for clearing a stuffed nose, while a tea made from rose hips (the fruit of the rose) is valued because of its high vitamin C content.

Russian children are served a nourishing custard-like drink that has rum in it whenever they feel a cold or other illness coming on. It has a silly made-up name that makes them laugh—*gogol'-mogol'* (GOH-gohl MOH-gohl)!

8

Wash up with soap and water.

People everywhere regularly wash their bodies to get rid of germs — and just plain old dirt!

Most cultures use soap for this. Indian soap has clove oil added to it, which is thought to kill bacteria. Olive oil, soothing to the skin, is a major ingredient in many Greek and Spanish soaps.

In many countries, washing up is accompanied with a good scrub. The dried insides of fibrous gourds called loofahs are used in the Middle East. You can grow your own loofah gourds. Lots of seed companies carry the seeds.

Which do you prefer — taking baths or showers? The box below describes some of the different ways kids around the world like to get clean.

WATERWORKS

Traditional Japanese families bathe in a tub full of hot water. One by one, everybody washes with soap *outside* the tub, rinsing off completely before getting into the soothing water. Some families bathe together (especially when the children are young); in other families, each person gets a turn to soak in the same water.

Many people in Greece use public baths. There are separate areas for men and for women (young boys usually go with their mothers). Some public baths are like a shallow swimming pool; others are private tubs enclosed within tiny rooms.

Finnish families in rural areas enjoy an invigorating cleansing in a *sauna* (SOW-nah, sow rhyming with cow), a small building filled with steam. It's very hot in a *sauna* and children usually don't stay long. Some hardy adults end a stay in a *sauna* by going outside and rolling in the snow!

9

Brush your teeth.

In countries like Zaïre, where refined sugar is rarely eaten, tooth decay is not a problem. But for most children, brushing teeth and visiting a dentist regularly is a life-long habit that begins in childhood.

Norwegian children fear *Tan-Verk Trollet* (tahn vairk TROH-let), the toothache troll, who is said to move into the mouths of sleeping children who haven't brushed their teeth regularly!

In exchange for baby teeth, children in many countries receive money and small gifts. These await children in the morning if a tooth was left under their pillow the night before. The Tooth Fairy makes this exchange in England, but Spanish children expect to be visited by *Ratoncito Perez* (rah-tone-SEE-toh PEAR-ace), or "Perez, the Little Mouse."

In China, children have a different custom. Upper baby teeth are buried in the ground, which is thought to encourage the new upper teeth to grow down. Bottom teeth are tossed onto rooftops, in hopes that the replacement teeth will grow up.

10

Propose a toast.

On special occasions in many countries, the host or head of the family proposes a toast before the start of a meal. With glasses raised, everyone listens while the occasion or someone present at the table is honored. Sometimes the toast is "to everyone's health."

At your next special family gathering or when you invite some friends over to share a meal with you, honor the occasion with a traditional toast from another country or culture. Here are a few that mean "to health!"

Na zdorov 'ye (nahz DROHV-yah) — **Russian**

Salud (sah-LOOTH) — **Spanish**

Skol (skohl) — **Danish**

Lechim (leh HIGH-em) — **Hebrew**

Fun in the Sun

In Thailand and Burma, the solar New Year is observed each April. As you'll see, people in that part of the world certainly have fun during this hottest part of their year.

You can have fun in the sun, too. Ahead are some ways to honor the closest star to our planet — the life-giving, warmth-making sun!

11

Pack a picnic basket.

For people around the world who normally eat their meals indoors at a table, a picnic is a real treat. Is it warm enough yet where you live to go on a picnic?

Take along some foods people around the world enjoy *alfresco* (ahl-FRES-koh), which is Italian for "in the open air." Pack a *baguette* (bah-GEHT), which is a long loaf of bread, and a selection of cheeses for a very French *picque-nique*. Load your basket with *empanadas* (em-pahn-AH-thus), which are baked or fried turnovers, for a Mexican-style picnic. Add chilled *flan* for dessert (for a simple recipe for *flan*, see March 29). A Lebanese picnic might include some *baba gannoujh* (bah-bah gah-NOOSH), a spread made from mashed chick peas and eggplant served with torn pieces of pita bread.

Pack your picnic basket with some of these goodies . . . and hope it stays sunny!

12

Play Shadow Tag.

In sunny countries such as Saudi Arabia, children sometimes play a version of tag called Shadow Tag. You're "out" once your shadow gets stepped on. When you become It, you must count to three to give everyone a chance to get away from you.

Spanish children play another version called "Moon and Morning Stars." This game is played near a large tree or building that casts a shadow. One player is chosen to be the Moon and that person must stay only in the tree's shadow (since the moon is visible in the dark sky). All the other players are Morning Stars. They run in and out of the shadow, taunting the Moon who tries to tag them. If the person who is Moon succeeds, the tagged Star becomes the next Moon.

The children who are Morning Stars chant this saying throughout the game:

> **The bright moon and the morning stars.**
> **The bright moon and the morning stars.**
> **Where the light shines gay,**
> **We dance and play,**
> **But who will dare the shadow?**

13

Splash water on friends for *Songkran*.

In Thailand, the New Year is celebrated in mid-April with a festival called *Songkran* (SONG-krahn). This is the hottest time of the year in Thailand, so it's not surprising that water is an important part of the festival. Everyone has great fun splashing water (even on unsuspecting strangers!), which is thought to wash away the evils of the past year. Who knows if it does — but getting a good soaking is certainly a memorable way to start a new year!

If you plan on splashing your friends with water today, be sure to give them plenty of warning, and tell them the reason behind your mischievousness. One thing is for sure. You had better be prepared to get splashed back!

14

Make fruit leather.

The sun is used to dry foods to preserve them in many countries. This is true where refrigeration is uncommon, as in Ethiopia where a seasoned sun-dried meat called *biltong* is eaten. Other foods are dried to change their character. In India, for instance, green peppercorns are dried on woven mats in the sun for seven to ten days before turning hard and the more familiar black color.

Children are often asked to help stir the spices and other foods spread out in the sun to speed the drying. Would you like to try your hand at drying some food? Make a batch of fruit leather to see how it's done. The instructions can be found in the box below.

SOLAR ENERGY

Fruit leather makes a naturally sweetened snack packed with energy!

It is best made with very ripe fruit. You can use thawed frozen fruit out of season, or wait until there are ripe berries, peaches, or apricots in your garden or at the market.

Peel and pit a pound (½ kilo) of fruit. Cut into small pieces and puree in a blender or food processor to make a smooth mush.

Cook the pureed fruit in a pan over low heat until it boils (have an adult help you at the stove). If the fruit sticks to the pan, add a little fruit juice or water.

Remove the pan from the stove and let cool. Meanwhile, wrap two or three plates in plastic wrap. Spread the puree on the plates, and place them in a shallow box. Cover with cheesecloth.

Place the box in the sun. It will take one to three days for the fruit to turn to "leather." Bring the box in each night, or if there are signs of rain. The leather is ready to eat when it can be pulled away from the plastic. Enjoy!

15

Read some legends about the sun.

Our ancestors may not have known as much about the sun as we do today, but they certainly understood how powerful it is. This is reflected in many of the myths and legends that have been passed down over the centuries.

Many early cultures thought of the sun as a god. Both the Japanese and Peruvian Inca believed the sun was a celestial being from whom all their rulers were descended. The ancient Egyptians thought the sun was a ship in which the sun god Ra carried the dead to their final resting place.

Many stories are told explaining the daily movement of the sun. The Aborigines of Australia have a story that tells how the sun is a bonfire lit each day to warm the earth. It goes out at night so that all may sleep, and is relit each morning.

If you didn't know what the sun was, how would you explain its light and warmth and movement across the sky?

16

Make a sun medallion.

The sun is used as a design in the artwork of many cultures. Make a sun medallion to hang on a wall in the style of Navajo sand paintings.

The Navajo of the southwestern United States create their sand paintings as part of healing ceremonies. They are made directly on the floor of Navajo homes called *hogans* (HOE-guns), from finely crushed rocks and pollen. The paintings are destroyed at the end of the ceremonies.

The traditional sun design below can be made on a piece of sturdy cardboard cut into a circle. Paint the cardboard with watered-down glue and cover with plain sand while the glue is wet. Turn the cardboard over and tap it to shake off any loose grains.

Now paint a design with glue and colored sands (made by mixing powdered poster paints with sand). Do one color at a time, shaking off any excess. Let dry completely before hanging.

Rainy Day Pleasures

It rains just about everywhere people live, although in some regions it's hardly measurable, while in others it never seems to stop!

Rainy days are good days to spend both outdoors and in. Here are a few ideas for making the most of a rainy day — wherever you want to be.

17

Take a walk in the rain.

Does it rain a lot where you live? The next time it rains, take a walk outside. Try to imagine what it must be like when it rains in other countries.

In the British Isles, for instance, it rains enough to make these countries very green. That's why Ireland is known as the Emerald Isle! While it doesn't rain everyday, kids always have their macs and brollies (raincoats and umbrellas) handy.

It does rain most every day in parts of Brazil. Children often shield themselves from the rain with a banana leaf held overhead!

In some parts of the world, it rains steadily for months on end. This comes as a relief after months of increasingly dry conditions. How do you suppose life is different for people in such places? You'll see in the box below.

IT'S RAINING, IT'S POURING

When the monsoons finally bring rain to India in late May, the ground is totally parched and even wide rivers have dried up completely. The rains are welcomed with much rejoicing!

It will rain everyday — very hard for a few hours, then the sun will come out and everything steams! It's off and on like this all day, for about three months.

In rural Laos and Vietnam, homes and other buildings are built on high ground or elevated on stilts to withstand the possibility of flooding. In cities, however, flooding can be a problem. In Thailand, for example, enough rain commonly falls so that it's ankle-deep. People simply roll up their trousers and lift their long skirts and walk right through the water. But when the floods raise the water level waist-high, everything comes to a stop!

In Nigeria and Tanzania, two African countries that also have a rainy season, there is no school during the rainiest part of the year. This is a good time for a vacation, since getting to school during heavy rains is not always easy.

18

Dance for rain.

Drought, or the absence of much-needed rain, is a real concern in the arid regions of the world. Many cultures still observe an ancient ritual to combat drought — dancing for rain.

The Pueblo Indians of New Mexico perform many such dances during the summer months. Many African peoples also have rainmaking dances at specific times of year and whenever drought threatens. One tribe in South Africa calls on its rainmaker, a woman whom they call "The Transformer of Clouds," to work her magic while the whole tribe dances. In parts of Uganda, rainmakers shake rattles as they dance, in imitation of the sound of falling rain.

Make your own rattle or shaker to shake in rhythm to a rain dance. Partially fill an empty frozen juice can (the kind with a pull strip that releases the lid) with dried rice or beans. Tape the lid back in place and cover the outside with a decorated paper "sleeve."

19

Look for rainbows.

Children everywhere look for rainbows in the sky once a storm has passed. In the Philippines, rainbows are believed to bring happiness, and children make wishes when they see one.

You might wish to find a pot of gold waiting at the end of a rainbow, a popular story that is told in Ireland. In Romania, children are told something else awaits them there. If they drink from the river where the rainbow ends, boys turn into girls, and girls into boys!

Not surprisingly, the rainbow is seen as a bridge in many cultures. In Japanese mythology, it was from this bridge that two gods cast the spear that created land. The Scandinavians once believed the rainbow was a bridge to the gods, a notion shared by many Native Americans. Native Siberians believed the rainbow was the hem of the sun god's giant cloak.

What does the multi-colored rainbow remind you of? Make up your own story about it.

20

Toss a rainbow flyer.

Here's an origami flyer you can make indoors when it's raining, to fly outdoors once it clears up!

You need eight squares of paper, in the colors of the rainbow (red, orange, yellow, green, blue, indigo, and violet) plus white. You also need white glue.

Start with the red square, placed color-side down. Fold in half, then fold the top left corner down so it meets the bottom edge (1). This creates a triangular pocket. Fold the bottom right corner up to the top edge (2).

This completes one section. Do the same with the remaining squares.

To assemble the flyer, insert the open-ended point of the red section into the triangular pocket of the orange section. Push in as far as it will go; secure with glue. Continue in this way, in the order of the rainbow colors, ending with the white section. Fit it into the red pocket to complete the circle. Let dry, then toss like a Frisbee® outdoors.

21

Make a Tangram.

Rainy days and puzzles go together! Here's a Chinese puzzle you may be familiar with called a Tangram. The Chinese call it *Qi-Qiao Ban* (chee chee-ow bahn) which means "the seven clever pieces." And clever they are! Using all seven geometric shapes, at least 1,600 different designs can be made.

You can make your own Tangram from a square of black paper. Using a ruler, measure and mark a grid of squares (these are the thin lines in the diagram). Mark the cutting lines (shown as thick lines). Cut along the cutting lines to make seven shapes.

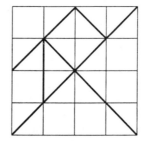

Can you assemble the pieces to make some of the designs shown here? What other configurations can you come up with?

22

Start a stamp collection.

Rainy days are also good for assembling collections indoors. Do you have a stamp collection? Now is a good time to start one!

Every country issues new stamps periodically, some commemorating people and events that have shaped those countries, others honoring wildlife and natural wonders. Collecting stamps is a great way to learn about places near and far. It's also a way to create a small-scale art museum, as postal stamps are truly miniature works of art.

Naturally, you'll save the stamps your pen pals send on their letters (see August 12 for more on international pen pals). Ask your relatives, friends, and neighbors to save interesting stamps for you. You can also purchase stamps from around the world at hobby shops and coin shops.

Where do some of your favorite stamps come from?

23

24

25

If I Were In Charge

When you were younger, your parents, and a host of other adults, did everything for you. Now that you're older, there is so much you can do for yourself.

Children in Turkey get a chance to see what it's like to run the government each year on Children's Day. Here's a chance for you to take on some adult roles, too.

Switch places with adults on *Milli Egemenlik ve Cocuk Bayrami.*

Turkish children look forward to *Milli Egemenlik ve Cocuk Bayrami* (meel-EE ay-gay-mahn-LICK vay choh-JOOK bye-RUM-ah), or "National Sovereignty and Children's Day."

Because Turks believe their country's future is closely linked to the prosperity of its youth, children are honored on this day. They are treated to many free entertainments, but even more special is the chance to experience what it is like to run the country.

Hundreds of young Turks take over the duties of civic officials in towns and cities. What do you think it would be like to be in charge of the community where you live?

Another way to see what it's like to play an adult's role is by switching places with your parents for part of a day. Or ask if you and your classmates can have a turn teaching a subject at school. You'll quickly appreciate how hard raising a family is, or teaching a classroom of inquisitive minds!

Compare job choices around the world.

What do you want to be when you grow up? Don't worry — you don't have to make up your mind yet! There are many options from which you may choose, whether you're a boy or a girl.

Is this true all over the world? It is becoming more so, certainly, as more and more women work outside the home. In some Middle Eastern countries, however, girls are still discouraged from going to school and later working. In Russia, on the other hand, the majority of doctors are women, a job many more men than women in North America hold.

In many rurals areas, traditional jobs for both men and women are slow to change. In Malawi, for example, farming is still a man's job, while making felt to cover yurts (tent-like homes) is a woman's job among the Turcoman of Iran.

Even where men and women are free to choose what they would like to do, there still exists an inexplicable difference in the amount of money men and women are paid for doing the exact same job. This is true in many countries including our own.

Work for pay.

You don't have to wait until you're grown up to be in charge of your own money. Do you have an after- (or before-) school job, or one that you work at during the summer months?

Perhaps you receive an allowance instead. Children in many countries are given money so that they can learn its value. Sometimes an allowance is tied in with doing chores at home, so it's almost like having a job!

Children in many regions of the world, such as in India and Peru, *must* work to help support their families. Often they must give up going to school as a result. While much practical experience comes from helping at the family shop or stall in the marketplace in Jordan, for instance, many children regret not being able to attend school. A girl in Angola may have to look after younger brothers and sisters, to allow her parents to work, also missing out on the opportunities going to school would offer her.

26

Make a money box.

Children around the world store their hard-earned coins or allowance money in all sorts of containers. Mexican children drop *pesos* (PAY-sohs) into pig-shaped banks; in China, banks are often in the shape of cats. In many places, however, money is simply put into a box.

You can keep your coins and other valuables in a box decorated in the style of the straw inlaid boxes of Belarus (formerly the Byelorussian Republic of the former Soviet Union). The instructions are in the box below.

A PENNY SAVED . . .

The straw designs of Belarus are made with flattened rye straw glued onto wood that has been dyed black. Solid areas are made from long strips of straw glued next to one another. Small squares, triangles, and thin strips are cut from straw to make mosaic-like decorations. The designs are usually of village scenes, people in costume, and animals.

Make your box from a small gift box painted black and decorated with narrow gift wrap ribbon in a golden yellow color (use the smooth shiny ribbon rather than

the ridged type). Hold the ribbon pieces in place with white glue, and seal the completed box with a coat of polyurethane if you like.

The traditional designs below should help you come up with your own designs for the top and sides of your box.

Start a collection of coins and paper money from around the world. Look for lira *from Italy,* won *from Korea,* pesos *from Cuba, Bolivia, and Argentina, and* dinar *from Yugoslavia and Jordan.*

27

Make a cord for your house key.

In many countries, from Chile to China, both parents are employed outside the home. This means many children let themselves into their homes after school. They are entrusted with a house key, which many wear around their necks for safe keeping.

You can make a decorative cord from cotton string to hang a key from, using a finger-knotting technique Swiss children learn when they're young.

Make a slip knot as shown (1). Hold the loop in your left hand; with your right hand, pull a bit of the continuous string up through the loop, pulling until a new knot forms next to the first knot (2).

Pull the continuous string with your right hand to reduce the size of the new loop. Continue making new loops and knots until the cord is as long as you like. Cut the string and put the cut end through the last loop. Pull tight; knot. Slip your key onto the cord and tie the ends together.

28

List some changes you might make.

If you really were in charge, what are some of the changes you would make at home or at school? Why?

Do you think kids everywhere have the same complaints? Children in Korea and Japan enjoy school and recreational activities but they feel pressured to excel. Their parents have high expectations for their children, and this takes some of the joy out of learning and playing.

Girls in such countries as Libya have the opposite complaint. They are discouraged from attending school and eventually from working outside the home. Some would like the opportunity to get an education and have certain freedoms girls in other countries have.

If you were really in charge, what would you like to see done to make sure there's enough food for everybody and medication for those who are ill? How might you solve global environmental problems? And what would you do to help bring about world peace? Who knows—some of your suggestions may be used someday!

Bringing in the May

While much of the Northern Hemisphere is already experiencing spring, the far northern reaches don't get a taste of it until now. No wonder May is such a joyous time in those parts.

May means flowers, and green grass, and an inexplicable urge to lie on one's back and stare at the clouds! Ahead you'll even find the perfect dance to usher in the month of May, too.

29

Pick wildflowers.

Children everywhere love picking wildflowers, one of nature's most appreciated gifts. What types of wildflowers are in bloom now where you live?

French children eagerly hunt for lilies of the valley this time of year. Small bunches of the bell-shaped flowers are traditionally exchanged on May Day. This flower doesn't grow wild in North America, but you may come across a plant known as the false lily of the valley. It's also called the Canada mayflower.

You probably won't have any trouble finding a patch of green grass growing nearby. In the Swedish countryside, some people still abide by an old folk belief. They sprinkle grass on their doorsteps on the last day of April. This supposedly keeps all the witches busy until morning (they can't resist stopping to count each blade of grass!), assuring the safety of the sleeping family.

30

Make May baskets.

In parts of England, some children observe the old custom of secretly delivering flowers to friends and neighbors on the first day of May. They leave a small basket of blooms on the stoop, or hang a bouquet from a doorknob.

This is something you can do. Shape paper semicircles into cones; glue or tape the seams. Punch holes in the sides for hanging ribbon. Before putting fresh flowers into the cones, wrap the stems with damp paper toweling, and enclose in a small plastic bag.

Can't find any fresh flowers? Make your own from colored tissue paper! Follow the instructions in the box below for some beautiful blossoms that never wilt!

BOUNTIFUL BLOOMS

For each bloom you need six 5" (12.5 cm) squares of tissue paper (all in the same color, or in an assortment of colors for a different effect). You also need a 3" (7.5 cm) length of florist's wire, florist's tape, and scissors.

Stack the paper and fold in half diagonally; crease well, then unfold. Fold into a rectangle, then in half to make a square. Unfold completely.

Refold the paper, pressing in the diagonally creased corners (1). Press flat, then fold in half (2).

Bend the wire at one end to make a hook, and staple that end to the bottom point of the paper. Cover the wire with florist's tape.

Cut the top of the paper in an arc (use pinking shears, or fringe the edge, to vary the flowers). Fold back all the layers, then one by one, pull the layers up toward the center, plumping them.

1.   **2.**

1

Dance around a maypole on May Day.

May Day traces its roots to ancient Rome, where a six-day celebration known as *Floralia* took place each spring. This was a time to honor Flora, the goddess of spring. As the Roman Empire grew, the custom took hold in the lands that later became part of it.

Today, May Day is observed in many European countries, although in France and Russia it is less a spring festival and more a day dedicated to working people.

Some towns in England still erect maypoles, decorated with flowers and long colorful ribbons, around which children and others dance. Attach some crepe paper streamers or ribbons to a pole stuck in the ground or a slender tree on your property. You and your friends can dance around it, singing:

**Now we go round the maypole high,
Maypole high, maypole high.
Now we go round the maypole high —
Let the colored ribbons fly!**

2

Drink some May punch.

Sweet woodruff is a low-growing herb that grows in shaded spots. It is especially sweet-smelling in May.

Known as *Waldmeister* (VAHLT-my-stuh), or "master of the forest," in Germany, the herb is used to flavor wine. The drink is traditionally served throughout the month of May.

You can flavor some juice in a similar way. Place a few sprigs of sweet woodruff in a container of juice overnight. The next day, pour the juice into a punch bowl. Add fresh strawberries, and serve!

3

Play games with plants.

Plants can be turned into toys and noisemakers (see March 1 and March 12 respectively). They can also be used to play a number of games.

In France, children play a guessing game using the closed buds of the poppy plant. They try to guess whether the blossoms-to-be are white, which they call *poulette* (pooh-LET), or "chick"; pink for *poule* (pool), or "hen"; or red for *coq* (coke), or "rooster."

The giant puffball, a round mushroom that can get as large as 24″ (60 cm) in diameter, is often used like a ball in those parts of Canada where it grows.

Petals can be plucked to make predictions about a future loved one's occupation. One rhyme from England that accompanies the counting goes like this:

Army, Navy, Medicine, Law, Church, Nobility, Nothing at all.

4

Look at the clouds.

Do you like to lie on your back and look for recognizable shapes clouds sometimes make? Puffy, white cumulus clouds make the best "pictures" (some people call them "cauliflower clouds" — and they do resemble that vegetable!). Clouds can even tell a story as they shift and change with the wind.

Cumulus clouds are generally fair weather clouds, unless the conditions change and they start to heap up. The Zuñi Indians of New Mexico say that when this happens the country of the corn priests (the earth) will soon be pierced with rain arrows.

Long ago, clouds were believed to protect the earth. This may have been because a cloud was the only thing that could block out the blazing sun — the same sun that was capable of drying up water sources and withering crops. Today, in many African countries, the clouds are summoned with dances when there is a drought (for more on rain dances, see April 18).

Sky High

Each May in Japan the skies are filled with flying fish. Not real ones, of course, but carp-shaped windsocks hung high from bamboo poles in honor of young boys.

Look to the pages ahead for some other high-spirited things you can make, including a kite and a delicious loaf of high-rising bread!

5

Make a windsock for *Tango no sekku.*

Japanese boys are honored each year during *Tango no sekku* (tahn-goh noh SEH-koo), or "Boys' Festival." Families hang carp windsocks (one for each boy) from tall poles placed outside homes. The carp, a fish that swims against the current, is a traditional symbol of determination, a quality the Japanese want their sons to have!

Make carp windsocks for the kids in your family. Fold a large sheet of tissue paper in half lengthwise. Draw the outline of a fish on it.

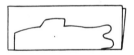

Cut along the outline and unfold the paper. Draw on features with a marker, or glue tissue paper pieces for scales, fins, and eyes.

Glue an inch-wide strip of stiff paper at the mouth opening, folding the tissue paper over the strip to hide it. Glue the ends of the strip to form a circle; glue the windsock along its upper edge.

Fold over Strip

WRONG SIDE

Tie string at either side of the mouth. Hang the windsock in a sheltered, but breezy, spot.

6

Name some regional winds.

No doubt the steady winds that blow over much of Asia inspired the invention of windsocks and kites. These winds, known as the monsoons, bring the region its two distinct seasons. (For more on monsoons, see the box on page 54.)

You may have heard of some of the world's other seasonal winds, so famous they have names! Everybody bundles up when the cold, dry *mistral* (mees-TRAHL) blows over southern France in winter. Egyptian children are grateful for the protection of long robes when the *khamsin* (calm-seen) whips across the desert, stirring up the stinging sands.

Siberians feel no love for the *purga*, which brings snow and violently cold temperatures to that region. A very different winter wind blows in the western United States. The *chinook* (from a Native American word meaning "snow-eater") is a strong, *warm* wind, capable of melting as much as two feet of snow in 24 hours!

7

Fold paper airplanes.

Kids around the world can thank the Chinese for both inventing paper and first folding it. Here's one of the best-known folded objects everywhere—the paper airplane!

Fold an 8½" × 11" (21.5 cm × 28 cm) piece of paper in half lengthwise; unfold. Fold the upper corners down (1); fold along the dotted line to make (2).

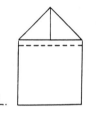

1.　　　　2.

Fold the upper corners down to make (3). Fold up the little triangular point; then fold the model in half so this shows on the outside (4).

3.　　　　4.

Fold one wing down along the dotted line shown in the last step; fold the other wing to match. Raise the wings so that they are at right angles to the plane's body. Launch with a gentle thrust of the arm.

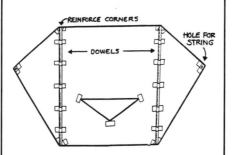

8

Go fly a kite.

The Chinese are also credited with inventing the kite, possibly as many as 3,000 years ago. From China, the know-how spread to other Asian countries where today many adults and children devote a lot of time to both making and flying kites.

Fighting kites are especially popular. A portion of string close to the kites is coated with glue and ground glass or porcelain. The kites are flown close to one another, each flyer guiding his own kite so that its string crosses and cuts his opponent's string. Children eagerly wait for the losers to fall, as it's the custom to award the kites to those who catch them on the ground.

Kites come in all sorts of shapes and sizes. Have you ever made your own kite? You'll find the kite below not only simple to make, but a breeze to fly!

HIGH-STRUNG

A plastic garbage bag can be turned into a high-flying kite in no time.

You need a white or light-colored bag that is at least 23½" × 29" (59 cm x 74 cm). You also need two ³⁄₁₆" (10 mm) dowels, tape, string, and permanent markers.

A Chinese riddle:
*What has eyes
and nose but
cannot breathe:
Can't get to
heaven, but
earth it must
leave?*

A dragon kite.

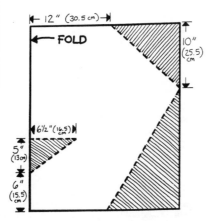

Spread the bag flat, and measure and mark the cutting lines as shown below. Cut along the lines, cutting away the shaded areas.

Open the bag and color one side of it with markers. Let dry.

Turn the kite over and tape the dowels in position. Use tape to reinforce the corners of the cut-out and the wing tips.

Poke a tiny hole in each wing tip, and tie one end of a 10' (3 m) piece of string through each one. This is the kite's bridle. Tie a loop at the end of the bridle, and attach your flying line to this.

9

Bake yeast bread.

Have you ever made yeast bread — the kind that is allowed to rise before it's baked? You'll really love this crunchy *pan cubano* (pahn coo-BAH-noh), or "Cuban bread," perfect for beginning bakers.

Pan Cubano

2 packages dry yeast
1 tablespoon (15 ml) salt
1 tablespoon (15 ml) sugar
2 cups (500 ml) lukewarm water
5-6 cups (600-750 g) all-purpose flour

Mix the first four ingredients in a large bowl. Stir in 4 cups (500 g) flour, one cup at a time. Remove the dough from the bowl, and knead it on a floured surface, adding more flour to make a firm dough. (To knead, push the dough down and away from you, then fold it back on itself; repeat.) Knead for five minutes, or until the dough is smooth and elastic.

Place the dough in a clean, greased bowl. Cover with a cloth and let rise in a warm place for one hour.

Shape the dough into two 14" (35 cm) loaves. Place them on a baking sheet sprinkled with cornmeal. Cut the tops with a knife; brush with water. Place the baking sheet in a *cold* oven; set the temperature at 400°F (200°C). Bake for 45 minutes.

Sing Out!

There's a wise old saying from Zimbabwe:

**If you can walk you can dance;
If you can talk you can sing.**

Here are some of the songs kids around the world sing — when they're alone, when they're with friends, when they are in school and in prayer. Join the global chorus and sing out!

Birthday songs can be found on May 27. For national anthems, see June 17.

10

Sing songs from other countries.

Some of the childhood songs sung in North America are found in other countries. Take *Frère Jacques*, for example, a song you may know in both French and English. Children in Spanish-speaking countries sing it like this:

*Fray Felipe, Fray Felipe,
¿Duermes tú, duermes tú?
  Tocan las campanas,
  Tocan las campanas,
Tan, tan, tan,
Tan, tan, tan.*

Do you know it in any other languages?
  Check a children's songbook for other examples of songs from around the world. You'll find the titles of some songbooks in the bibliography. If you don't read music, have someone who does play the basic melodies on a piano or recorder, so you can learn how the songs go.
  You can also learn new songs by listening to recordings. Many children's recording artists include international favorites in their repertoire. Your friends from other cultures can also teach you some of the songs they know. Teach them one of your favorites in return!

11

Sing some rounds.

It's fun to sing by yourself, but it's even more fun when you're part of a group that is singing. And what better way to get everybody in on the act than by singing rounds!
  Lots of popular rounds originated in other countries. *Kookaburra* is a rollicking round from Australia. *Hey-Ho, Nobody Home* is an old English round. Even the French song *Frère Jacques* works well when sung in parts.

One lovely French round that is simply a string of names of French cathedrals has a rather haunting melody. Two people or groups can sing this round, or as many as six can (each coming in after 2 measures). Sing it slowly, or fast, for different effects. You'll find the words and the music in the box below.

ROUND & ROUND

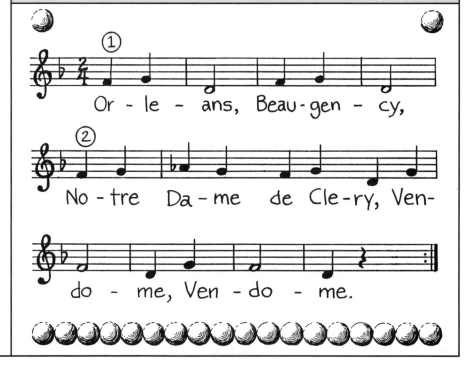

12

Play a singing game.

Some songs are sung as an accompaniment to games. What singing games do you and your friends enjoy playing?

Mexican children sing a song called *Naranja Dulce* (nar-AHN-hah DOOL-say), or "Sweet Orange," while they play a simple game. The children join hands to form a circle, surrounding one child who is the *soldaje* (sohl-DAH-hay), or "soldier." As they sing the song, the *soldaje* chooses a "sweetheart" from the circle. The two leave the game, and a new *soldaje* is chosen. This continues until no one is left in the circle.

Chant the words below, or sing them to a tune such as *Twinkle, Twinkle, Little Star.*

Naranja dulce,	Sweet orange,
limón partido,	Lemon slice,
dame un abrazo	Give me a hug
que yo te pido.	I ask of you.
Si fuera falso	If I'm untrue
mi juramento,	My dear,
en poco tiempo	In no time
se olvidará.	You'll forget me.
Toca la marcha	Play the march—
mi pecho llora;	My heart weeps.
adios, señora,	Goodbye, lady,
yo ya me voy.	I am off now.

13

Sing a lullaby.

Do you remember any of the lullabies your parents sang when you were little? How do they go?

One of the best-known lullabies in the English language is *Rock-a-Bye Baby.* British and Australian children, however, grow up hearing this sung to a different melody than the one Americans know. It is said that the American tune is actually a Native American melody heard and admired by an early English settler.

Lullabies that promise a restless child something in return for sleep are common everywhere. Greek children are soothed with a song which promises first the city of Alexandria made entirely from sugar, then all of Cairo filled with rice. The final prize? Constantinople, where the cooperative baby shall reign for three years!

Ask your friends from other cultures to sing you one of the lullabies they remember, or that their parents may recall. Are they similar to any of the songs you know?

14

Sing a spiritual.

Songs and singing are a part of many religions, but are particularly important for many Black Americans who share a rich legacy of songs known as spirituals.

Many spirituals are believed to have been written during the early days of slavery. Here's an uplifting one you may know called *In His Hands.*

**He's got the whole world in His hands,
He's got the big round world in His hands,
He's got the wide world in His hands,
He's got the whole world in His hands,**

There are other verses, such as

**He's got the wind and the rain . . .
He's got the little bitty baby . . .
He's got you and me brother . . .**

Make up some new verses of your own, too!

15

Listen to a singing cricket.

Crickets are kept as pets in many Asian countries, including China and Vietnam, where they are thought to bring good luck. Their singing, or chirping, is also highly valued. Only the male crickets sing, which they do by rubbing their wings together, drawing one across the other like a bow across a fiddle.

You can catch a cricket to keep as a short-term guest. When the weather warms in your area, listen for the insects outdoors (you may also find them in your house). Finding the insect's exact location may prove a little more difficult!

Make your cricket comfortable in a box or large jar containing some soil, rocks, and leaves. Be sure to cover the top of this cage with a piece of screening. Feed your guest bits of fresh vegetables and crumbs, and you'll be amply rewarded with song! After a day, return the cricket to the same place you found it.

With Rake & Hoe

There's something truly magical about gardening. After all, just think how a single tiny seed can turn into a carrot, a daisy . . . even a tree!

Many of the vegetables and flowers found around the world are available to home gardeners. You don't even need a lot of room to grow some of them — many are perfectly happy in soil-filled containers. So, put a little magic in your life. Plant a garden!

16

Plant an international food garden.

This is easy! Most home gardens are filled with plants from around the world. The tomato, for instance, was probably first grown in Peru; spinach is thought to have originated in Persia (modern day Iran).

This year be a little more adventurous, and make room for some varieties you may never have heard of or tasted. The box below offers some suggestions for international favorites you'll find rewarding to grow, as well as delicious!

GARDEN OF EATIN'

Mix the seeds of several types of lettuce and salad greens and sow thickly in the garden or in a container of potting soil. This type of mix is called *mesclun* (mess-CLOON) in parts of France, where the leaves are snipped off with a pair of scissors when just a few inches high. Best thing is, in a week or two you can come back for more!

There's nothing like peas fresh from the garden, but it's a lot of work shelling them (and you aren't always left with a whole lot of peas!). Grow snow peas, the type that are eaten pod and all. These are delicious in Asian stir-fry dishes.

Grow a few *tomatillo* (toe-mah-TEE-yoh) plants, which look like tiny green tomatoes inside papery husks. Add some to Mexican *salsa* for a distinctive taste.

Make room for zucchini (zoo-KEY-nee), as the green summer squash are called in Italy. The plant's large flowers are also edible. Dipped in batter and fried, squash blossoms are considered a delicacy in many Latin American countries as well as by Native Americans living in the southwestern United States.

Several companies package some of the more unusual seeds. Request a catalogue from the source listed on page 145.

17

Grow plants from kitchen scraps.

Wait, don't throw those food scraps away! You can brighten a windowsill with plants grown from some international foods. They won't yield anything edible, but the plants are nice looking.

Sprout an avocado seed, from the delicious fruit native to Central America. Stick three toothpicks into a washed pit and suspend it (fat end down) over a jar of water. The pit will eventually split open and send down roots, followed by a green stem from the top. Be sure to replenish the water as it evaporates, and pinch the plant back often to encourage it to branch out.

Grow a lush plant from a small piece of ginger root, which is used extensively in China and India as a spice and for medicinal purposes. Partially bury a bit of root into a pot of store-bought potting soil. Keep the plant warm and watered well and it will reward you with a tangle of growth.

18

Grow some herbs.

Herbs are among the easiest plants to grow. Few are bothered by insects or disease and most can tolerate neglect, a boon for beginning gardeners!

Grow some coriander, a plant that produces sweet-smelling round seeds used in Middle Eastern cookery as well as in many European baked goods. When the green leaves are used fresh in Chinese and Mexican cooking, the pugent herb is known as Chinese parsley or *cilantro* (see-LAHN-troh).

Sow some dill. In Scandinavian countries, fresh dill leaves are eaten with just about everything! Dill's name comes from the Old Norse *dilla,* meaning "to lull," and was once given to babies to help them sleep. Stuff a small pillow with dill seeds and see if it improves your sleep!

Savory is know as the "bean herb" in Germany because its flavor goes well with beans. Sage is one of the herbs found in many sausages. Long ago it was believed to promote longevity, or long life. An Arab proverb asks, "How shall a man die who has sage growing in his garden?"

19

Sow some flowers.

Make room in your garden for a few flowers that originated in, or are associated with, different countries.

Geraniums are native to South Africa. You are probably familiar with the geraniums that have showy blossoms. There are dozens of others valued for their scent. Amazingly, there are geraniums that smell just like coconut, nutmeg, lemon, and even chocolate mint!

Grow some dahlias or marigolds, both Mexican natives. Their bright colors will add some *fiesta* spirit to your garden!

In the fall, plant some spring-flowering tulips, the Netherlands' famous flower. Actually tulips are native to several central Asian countries, including Turkey. The name tulip, in fact, is thought to have come from *dulban,* the Turkish word for "turban." You can see why they'd be named that!

20

Eat some flowers.

Some flowers are enjoyed not only for their beauty or their sweet scent but because they are good to eat!

Roses are highly valued in the Middle East, where legend has it the first rose grew from a bead of sweat which fell from the prophet Muhammad's brow. The flowers are an essential ingredient in many foods. Roses flavor a yogurt soup eaten in Iran, as well as many Tunisian dishes. Rose water, (distilled from fresh petals) is sprinkled over desserts and fresh fruits throughout the region.

Look for rose water in the gourmet section of your market and use it to flavor baked goods (substitute it whenever vanilla extract is called for). You can also eat fresh rose petals, right off the bush! (Don't eat *any* roses that have been sprayed with chemicals, however, so ask before you eat.) Make a rose petal sandwich by spreading a layer of petals on buttered bread. Smells and tastes good, too!

21

Make a scarecrow.

Gardeners and farmers all over the world attempt to protect newly-sown seeds from hungry birds. What do they do? They try to scare birds away with — you guessed it! — scarecrows.

Hopefully, your garden won't be bothered by birds, but you can make a scarecrow just for decoration. Make a figure from old clothing stuffed with dried grass or straw and lash it to a tall pole stuck in the ground. Draw a scary face on your scarecrow in keeping with what the French call theirs — "the terrifier!"

Or make a Japanese-style scarecrow wearing a *kimono* (key-MOH-noh), or sashed robe, and a conical straw hat. Some scarecrows hold a bow and arrow, made from bamboo.

Alphabet Soup

When you think of alphabets, you probably think of the roman alphabet — the one used in this book. But did you know there are lots of other alphabets in use around the world today?

Here's a small sampling of these writing systems, plus a few fun ways to play with the 26 letters of our alphabet!

22

Look at different alphabets.

If you've ever glanced at some of the international newspapers sold in North America (as well as those that are published here for people who speak other languages), you've seen some of the world's alphabets. Some of these alphabets look familiar, but others are definitely different!

Most European languages, as well as Vietnamese and Somali (a wide-spread African language) are written using the roman alphabet. There may be tiny symbols over, under, and through some of the letters, but by and large the letters look much like those used to write words in English.

Other alphabets may look like nothing you've ever seen before! There is tremendous variety in the world's alphabets, and many are extremely beautiful, as you can see in the small sampling in the box below.

Do you think it would be hard to learn to read a different alphabet? Children do it all over the world when they learn a foreign language! In fact, in China, children are taught to write their own language in two completely different ways. They learn not only how to write Chinese characters, but also *pin-yin* (peen yeen), a much simplified method of writing the language using roman letters to represent Chinese sounds.

As you may have already guessed, the Chinese words in this book have been written in *pin-yin*. Otherwise, for example, you would have to be able to read

to know it said *Chun Jie*. (For more on this best-loved Chinese festival, see February 18.)

LETTER PERFECT

The Arabic alphabet is made up of sweeping symbols, written right to left. It is used to write Arabic as well as Kurdish and Persian.

The Buginese alphabet, used on the Indonesian island Sulawesi, has short, wavy symbols.

The Thai alphabet has separate symbols for long and short vowels. The Thai language is spoken in Thailand and throughout Southeast Asia.

ၓ-ၓ | ၐ-ၐ | |

The Burmese alphabet of Myanmar (formerly called Burma) is made up of many circular and semi-circular shapes.

The Tibetan alphabet is used to write Lhasan, the language spoken in Tibet's capital city, Lhasa. It is modeled after an Indian alphabet, which it resembles somewhat.

For more on languages around the world, see pages 90 and 91.

23

Write some Chinese characters.

All alphabets are writing systems that use symbols to represent spoken sounds. The Chinese don't use an alphabet as such. They write what we call characters, symbols which may stand for sounds, syllables, words, and even whole ideas.

The Chinese write everyday characters with pens and pencils, but fine calligraphy done with a brush is a centuries-old art. Try your hand at writing the characters for "friendship," shown below. You need a 1" (2.5 cm) brush that comes to a point, black ink or paint, and inexpensive paper in large sheets, such as newsprint.

Dip the brush in the ink and hold it upright. Make thick and thin lines by varying the pressure on the brush. Follow the order and the direction of the strokes as shown. You'll find it gets easier with practice!

24

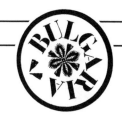

Make a poster for *Den Na Bratyata Kiril e Metodii*.

Bulgarians honor two Greek brothers each year on *Den Na Bratyata Kiril e Metodii* (den nah BRAHT-yah-tah key-reel ee may-toe-dee), or "Brothers Cyril and Methodius Day."

In the late 9th century, these two men revised and refined the Greek alphabet to make an easier writing system to use with the Slavic peoples they were converting to Christianity. The alphabet was a great success and soon spread to other regions. The Cyrillic alphabet, as it's now called, is used to write Bulgarian, as well as Russian and a number of other Slavic languages.

In recognition of the world's different writing systems, design an alphabet poster. Choose an alphabet of particular interest to you, and write something in that alphabet, or make an abstract design using letters and symbols from around the world. Your friends from other cultures can help you with those alphabets you are not familiar with.

25

Create a rebus.

Puzzle your friends by sending them messages written in rebus form, a crazy way of writing words using a combination of letters, pictures, numbers, and other symbols. Here is an example:

Can you figure it out? It says, "Dear Sam, Be at my house at 7:00. Your pal, Fred."

Notice how some of the words are formed. Letters may be added to (or subtracted from) a picture that represents part of a word's sound. Certain pictures may stand for whole words (treated like homonyms). Rebuses are made in different languages all over the world in the same way. If you speak another language, try your hand at making a rebus in that language, too.

Have fun assembling your rebuses. Cut pictures and letters out of old magazines. Use rubber stamps and stickers to add a little pizzazz. Be as creative (and sneaky!) as you like.

26

Send messages by Morse code.

There are lots of ways of spelling out words that don't require paper and pencil. Sign language is one of these (see July 31); semaphore signaling with flags is another. The Morse code is a third.

The American artist and inventor, Samuel Morse, devised this code in 1832 as a means of sending messages by telegraph. You can tap messages to a friend using the International Morse Code alphabet Samuel Morse invented. Rap on heating pipes in your home (the sound really carries!), or use a flashing mirror outdoors on a sunny day. You can also signal at night with a flashlight. Just pass your hand across the beam — fast, then slow — to differentiate the dots and dashes.

Have you ever wondered why the "e" is one dot, and the "t" one dash? These are the most frequently used letters in English, so Morse made them the simplest signals.

A ·—	J ·———	S ···
B —···	K —·—	T —
C —·—·	L ·—··	U ··—
D —··	M ——	V ···—
E ·	N —·	W ·——
F ··—·	O ———	X —··—
G ——·	P ·——·	Y —·——
H ····	Q ——·—	Z ——··
I ··	R ·—·	

Many Happy Returns

Most children would agree — birthdays are the best days!

In some countries, such as Italy and Mexico, some children celebrate not only their birthdays but their saint's days. They get to have two parties every year!

Here are some of the songs, foods, and customs that make birthdays special days all over the world.

27

Sing a birthday song.

Did you know that in almost every country in the world *Happy Birthday to You* is the most popular birthday song? The 100-year-old American song is often sung in different languages, of course, and the meaning is sometimes slightly changed, but the melody and the sentiment are the same!

Many countries do have their own traditional birthday songs as well. Mexican children are serenaded with a song called *Las Mañanitas* (lahs mahn-yahn-EE-tahs), or "Early Mornings." In Venezuela, *Hoy Es Tu Día* (oy ess too DEE-ah), or "Today Is Your Day," is sung.

Children in the Netherlands are honored with a song entitled *Lang zal zij (hij) leven* (lahng zahl zay (hay) LAY-vehn), which means "Long May She (He) Live." Israeli children are seated in a decorated chair, crowned with a wreath of flowers, and lifted high in the air (chair and all!) while a special birthday song describing all these actions is sung.

28

Light a birthday candle.

Long ago, smoke was believed to transport prayers and wishes to the gods in the heavens. So naturally, fire was an important element during birthdays. We can thank the Germans for including birthday candles on a cake — one for each year and "one to grow on" — a tradition adopted all over the world today.

Some German children also receive a special birthday candle as a christening present when they are babies. It's a large candle marked off with lines and numbers (usually twelve). On each birthday, the candle is allowed to burn to the next mark.

Make your own birthday candle. Mark off as many years as you like on a fat, flat-bottomed candle. Draw on lines with a permanent marker, or press on stickers or decorations made from wax. Special decorating wax that comes in thin sheets (and lots of lovely colors!) works especially well. Knead the wax to warm it; then roll, pinch, and sculpt shapes that can be stuck directly onto the candle.

29

Serve a special birthday food.

The birthday cake is thought to have originated in Germany several hundred years ago. It was once customary to bake small items in the cake. Each guest's slice was used to predict the future. Someone with a coin in his slice was sure to look forward to great wealth, while the person finding a thimble would never marry!

In Russia, birthday pie is more common than cake. The birthday child's name is written on the pie, along with a birthday greeting, by pricking tiny holes in the crust before it is baked.

Several sweets are customarily served on birthdays (and other special occasions) in Iceland. One of the most popular is *pönnukökur* (PAHN-er-KER-kuh), or "pancakes." These thin pancakes may be sprinkled with sugar and rolled up, or spread with fruit preserves and whipped cream and then folded into wedge shapes.

30

Play some party games.

In Central and South America, the highlight of many birthday parties is the breaking of the *piñata* (peen-YAH-tah).

A *piñata* is a decorated container filled with sweets and party favors (or fruit, as is the custom in tropical regions). The *piñata* is hung in an open area, and each child is blindfolded, twirled around a few times, and given a chance to break it with a stick. To make it even harder to hit, the *piñata* may be raised or lowered by means of its rope. When the *piñata* finally breaks, everyone races to gather up its spilled contents.

Bli Yaadaim (blee yah-DIE-eem), or "Without Hands," is a popular party game in Israel. Team players stand in rows holding onto a long rope with both hands. Hats are placed on the ground in front of the players. At the signal, the teams attempt to put the hats on their heads without using their hands! Team members may help one another with their feet, heads, and teeth. The first team to put on all its hats is declared the winner.

BEST WISHES

Just as friends are thought to bring luck on the first day of the year (see January 1), their presence at birthdays is an ancient tradition in many cultures around the world.

Many of the customs surrounding birthdays are also very old. Pinching or spanking the birthday child harks back to a time when it was thought you could scare off evil spirits. In England and Ireland, children are lowered to the ground with a hard bump; in Scotland, a birthday punch is more common. In Belgium, harmful spirits are sent packing with a needle prick first thing in the morning!

Ouch!

Certain party games are also relics from our superstitious past. Pin the Tail on the Donkey (or *Rabbit* in Brazil and *Pig* in Denmark) evolved from an ancient ritual used to predict a person's future. The placement of the tail or other object would be interpreted by those claiming to be able to "read" into the future.

Hindu children pray for the future on their birthdays. They visit temples early in the morning, where priests mark the children's brows with a spot of red or black to insure the prayers will be answered. Later that day, there may be a party with games and presents from family and friends. Well-to-do families might include orphaned children in the celebration, because Hindus believe this is a time to remember less fortunate people as well.

31

Make a birthday banner.

In Denmark, the national flag is used as a decoration on birthdays. Flags are hung from windows and porch railings (you can always tell who's having a birthday!). They are also used inside the home. A large flag might be draped over the dining table, and little paper flags stuck into the birthday cake.

Design your own flag or banner to proclaim your birthday. Choose some symbols that are meaningful to you, or write the words "Happy Birthday," in another language. Make a paper banner from newsprint and paint or markers, or craft a colorful felt banner that has a pocket for a hanging rod (use a fat dowel or broomstick for this). Use your banner as a decoration in your room, or hang it outdoors so everyone invited to your birthday party will be able to find your house easily!

The Good Earth

Saving our earth begins at home, and in schools and businesses in our own communities. We need to look beyond our own backyards, however, to do our part to help the earth as a whole.

Make World Environment Day the focus of some of your environmental activities where you live. You'll be joining millions of people around the world who are working together to bring about positive change.

1

Conserve and recycle at home.

There are lots of ways to save the earth—while saving you and your family money—right at home.

Let's start with the food you buy. Do away with wasteful packaging by purchasing food in larger quantities rather than in individual servings. Fill your own containers with food from bulk bins. Bring your own bags when you shop (for a bag you can make yourself, see June 2).

Conserve electricity by turning off lights; save heating fuel by setting the thermostat lower and putting on a sweater. Check for leaky faucets, and remember not to let the water run while you're brushing your teeth!

Recycle every bit of packaging you can, as well as newspapers and white paper. In Japan, *chirigami kokan* (cheer-ee-GAH-mee KOH-kahn), or "toilet paper exchangers," go door-to-door collecting paper for recycling in exchange for toilet paper.

Recycle other things, such as clothes you've outgrown or toys you no longer play with. Donate these to a charity organization in your area. You'll be making other children happy and saving the earth at the same time!

2

Stitch a carrying bag.

One way to reduce waste is to take along your own reusable bags whenever you go shopping. French families tote net bags, which take up no room at all when they are empty, but expand to hold a surprising amount!

You can make your own drawstring bag in a size to suit you. Cut a sturdy piece of fabric into a rectangle; fold over one long edge and stitch a casing for the drawstring.

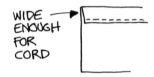

WIDE ENOUGH FOR CORD

Fold the fabric in half (with the right side of the fabric to the inside) and stitch along the side and bottom, taking care to leave an opening at the casing. Turn the bag right side out and thread a thick cotton cord through the casing. Knot both ends of the cord so it can't accidentally be pulled out of the casing.

3

Turn your school "green."

Schools all over the world are joining the crusade to save the earth. What types of programs do you have at your school to encourage recycling and conservation?

Here are just three ideas for making your school "green":

Make recycling boxes for white paper for each classroom.

Urge your principal to ask the school board to look into purchasing more energy-efficient light bulbs.

Suggest vegetable scraps from the cafeteria be composted in bins on school grounds. Making the bins is another good school project.

There is plenty more you can do. How about planting a garden? In Niger, schoolchildren in many areas grow rice and millet and vegetables. The kids do all the work themselves, from clearing the land to harvesting. Gardening is also a part of the curriculum in the Netherlands.

Create a nature area on school property. In Australia, children "adopt" trees on school grounds that they care for and spend time learning about.

4

Boycott products.

Boycotting, or refusing to have anything to do with certain goods or items, is an effective way to bring about change.

Tell your mom you no longer want to drink juice in juice boxes. The aluminum, plastic, and paper that are bonded together to make boxes can not be separated for recycling. You'll also be helping conserve valuable bauxite (the ore from which aluminum is extracted), an important resource found in Australia and Guinea in West Africa.

Refuse to purchase tuna that has been caught in large nets that also unnecessarily snare and kill hundreds of thousands of dolphins each year. How can you know which companies are now being supplied with tuna from responsible fishermen? Look for the label that says "Dolphin Friendly," or a similar statement.

If enough people stop buying these and other harmful products, the companies will take notice and eventually stop making and marketing them.

5

Plant a tree for World Environment Day.

The nations of this earth have united forces to help save the earth we all share!

On June 5, 1972, the United Nations established the United Nations Environment Programme, or UNEP (pronounced you-nep). With headquarters in Nairobi, Kenya, UNEP's responsibilities include keeping a watch on the global environment as well as helping countries work together to solve regional problems. The agency's work is honored each year on this day, and children everywhere take part in events that will shape our planet's future.

Many countries participate by planting trees on this date (or whenever it's the best time for planting). Plant a tree on your property, or join with classmates and plant trees at your school or in your community. Or do as some Czechoslovakian children did one year and send saplings to a school in a developing country.

A local nursery can help you choose suitable trees and offer planting instructions.

TREE-MENDOUS!

Many trees are an important part of national heritage around the world.

The white birch, which figures in so many Russian stories and songs, is the national tree of that country.

Bamboo — actually a grass with a woody stem capable of growing 70 feet (21 m) high! — is treasured throughout Asia. It's no wonder bamboo is considered sacred in Japan, where it's used for everything from food to building materials.

In some parts of Switzerland, a tree is planted when a child is born. Pear trees are traditionally planted for girls, apple trees for boys.

The baobab is an impressive tree that grows in the hot, dry grassy plains of Africa. Its leaves, fruit, seeds, and roots are all edible. Its massive trunk can be hollowed out for storing water, as well as serving as a cool spot in which people can escape the heat of the midday sun!

6

Join an environmental group.

One way to join the international environmental movement is to become a member of one of the organizations that specialize in world-wide concerns. Kids just like you are making a big difference in this way!

Your membership dollars help to fund all sorts of things. The money pays trained people to demonstrate more effective farming methods in Ethiopia. It funds programs in Brazil that enable people there to make a living from the rainforests without cutting down trees. It even helps children in disadvantaged countries learn about environmental issues.

You'll find the names and addresses of some environmental organizations that are especially interested in kids on page 143. Write to some of them to learn more about what they are doing to help our earth, and how *you* can help!

In Zambia, children between the ages of seven and fourteen are encouraged to join Chongologo Clubs, which stress animal conservation.

Trade Winds

If your family car was made in Korea, or the grapes your mother picked up at the market were imported from Chile, you have first-hand knowledge of world trade.

Trading goods with people in other parts of the world is nothing new. Ahead you'll see how trade once inspired world exploration, plus you'll get a delicious taste of some of the first foods to be in global demand!

7

Learn how trade led to world exploration.

The first known explorers were from ancient Babylonia (in modern-day Iraq) and Egypt. They ventured far from their homelands as early as 2500 B.C. in search of people with whom to trade goods. It wasn't long before trade was established between this region and Asia. Spices, especially, were highly prized.

Silks, spices, and other goods were eventually introduced to Europeans. These desirable items from faraway lands spurred the burst of European exploration in the 15th and 16th centuries.

It was during this time, of course, that Christopher Columbus accidentally landed in the Americas. He was actually seeking an alternative route to spice-rich Asia. (He was not the first to land on this continent, however. For more on this, see October 12.) An amazing thing happened as a result of Columbus's "discovery" of the Americas. The food that people around the world ate was to change forever! Many food plants native to the Americas would be adopted by peoples on other continents (and some Old World plants introduced to the Americas). The box below describes some of these.

TASTY TRADES

Can you imagine a typical Italian meal—say, a plate of spaghetti—without tomato sauce, or an Irish meal that doesn't include potatoes?

Although Columbus did not personally bring back all the plants, his landing in the Americas made possible the widespread distribution of native plants such as tomatoes, potatoes, corn, *chile* peppers, and the cacao bean (from which chocolate is made).

In return, many plants from Asia and Europe (and later Africa) were soon grown throughout the Americas. These included wheat, barley, citrus fruits, and sugar cane.

8

Bake a spice cake.

In honor of some of the first foods that fueled world exploration and international trade, bake a spice cake. Here's a recipe for a type of cake Germans fondly call *Blitzkuchen* (BLITZ-koo-shun), or "lightning cake," because it's so quick and easy to make!

Spice Cake

½ stick butter or margarine, melted
1 egg
⅔ cup (200 ml) milk
1½ cups (200 g) all-purpose flour
½ cup (100 g) sugar
2 teaspoons (10 ml) baking powder
½ teaspoon (2.5 ml) cinnamon
½ teaspoon (2.5 ml) ground cloves
Pinch of nutmeg and salt

Place the first three ingredients in a mixing bowl; beat with an electric beater for 1 minute. Sift the remaining ingredients together and add to bowl. Beat until smooth. Pour into a greased 8" (20.5 cm) square pan. Dot with bits of cold butter and sprinkle with sugar and cinnamon, if desired. Bake in a preheated 375°F (190°C) oven for 25 to 30 minutes, or until golden brown.

9

Prepare for a journey with a *baci.*

A *baci* (bah-SEE) is a traditional Laotian good luck festival that is held whenever someone is about to leave on a long journey or has just returned from one. Visitors from foreign countries are also honored in this way, as well as newborn babies and their mothers and people recovering from illnesses.

Friends and relatives are invited to a *baci*, where they welcome the honored guest with poetry and prayers to bring good fortune. It is believed that each person has 32 souls that protect each part of the body, and these are summoned during the ceremony. A string is wrapped around the guest's wrists, tying them together, which symbolizes the uniting of the souls with the body.

The next time you and your family are planning a long trip, think of the Laotian *baci*. You might want to tie a bit of string around your wrists for extra good fortune, too!

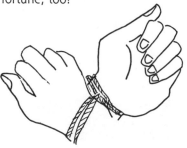

10

Make up a story about a fabled land.

Throughout history, explorers have searched for lands that may never have actually existed!

In 1540, for instance, the Spanish explorer, Coronado, feverishly searched northern Mexico and the southwestern part of the United States for the "Seven Cities of *Cíbola*" (SEE-boh-lah), rumored to be stockpiled with gold. He never found any of the fabled riches.

Countless explorers have been intrigued by accounts of Atlantis, an island that supposedly sank to the bottom of the Atlantic Ocean in 8498 B.C. near the Azores (off the coast of Portugal). Legend has it the people who lived in Atlantis were superior human beings in every way. The civilization vanished without a trace when an earthquake (or meteorite, as some believe!) rocked the region.

Create your own story about an imaginary land full of wonders. You can even make a map to go with your story (for a clever way to fold a map, see June 11).

11

Fold a map.

Exploration and maps go hand in hand! Here's an ingenious way of folding a map that is used by a Dutch mapmaker. Use it to fold any size rectangular map. Make the folds carefully and crease them well for best results.

Fold the paper in half from the top (1). Fold the corners down so they meet in the middle (2).

Unfold the corners. Push the top left-hand corner down and over (3). Turn the paper over and do the same on the other side (4).

Push the top layer of the bottom left-hand corner in, overlapping the center slightly (5). Do the same with the right-hand corner (6).

Turn the paper over and repeat the last two overlapping folds. To open, pull apart at the outermost folds. The map will spring open almost magically!

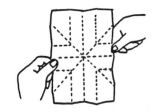

Explore some of the neighborhoods in your town or city! Perhaps you have ethnic neighborhoods where you can buy foods from around the world, or that you can visit when there are street fairs and other festivals taking place. You may not have to travel far to get a sense of some of the world's diverse cultures.

One Nation . . .

Today, there are about 170 officially recognized nations in the world. Each has its own flag and national anthem.

But what is it that really holds these nations together? It's people — many of whom share common traits, such as language, as well as the desire for a good life. Let's examine what makes a nation, and take a look at some of the outward symbols, too.

12

Describe what makes a nation.

Most nations are characterized by certain things its people have in common, such as history, language, and culture. But in recent years, the makeup of nations has been changing rapidly.

Some countries, such as the former Soviet Union have split into smaller nations (each now representing its own cultural heritage). Western European countries have done just the opposite. They've joined together for their mutual benefit, forming something known as the European Community.

Many countries, including the United States and Canada, are becoming increasingly multicultural. This is leading to a very exciting exchange of ideas and traditions, but people have to respect one another to make it work well for everyone.

Perhaps there will come a time when there are no longer nations. This isn't so far-fetched. After all, grouping people by nation only dates from the late 1700s. Before that, people pledged their allegiance to rulers or religions. Who knows what the future will bring?

13

Write your own constitution.

In order for a nation to prosper, its people must work together to assure the safety and well-being of everyone. This is where government comes in. Most countries have a plan, sometimes called a constitution, by which the people govern themselves.

A constitution often lays down the rules by which leaders are chosen. In a democracy, for example, leaders are elected by a majority vote.

A constitution might outline how property is divided, as in communist countries where land and houses are owned by the government itself in an effort to make things equal for a great many people. In theory this sounds good, but in practice many people resent the lack of freedoms, including being unable to publically criticize the government.

What sorts of rules would you make if you were in charge of keeping a group of people happy? Write a constitution for your family or classroom. Do you think any of your ideas would work on a larger scale?

14

Uncover the origins of names of nations.

Forming groups of people into nations led to the naming of countries. Have you ever wondered how some countries got their names? Do a little detective work (with the help of an encyclopedia) and see what you can discover about the origins of some national names.

Austrians call their nation *Österreich*, which is German for "eastern kingdom." One thousand years ago, what we now call Austria was just the northeastern part of a vast empire.

Ecuador takes its name from the Spanish word for "equator." Just remember this and you'll always be able to find Ecuador on a map!

Zimbabwe's name honors the Great Zimbabwe — the stone ruins of a center of commerce that flourished near the modern capital city of Harare for centuries, ending around the 1600s. Zimbabwe is the Bantu word for "stone house."

Syria is thought to get its name from *suri*, a type of rose that once grew in abundance in that region.

If you could name a country, what would you choose, and why?

15

Draw national flags for *Valdemars dag.*

The Danes feel strongly about their flag, especially on *Valdemars dag* (VAHL-duh-mars day), or "Valdemar's Day." This day commemorates an event which took place in 1219 when the Danes were at war with Estonia. Legend has it the Estonians had the upper hand in the battle when a red flag emblazoned with a white cross fell from the sky! King Valdemar II hoisted the flag above his troops, so heartening them that they won the battle.

While the story may stretch the truth a bit, it's true that the *Dannebrog* (DAHN-nuh-broh), as it's called, is the oldest national flag in the world.

How many national flags can you identify? Draw some of them to display in your room. You'll note that many share common traits, as described below.

STARS & STRIPES

The majority of the world's flags are striped. The stripes may be narrow or wide, and run either horizontally or vertically.

Thailand

Many flags feature a star or stars. Some show a crescent moon and star(s). The crescent moon is a symbol of Islam and is found on many of the flags in the Middle East.

Algeria

The cross is a common flag design. The flag of the United Kingdom combines three crosses, one for each of the three separate countries that make up the U.K. — England, Scotland, and Ireland.

United Kingdom

Some flags have unique emblems. Lebanon's flag has a cedar tree on it. Shields and spears are pictured on the flags of both Kenya and Swaziland.

Kenya

16

Design a national emblem.

Many countries have other recognizable symbols in addition to a flag. The kangaroo, for instance, is one of Australia's treasured symbols, just as the great pyramids are uniquely representative of Egypt.

Some national symbols have an interesting story behind them. Take Scotland's emblem, the purple thistle. As legend has it, the Picts (forebears of the Scots) were once the target of a surprise Danish raid. One of the Danes who came ashore stepped into a thistle, shouting out in pain. His cries served as a warning to the Picts, and the prickly plant became the beloved symbol it is today!

Design an emblem for a country of interest to you. How about a decorated egg to represent Ukraine, or a traditional wood carving for Ghana? What animals might you choose to represent Peru or New Zealand? Most countries have such a rich cultural heritage it may be hard to choose just one symbol!

17

Listen to some national anthems.

Every nation has a song, or anthem, that is sung during ceremonial occasions. (Some countries have several anthems.) Which have you heard?

Check your library for a recording of national anthems. You'll hear how some honor a monarch, such as Japan's national song entitled *Kimi-ga-yo,* or "The Emperor's Reign." The British royal anthem is *God Save the Queen* (or *King* when a male is on the throne).

Some anthems are dedicated to the homeland. The Finnish anthem *Maamme* means "Our Land." Costa Rica's anthem is entitled *Noble Patria,* or "Noble Country."

Most national anthems are uplifting. The Israeli anthem is optimistic, and appropriately called *Hatikvah,* or "Hope." Peru's anthem proudly proclaims *Somos libres,* which means "We are free."

. . . And the Livin' is Easy

Ah, summer! These are happy days for many kids living in much of the Northern Hemisphere.

Summer means no school for a while, plus all sorts of seasonal treats. Care to relax a while in a hammock, popping ripe berries into your mouth? Ahead are plenty of ways to make the most of your summer!

18

Hang a tree swing for *Tano.*

Korean girls look forward to *Tano* (TAH-noh), a festival during which traditional swinging contests are held for girls.

The girls compete for prizes while standing on swings hung from tall trees. It is thought that this type of swinging goes back to the days when girls were not allowed outside the confines of walled settlements. Standing on the swings, the girls were able to catch a glimpse of the world beyond their homes.

Do you have a tall tree with sturdy branches you can hang a rope swing from? Have your parents help you hang it and test it for strength. While you're swinging, you can think of these words from an ancient Korean poem that describes what it feels like when you're in the air:

**Not in heaven, not on earth,
But you are in mid-sky.
Blue hills and green waters
Seem to swing to and fro.
You come as falling flowers;
You go as skimming swallows.**

19

Put up a hammock.

Stay cool this summer in a hammock hung in the shade!

Did you know Columbus was so impressed by the hammocks he found the natives using in the Americas that he outfitted his ships with similar net beds? This idea was borrowed by other seafarers. Today, many people enjoy relaxing in hammocks, and they are still used as beds by native peoples in parts of Brazil.

Make your own hammock from a beach towel, two thick hardwood dowels 3 feet (1 m) long, and two 8-foot (2.5 m) pieces of sturdy rope. Stitch pockets for the dowels at either end of the towel; slip the dowels in place. Tie a piece of rope to both ends of each dowel.

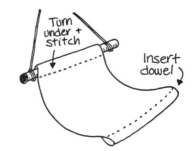

Turn under + stitch

Insert dowel

Tie the hammock to two shade trees or porch posts with more rope. Hop in!

Note: This hammock is designed to support the weight of just one child at a time.

20

Do some summer reading.

Once school is out, you'll probably have more time to read for pleasure. Get yourself some good books and head for your hammock!

Libraries all over the world encourage children to read not only during the summer months, but year-round. In Sweden and Israel, libraries sponsor programs offering everything from reading contests to visits from authors of children's books.

Does your library have a summer reading program? Join up this year and read some books written about other countries and cultures. You'll be touched by *Sadako and the Thousand Paper Cranes*, delight in the *All-of-a-Kind Family*, and sympathize with Miguel in . . . *And Now Miguel.* Of course, there are also many folk tales from around the world (some of these are listed in the bibliography starting on page 147).

In China, schoolchildren are often given homework and a required reading list to be completed over the summer break (which may be only six weeks long). So . . . enjoy the time you have, and put it to good use. Read!

21

Watch the sunset on the first day of summer.

The first day of summer is the longest day of the year, at least in the Northern Hemisphere. (It's the first day of winter south of the equator.) Ask your parents if you can watch the sun set tonight. Choose a special place, such as the top of a high hill, to view it from. What time does the sun finally disappear from sight?

If you lived close to the Arctic Circle, in one of the Scandinavian countries for example, you would be up all night! For several days around the beginning of summer, the sun never sinks below the horizon. For many weeks after that the sun is still visible well into the night. No wonder they call it the Land of the Midnight Sun!

In some places in Japan, specially raised fireflies are released on the evening of the first day of summer.

22

Decorate a *majstång*.

As you might expect, beginning-of-summer festivities are especially popular in the Scandinavian countries.

Many Swedish villages put up a *majstång* (MY-stung), or "maypole," on the village green. (The word doesn't come from the month of May, but from the Old Swedish word *mayar*, meaning "to adorn with branches or leaves.") Swedish maypoles are usually quite large and shaped like a cross with rings at either end of the horizontal piece, much like the one shown below.

Make your own *majstång* from two sticks bound together with rope or twine. Wrap vines around the sticks, or simply tie bunches of grass, flowers, and leafy branches to the poles with bits of colored yarn or ribbon. Everybody helps decorate the *majstång* in Sweden, so invite your friends to join in on the fun!

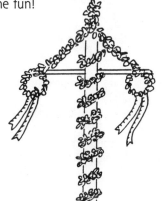

23

Make berry jam.

With summer finally here, berry-picking can't be far behind!

There's nothing like a handful of fresh bilberries (as blueberries are called in England) or lingonberries (a favorite in Scandinavia and Russia).

When you've had your fill of fresh berries, why not make some berry jam? It's a great way to capture the flavor of summer in a jar. The box below outlines the steps to follow to make the best-tasting jam ever!

JAM PACKED

Making jam is as easy as one, two, three! This recipe makes about two 8-ounce (250 ml) jars of jam. Use any type of berry, such as strawberries, raspberries, or blueberries, alone or in combination. Be sure to have an adult help you at the stove.

1. Sterilize two canning jars with two-part lids (the kind with a rubber-backed disk held in place with a screw band). Boil the jars and bands in water for 20 minutes; put the disks in a bowl, cover with boiling water, and set aside.

2. Meanwhile, place four cups (500 g) of washed berries and one apple cut into tiny pieces in a heavy-bottomed pan and cook until soft. Add three cups (600 g) sugar, stirring to dissolve. Bring to a boil, then reduce the heat and cook, uncovered, until the jam begins to thicken. This will take 20 to 30 minutes.

3. Spoon the jam into the empty, hot jars, leaving about ½" (1.5 cm) of space at the top. Place the disks on the jars and screw the bands in place. Turn each jar upside-down to seal the jars. Let cool completely.

Leave ½" (1.5 cm) space

Spiritual Upbringing

Religion plays an important role in many people's lives around the world. Religious beliefs differ considerably, however, from faith to faith.

Just what are some of these differences? Read on to find out. Here are also some ways to gain an appreciation for the world's religions through their art.

24

Name some of the world's religions.

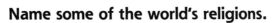

There are dozens of different religions practiced throughout the world today. They range from the so-called tribal religions of Africa and the Americas (many of which have a very small following) to the world religions such as Islam and Judaism, both of which claim millions of followers in many countries throughout the world.

Five well-known world religions are briefly described below. What other religious beliefs can you add to this list?

BELIEVERS ALL

The oldest world religion, founded 4,000 years ago, is Hinduism. Hindus worship many gods and goddesses, all thought to represent a supreme unknowable God. Hindus believe in reincarnation, or rebirth after death. By living a good life, a person will, Hindus believe, be reborn into an even better life.

Buddhism was founded about 2,500 years ago by a Hindu prince named Siddhartha Gautama, who came to be known as Buddha, or "the enlightened one." Buddhists also believe in reincarnation, hoping to eventually reach nirvana, a state of being free from pain and suffering.

Judaism is a 3,000-year-old religion whose followers believe in just one God. There are several branches of Judaism. Orthodox Jews are considered the most strict. They prepare their food according to certain dietary rules, and do no work on the sabbath (from sundown on Friday until sundown Saturday). Other branches of the religion observe many of the same traditions but have relaxed some of the rules.

Christianity takes its name from Jesus Christ, born nearly 2,000 years ago. Jesus, who was Jewish, felt many Jews did not understand the meaning of God. After his death, his followers carried on his work, convinced that Jesus was in fact the son of God.

Islam was founded nearly 1,500 years ago by an Arab named Muhammad who claimed he was the prophet of the one god called Allah. Muslims, as followers of Islam are called, must do five things. They must declare their faith in Allah; they must pray five times a day facing Mecca (located in Saudi Arabia); they must fast during the month of Ramadan; they must give money to the needy; and they must make a pilgrimage to Mecca once in their lifetime.

25

HINDU HOLIDAY

Draw religious symbols for *Rath Yatra.*

Rath Yatra (rahth YAH-trah) is certainly one of the most spectacular of the Hindu holidays. People line streets to watch as a procession of enormous floats are wheeled by. The floats are actually models of Hindu temples, complete with images of gods and goddesses (some with several pairs of arms and legs).

Many religions are characterized by certain symbols that are slightly mysterious and certainly awe-inspiring. A Buddhist temple may have several towering statues of Buddha in it, some showing him sitting cross-legged, others lying down. Imagine the wonder this inspires in young children when they visit a temple!

Draw some of the symbols of different religions, such as the six-pointed Jewish star of David or scenes from the life of Jesus that are depicted in stained glass in some churches. Studying these symbols will give you a sense of the beauty and wonder that are a part of many religions.

26

Write a prayer or blessing.

Spoken prayers and blessings are a part of many religions. Many appeal to a higher being, be it a god, or in the case of many Native American religions, nature. This Tewa prayer from New Mexico is an example of the latter:

> **Weave us clothing of great brightness**
> **That we may walk where birds sing and grass grows green,**
> **Oh, our mother the earth,**
> **Oh, our father the sky.**

Buddhists recite an ancient prayer each day which starts like this:

> **May all beings have happiness and the cause of happiness.**
> **May they be free of suffering and the cause of suffering.**

Write your own words to describe your hopes for humankind, or the thanks you feel for the food on your table and the love of your family and friends. Recite your prayer or blessing at mealtime, or at the start of your day.

27

Design a prayer rug.

Many Muslims kneel on a mat or rug when they pray. The rugs have a special feature woven into the design. One end of the central design comes to a "point" that is positioned to face the direction of Mecca.

In the spirit of these and other beautifully patterned rugs made in the Middle East and central Asia, paint a piece of canvas to look like a woven rug. Turn under the hem of a small rectangle of canvas (fabric stores stock inexpensive canvas); glue to secure. Sketch a design on the canvas in pencil. Use the rug illustrated below as inspiration, or check your library for books with color pictures of rugs.

Outline your design with a permanent marker; then color both the background and inside the designs, using acrylic paints. Use as a rug on the floor, or hang on a wall as decoration.

28

Make an *Ojo de Dios.*

The *Ojo de Dios* (OH-ho day dee-OHS), or "God's Eye," is an ancient symbol made by the Huichol of Mexico. The central "eye" is made when a child is born. Each year a bit of yarn is woven around the sticks, until the child turns five, when the *Ojo* is completed.

Make your own *Ojo* from two straight twigs and a selection of colored yarns. Cross the sticks and lash them together by wrapping yarn over them diagonally, first one way and then the other. Do this until there's a rounded hump, which is the "eye."

Tie a new length of yarn to the old and, bringing it from behind, wrap it completely around one of the spokes of the cross. Carry the yarn to the next spoke and do the same. Continue in this way (changing colors as desired), turning the cross as you go from spoke to spoke. Knot securely to finish.

Growth Spurt

Have your parents ever said to you, "Enjoy being a kid. It doesn't last forever!"?

All kids are anxious to grow up, and for some it comes sooner than others. Depending on the culture, a child might be considered an adult as young as 11 or 12 years of age. Marriage may follow close behind.

Here are some of the ways these milestones are observed around the world.

29

Count the years until you are "of age."

When do kids stop being children and start being adults? It all depends on the culture, and whether you're talking about being "of age" according to a religion, to the law, or to the customary age when marriages take place.

Jewish boys all over the world, for instance, are considered adults, according to their faith, once they have been initiated with a *bar mitzvah* at age thirteen. They are still children for a few more years, however, according to the laws of the countries where they live, and they probably will not marry until they are much older.

In most cultures, coming of age happens at puberty (a time when bodily changes occur). This transition to adulthood is celebrated with great fanfare in some places, as you'll see in the box below.

GROWING, GROWING, GROWN!

Getting ready for the leap to adulthood is an exciting time in many cultures. In many places, boys and girls are isolated from others when they are close to their coming of age. This may be for a period of several months, as it is for Efe girls in Zaire, and for Basari boys in Senegal. During this time, the almost-adults are taught many things by their elders. Girls will learn about the responsibilities of marriage and raising a family; boys might be required to pass many tests of endurance, such as going without food in the wilds for five days.

After this time, there is usually a village-wide celebration that lasts for many days in honor of the young adults. In many rural African communities, the girls are now eligible for marriage.

Navajo girls in the southwestern United States are honored with similar festivities. Their initiation ends with an all-night singing session led by tribal medicine men and the baking of a special cake in a large hole dug in the ground.

30

Learn some proverbs.

The wisdom of elders is passed down from one generation to another in many ways. One of these is through proverbs — sayings that serve to guide people in their everyday lives.

One Japanese proverb, for example, states:

A protruding nail is hammered down.

This is a clever way of saying that it is best to conform and not stand out.

The Vietnamese remind their children that

A drop of blood is better than an ocean of water.

What do they mean by this? That family ties are the strongest bonds. The Berbers living in northwestern Africa say:

Follow the path of your father and grandfather.

This is another reference to the importance of family.

One Italian proverb is a colorful reminder that it is sometimes best to keep your opinions to yourself. Remember this the next time you're not sure if you should speak up:

Flies don't get into a closed mouth.

1

Put on a veil.

In many Middle Eastern communities, once a girl reaches puberty she must wear a veil whenever she's in public. This is an ancient custom thought to have originated in India and Persia (modern-day Iran), and later adopted by the nomadic peoples throughout the Middle East.

Some veils, such as the *yashmak* (YAHSH-mahk), cover just the head, face (except for the eyes), and upper body. Other veils are more like cloaks, concealing the entire body except for the face. Young girls usually wear veils that are not so restricting, such as a headcovering of some sort. Some girls in Saudi Arabia start wearing these when they are as young as six years old.

To get a sense of what it feels like to wear a veil, tie an oblong scarf around your head so that one end drapes down over your forehead and the other end covers the lower part of your face. Or tie a scarf over your head to create a head-covering.

2

List the contents of a dowry.

When women in India, Italy, and Arab countries marry, their families present the husbands with a dowry, or valuables such as money, property, and useful goods. This is meant to compensate the husband for taking on the financial burden of a wife and family.

The Gisu of East Africa do just the opposite. Because a wife is considered such a valuable asset, her prospective husband gives the bride's family livestock in exchange for the young woman's hand in marriage.

Try to imagine what might be included in a dowry in a particular culture or country. What, if anything, would you want your future husband or wife to contribute in the way of a dowry?

3

Compare wedding customs.

Different cultures and countries have their own wedding customs that have been handed down over the years. Here are just a few ways people begin a life together.

Jewish couples are married under a *huppah* (HOO-pah), a canopy held up by four poles. In Israeli communes, the *huppah* is sometimes made from an Israeli flag supported by farm tools.

In Japan, the bride and groom share a cup of wine, exchanging the cups nine times to symbolize the bond of marriage.

When an Ibo woman of Niger is born, she is "claimed" by a villager who brings gifts to her parents each year thereafter in exchange. Her wedding day is simply the day on which she moves into her husband's house.

In Vietnam, a bride steps over a small stove full of burning coals when she enters her husband's home on the day of her wedding. This is believed to banish any evil spirits and purify her for her new life.

4

Make a wedding crown.

Couples in Myanmar (fomerly Burma), Greece, and parts of Eastern Europe are treated like royalty on the day of their marriage. In keeping with this, they traditionally wear crowns during the wedding ceremony.

Just for fun, make a wedding crown you can wear. Shape a strip of poster board with scissors, then decorate with traditional designs from a culture that is of interest to you. Use markers, crayons, or paint, as well as glitter and glued-on sequins, if you like. The crown illustrated below is decorated with the tree of life, an important symbol found at Ukrainian weddings.

Let your crown dry completely before stapling or gluing it into a circle to fit snugly on your head.

In Thailand, the bride and groom wear string crowns, attached to one another with a sacred thread.

Night Vision

Did you know that the stars you see at night are not the same as those seen by children in Argentina and Australia? In the Southern Hemisphere, a different set of constellations is visible once the sun goes down.

Ahead, you'll discover some constellations have different stories to explain their presence in the sky. And don't forget the moon! It is important to many cultures around the world, too.

Look for Polaris, or the North Star. This star is known as the Great Imperial Ruler of Heaven in China. The Navajo refer to it as Star That Does Not Move.

5

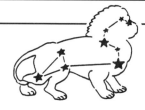

Identify some constellations.

The Big Dipper is certainly one of the best-known star formations in the Northern Hemisphere. It does look like a ladle, doesn't it? (The seven stars are actually part of a larger constellation called *Ursa Major,* Latin for "big bear.")

The Big Dipper isn't visible everywhere, however. The favorite constellation of kids living in Australia, South America, and parts of Africa is one known as the Southern Cross.

How many constellations can you identify? Someone who is familiar with different constellations can help you find them in the night sky, or you can study a star chart. Do this before you head outdoors so you know what you're looking for.

The following hints will make your star search more enjoyable:

 Lie down on a blanket or reclining chair (it's a lot easier on your neck).

 Dress warmly!

 If you refer to a star chart outdoors, cover your flashlight with some red cellophane. That way your eyes won't have to continually adjust to the light changes.

6

Learn some legends about the sky.

Explanations about the appearance of stars, planets, and other celestial objects often reflect what was important to the people who invented their names and stories. Take the constellation known as the Northern Crown, for example.

This cluster of seven stars was named by European stargazers long ago. They called it *Corona Borealis,* which is Latin for "northern crown," because it looked like a crown to them.

To ancient peoples living in England, this constellation looked more like a castle with an open door. The moon goddess was said to live there. The Arabs in the Middle East thought the constellation resembled a beggar's bowl.

Certain Native Americans believed the stars were a group of dancing sisters. The gap in the circle was thought to exist because one of the sisters had been carried off by a hunter.

What sorts of stories might you make up to explain what is visible in the night sky?

7

Make paper decorations for *Tanabata.*

Tanabata (tah-nah-BAH-tah) is a popular Japanese festival based on an ancient Chinese myth. As the story is told, there once was a star princess who was a weaver (she is represented by the star we call Vega) who fell in love with a cowherd star (Altair). The two were so in love that they neglected to do their work, and so were sent by the princess's father to opposite ends of the Milky Way. They were allowed to meet just once a year on the seventh day of the seventh month, crossing the heavens on a bridge made of birds.

Today, Japanese children write poems on long strips of paper and tie them to the branches of trees. Festive paper streamers representing the Milky Way decorate the streets all over the country.

You can make a traditional *Tanabata* decoration to hang in your home. Just follow the simple directions in the box on the facing page.

8

Name the full moons.

There is nothing quite so awe-inspiring as the moon when it's full. Have you ever watched as it slowly rises into the night sky?

While the pattern of the moon's craters may remind you of a face, Japanese children look at the full moon and see a white rabbit pounding rice into rice cakes and dumplings. The next time the moon is full, take a good look. Do you see it?

Many Native Americans have names for the different full moons during the year. You may have heard September's full moon called the Harvest Moon. The Zuñi Indians of New Mexico and Arizona call the full moon of July the Corn Moon because it appears when the corn is beginning to ripen. Several tribes refer to the full moon that rises in January or February as the Hunger Moon, because traditionally that was a time when game was scarce and stored grains would be running low.

What names might you give to some of the full moons during the year? Why have you chosen those particular names?

STAR STREAMERS

Gather lots of paper squares (use origami paper or cut your own from gift wrap), a stick about 2 feet (60 cm) long, a needle with a large eye, and some thin string.

To make one unit, fold a paper square (colored side up) in half to make a rectangle; fold in half again to make a small square. Unfold completely.

Fold the paper in half diagonally, then in half diagonally again. Unfold completely.

Refold the paper into a rectangle, pushing in the two sides to form a triangular shape.

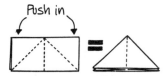

Make as many of these triangular units as you like. String them in long strands, using the needle and thread, knotting the string after each addition so the triangles stay apart. Tie several strands to the stick and hang.

9

Bake crescent cookies.

Did you know the crescent moon was the model for the French *croissant* (kwah-SAHW)? The flaky pastry actually got its start in Austria. To celebrate a victory over Turkish troops in the 1600s, Viennese bakers made bread in the shape of the crescent on the Turkish banner.

Many countries include crescent-shaped cookies among their traditional sweets. Use the following recipe to make your own.

Pecan Crescents

1 cup (125 g) flour
½ cup (125 g) butter or margarine
1 cup (125 g) finely chopped pecans
2 tablespoons (30 g) sugar
1 teaspoon (5 ml) vanilla
Pinch salt
Confectioners' sugar

Combine the first six ingredients, mixing well with your hands. Chill in the refrigerator for 30 minutes.

Shape walnut-sized pieces of dough into crescents. Place on ungreased baking sheets and bake in preheated 375°F (190°C) oven for 15 to 20 minutes. Let stand for one minute before removing from the sheets. Cool for an additional five minutes, then roll in confectioners' sugar. Makes about 20 cookies.

10

Learn your astrological sign.

Astrology is a branch of astronomy that is concerned with the supposed influence of the planets. According to astrology, how the planets were positioned when you were born determines what kind of person you are and can also be used to predict your future.

Astrology is a guiding force in such countries as Bhutan, where astrologers are consulted often to determine the best time to plant crops, make a journey, or marry. Many people in other Asian countries also rely on astrology, while millions more around the world have a passing interest in it.

Do you know your astrological sign? Look for the horoscope, or astrological forecast, in your local newspaper. There you'll find the twelve signs and the dates they cover. You'll also find what supposedly will happen to all those born "under" those signs. Is there any truth to what it says will happen to you today?

ARIES

BELGIUM

Getting Around

When you want to go somewhere, what do you do? Do you hop in the family car, or reach in your pocket for a subway or bus token? Maybe there are some places you walk or ride your bike to.

Children around the world move about by many different means. Here are just a few of these ways.

11

Take a walk for *Ommegang.*

Each year in July, the people of Brussels, Belgium enjoy a spectacle known as *Ommegang* (OH-meh-gahng), which is Flemish for "walk around." This colorful pageant is a reenactment of the medieval custom of walking around the perimeters of buildings (or entire cities) to offer them protection.

Even if you don't believe walking around a town offers magical protection, there is something magical about walking! It's the best way to really get to know an area (and it's great exercise!). You have time to notice all the little things you might otherwise miss, and you can stop and say hello to the people you meet.

In many countries, including Bhutan, Laos, and Peru, people walk great distances everyday. That is the only way for them to get around. As you can imagine, a lot of time is spent just getting from one place to another. Think about that when you're on foot, and take a moment to enjoy the slower pace of life made possible by walking.

12

Ride a bicycle.

Do you have your own bicycle? Lots of people ride bikes for fun and recreation, but did you know that in many parts of the world bikes are a major form of transportation?

China is one country that relies heavily on bicycles. Both adults and children ride them regularly. It's not always easy purchasing a bike in China, however, because they are expensive, and there is often a waiting period involved when buying one.

Bikes are popular in the Netherlands, where even cities have bicycle paths that are used by those who cycle to work as well as by those who ride for pleasure.

In many Asian countries, including India and Malaysia, bicycles are used to pull rickshaws—hooded carriages that seat one or two persons. Rickshaws were once pulled by people running on foot. People still, of course, supply the pedal power!

13

Name some of the world's cars.

In some countries, such as Germany, many people rely on cars for their transportation needs. Most industrialized nations produce their cars, but there's also a good deal of international trade in automobiles. How many cars manufactured in other countries can you name?

Names that are given to cars are quite interesting. Sweden's Volvo, for instance, is the Latin word for "I roll," referring to the ball bearings that were the trademark of this car early on. The Volkswagen (pronounced FOHLKS-vah-gen in German) means "people's car" and was named that because the first models were inexpensive enough for everyone to afford.

Many companies also name the various models they produce. Occasionally a particular model is renamed for sale in another country. The Chevrolet Nova, named for a type of star, didn't inspire confidence among Mexican car buyers. No wonder! *"No va"* in Spanish means "doesn't go"!

14

Use public transportation.

Cars are too expensive for many people around the world to own. Not only that, many cities are already choked with traffic, and many rural areas have rough roads (and few mechanics!).

So how do people travel those distances that are too far to walk? They use public transportation. If you ride the subway or bus where you live, you can appreciate some of the benefits of public transportation. With many people sharing one bus or train, there is less congestion and, more importantly, less pollution.

Which of the types of mass transit described below are you familiar with?

ALL TOGETHER NOW

If a regular bus can hold dozens of people, imagine what a bus twice the size can hold! In Great Britain, there are many buses like this that are known as double-deckers.

Buses in Haiti are often very crowded. It's not uncommon for passengers to actually sit on the rooftops. Buses are affectionately called tap-taps, because the riders on the roof tap when they want to be dropped off.

Many large cities around the world take advantage of the space beneath the streets and run underground trains. Children in Paris, Mexico City, and Tokyo may use the subway system to get to school or to visit friends in other neighborhoods.

Both the Japanese and French have developed high-speed trains to link various cities. While electric trains in North America average 80 mph (130 kph), the French TGV (for *train à grand vitesse*, "high-speed train") is the world's fastest, averaging over 170 mph (270 kph)!

15

Make a pair of stilts.

The Bajau Laut who live on boats in the Philippines sometimes walk through the water on stilts. You can imagine what happens when someone loses his or her balance!

In other parts of the world, stilts are mostly just for fun. Kids everywhere make their own, and so can you.

You need two lengths of lumber, say 2 × 3s—a little longer than you are tall. Make foot rests from a 6" (36 cm) piece of a 2 × 4 cut in half as shown.

Drill two holes in each foot rest and a series of holes along the lower length of each stilt. Attach the foot rests with long screws (start low!). Sand the edges and any rough spots.

To use your stilts, stand on a step, tuck the stilts under your arms, and step onto the foot rests. Keep your feet snugly against the stilts and think of them as an extension of your legs.

16

Make toy vehicles.

Children all over the world are fascinated by cars and trucks and other things that "go." Wherever ready-made play vehicles aren't commonly available, children make their own from whatever is on hand.

Boys in Haiti create clever vehicles from vegetables and fruits. They might slice an orange to make wheels for a car made from a whole papaya.

!Kung children in Africa work together to make pretend cars and trucks. A group of kids support a frame made from bent sticks on their shoulders (there is sometimes a separate steering wheel). They take turns "steering," while the whole group moves together as one. With everyone making the revving sounds of an engine, it sounds almost like the real thing!

These are just two ideas you can use to make some toy vehicles of your own. What other ideas can you and your friends come up with?

The Sporting Life

One dictionary defines sport as "physical activity engaged in for pleasure." That's an important point to keep in mind. Winning isn't nearly as important as having a good time!

Kids around the world enjoy playing organized sports after school, as well as more casual games with a few friends and a ball. Here are a few sports played around the world, as well as the biggest international sporting event of them all—the Olympics!

17

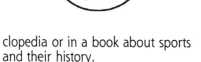

Research the origins of sports.

Many of today's popular sports trace their origins to various countries and cultures around the world. Pick a sport you enjoy playing, or watching, and see what you can discover about its origins. Look for information in an encyclopedia or in a book about sports and their history.

The box below describes some of the sports played around the world, and the reasons they were first played.

BODY BUILDERS

Some sports are thought to have originated as religious rites. Running is one of these. In fact, foot races, usually run barefoot, are still run by the Pueblo Indians of New Mexico and the Maya in Guatemala for religious reasons.

Other sports were used to train young men in the ways of war. Lacrosse originated in Canada where native peoples used it as an exercise in combat. The game was known as baggataway (and was quite a brutal game), until French missionaries started calling the stick la crosse because it resembled a bishop's staff.

Some of the sports that are especially popular in certain countries got their start in other parts of the world. Curling, a popular Scottish sport where large round stones are hurled across ice, is thought to have originated in the Netherlands (home of many ice sports). Tennis probably got its start in France, where it was played with a bare (or gloved) hand for centuries before the long-handled racket was invented around 1500. Field hockey is believed to have originated in Asia. This may explain why there are many ancient Native American games that are like hockey. The first Americans made their way to this continent from Asia around 24,000 years ago.

18

Play ball.

Without a doubt, the most popular sport in the world (to both play and watch) is soccer, or football, as it's known around the world. Did you know there is also a sport called Gaelic football, which is played in Ireland, as well as Australian, American, and Canadian football? In these versions, players not only kick the ball but pass and catch it with their hands.

Malaysian boys and men enjoy a sport called sepak raga, played with a small ball made from interwoven rattan strips. The players stand in a circle and pass the ball to one another using every part of the body but the hands. In another version of the game, the ball is volleyed over a net.

Team a ball with a bat and you've got baseball, as popular in Japan today as it is in North America! The British prefer another sport where the ball is batted—cricket. Spectators politely clap for both teams during matches. From this display of fair play comes a popular expression. Kids in England often describe something that is unfair as "not cricket."

19

Run a relay race.

Relay races are fun for everyone because they don't require any fancy equipment or skills, and team effort really counts!

You and your friends can run relays even in small areas, by racing to a turnaround point and going back to the start where another runner is tagged or handed an object such as a small stick.

Try some international versions of relays, such as the William Tell relay. (William Tell was a Swiss man who refused to pay his taxes and was ordered to shoot an apple from his son's head with a bow and arrow. Happily, his aim was perfect!) Runners in this relay are given apples, which they balance on their heads while *walking* to the turnaround point. They then hold the apples in place and run back to the start.

An Oasis relay is perfect for a hot day when you can imagine you are in the desert in Egypt or Algeria. Each team is given a cup full of water to carry while running. The team with the most water in its cup at the end of the race is the winner.

20

Try some Olympic sports.

Athletes from all over the world—each representing his or her own country—come together to participate in the Olympics, a sporting event that traces its roots to ancient Greece.

The first Olympic Games were held in Olympus, Greece in 776 B.C. Not much is known about those early games, but they were regularly scheduled every four years until they were banned by a Christian emperor in 393 A.D. A modern version of the competitions was revived over 1,500 years later in 1896.

The events today are open to athletes no matter where they come from. Occasionally, someone from a tropical climate will represent his or her country in a winter event such as skiing!

Which Olympic sports have you tried? Perhaps you enjoy gymnastics, swimming, and running—all Olympic sports. Try throwing a javelin (use any long, slender stick), or practice the long jump. Come winter, pack a narrow trail down a snowy hill and sled down it, pretending it's a luge run!

21

Host a neighborhood Olympics.

Get a group of your friends together and put on a neighborhood Olympics. Have everybody represent the country of his or her choice. You can even make tiny paper flags for everyone to pin onto their clothes!

Organize events that are similar to those that take place either during the summer or winter Olympics. Scale the events down to suit the kids who are participating as well as the area you have to work within. You can adapt a swing set or jungle gym for various gymnastic events, for example, or substitute something like roller skating (which is not an Olympic sport) for speed skating (which is).

Or come up with your own crazy events, such as a backwards race or soccer played on stilts (make your own stilts as described on July 15). Plan both individual events as well as some team sports. Just remember, like in the real Olympics, it's the spirit of friendly competition that counts!

22

Make award medals.

Honor the athletes who participate in your neighborhood Olympics with some eye-catching medals!

One way to make these is with frozen juice can lids (the kind held in place with a plastic strip), permanent markers, and ribbon.

Hammer a hole in each lid near the edge with a fat nail. Turn the lid over and flatten the hole's jagged edges with the hammer. Decorate the lids with the markers, writing some with the words "gold," "silver," and "bronze," if you like, or making them all the same. Make enough so everybody gets a medal.

Cut the ribbon into 30" (.75 m) lengths and thread a ribbon through the hole in each lid. Tie the ends securely.

During the awards ceremony you might want to play a recording of Aaron Copland's *Fanfare for the Common Man*, which is the familiar Olympic musical theme, or a selection of national anthems.

A Hero's Welcome

Thanks to the heroic efforts of men, women, and children everywhere — who put the needs of others before their own concerns — the world is a better place in which to live. But a lot still needs to be done!

Ahead you'll meet some national heroes and some religious ones, as well as discover what it takes to be a hero or heroine!

23

Define heroism.

In fairy tales and fantasy films, heroes and heroines are unbelievable characters who battle evil and conquer foes singlehandedly. In real life, of course, it's not quite like that!

A hero is a man, and a heroine is a woman, who are noted for their outstanding achievements, their courage, or their kindness and thoughtfulness towards others. Soliders who fight for their countries are heroes; so are scientists who discover cures for diseases. Heroes include many people who have stood up for what they believed was right.

Does everyone agree on who is a hero and who is not? No, because there are often two sides to every story. Today many people regard Christopher Columbus as more of a villain than a hero because his landing in the Americas 500 years ago forever changed life on these continents. People's perceptions change, however, and you have to look back in history to understand that what Columbus did was acceptable at the time.

24

Name national heroes for *El Nacimiento de Libertador Simón Bolívar.*

Heroic men and women have played important roles in shaping many of the countries of the world.

Venezuelans honor their greatest national hero with parades on *El Nacimiento de Libertador Simón Bolívar* (ell nah-see-mee-EN-toh day lee-bear-tah-DOOR see-MONE boh-LEE-vahr), or "Liberator Simón Bolívar's Birthday."

Bolívar was born on this day in 1783, into a wealthy family. He gave all that up to fight for South America's independence from Spain. This proved to be a struggle that outlived him, but which earned him the nickname "the George Washington of South America." He is considered the father of not one but five countries — Venezuela, Ecuador, Colombia, Peru, and Bolivia (once called Bolívar). He also layed the groundwork for the freeing of slaves, which was enacted nine years earlier than in the United States.

Can you name some national heroes and heroines from your country? How is your life affected by what they did?

25

Celebrate a saint's day.

The Christian church has honored some of its heroes and heroines by making them saints. Each saint is remembered on his or her feast day. Christian children who are named after saints are often honored on these days instead of on their birthdays. This is true in Mexico and Greece, although it is becoming common to celebrate *both* a child's birthday and name day! Do you share the same name with any of the saints? When is that saint's feast day?

Certain saints are associated with different countries. St. Olaf is the patron, or protecting and guiding, saint of Norway; St. Joan of Arc, the patron saint — and national heroine — of France.

There are even saints that are said to look after the needs of children. It probably comes as no surprise that St. Nicholas (you may know him better as Santa Claus) is the patron saint of all children!

My name is Patrick!

26

Illustrate a hero's deeds.

Japanese children are familiar with the life and adventures of the *Kyokaku* (kyo-KAH-koo), or "hosts of heroism," who helped the common people during a time in Japan's history when there was a lot of corruption. There are many songs, plays, and even comic books, featuring some of these courageous heroes.

Draw a picture or storyboard (a sequence of pictures like a comic strip) to illustrate a real life hero from a country or culture of interest to you. You might illustrate the life of St. Patrick, Ireland's beloved saint, or that of Moshoeshoe, a young chief who united the Basotho people of modern-day Lesotho in the mid-1800s.

Or choose someone who is alive today, such as Lech Walesa who has done so much for the Polish people, or Mother Teresa, the Roman Catholic nun who aids the poor and suffering throughout the world. If you don't know the true story of his or her life, draw it the way you imagine it might have been.

27

Stage a shadow puppet show.

You can also tell a hero's story with puppets. In Java, shadow puppets have been used to perform shadow plays called *wayang kulit* (WHY-anhg koo-lit) for nearly a thousand years. The Hindu stories they tell originated in India. One popular epic is called the *Ramayana* (rah-mah-YAH-nah) and tells of the exciting adventures and good deeds of King Rama, Queen Sita, and the king's brother, Lakshmana.

The flat puppets (called *wayang*) are made from intricately cut and chiseled water buffalo skins. The arms are often hinged at the elbows and shoulders, and are moved with stiff wires. The puppeteer positions himself behind a screen which is lit from behind, so just the silhouetted figures are seen.

Put on your own shadow puppet show of real or imaginary heroes and heroines! The basics are outlined below.

PUPPET PRIMER

Simple shadow puppets can be made from poster board, two straightened wire coat hangers, paper fasteners, and tape.

Sketch the outline of each figure on the poster board, making the arms separate and in two sections. The joints at all moving parts should be at least ½" (1.5 cm) wide to accommodate the fasteners. Cut out each figure, adding interior details with an X-acto knife or paper punch.

Punch holes in the shoulders and in the shoulder and elbow joints of the two arms. Assemble all the parts with the fasteners, making sure they aren't too tight — there should be a little play so the arms move freely.

Bend one hanger to conform to the figure's shape. Tape it to the back. Cut two wires about 18" (45 cm) long for the arms. Tape one end of each wire to each hand.

Punch holes for fasteners

Stretch a white sheet across a doorway, placing a lamp behind it, or use a conventional puppet stage.

28

Be a hero or heroine.

All heroic men and women were once children! Many of them probably learned something about being thoughtful and helpful when they were young.

Have you ever helped a frightened kitten out of a tree, or taken on extra responsibilities without complaint to help your family in some way? Have you ever spoken up for something you really believed in, even though it wasn't popular? Then, in a small way, you have been a hero.

Just remember, all the little things you do add up. Making friends with a new kid in class, offering to run errands for a housebound neighbor, raising money to send as a contribution to a struggling country — things like this mean a lot. Heroes aren't superhuman characters found in comic books, with special powers and big muscles. Heroes are real people just like you . . . with big hearts.

Native Tongue

It is not known exactly how many different languages are spoken throughout the world. Most references say there are somewhere between 4,000 and 5,000. Amazing!

No one could ever learn to speak even a fraction of that number of languages, but many people around the world are fluent in several languages. Learning a new language is said to be easiest for children. So, don't put it off any longer — learn a new language today!

For more on alphabets, see pages 66 and 67.

29 Learn a foreign language.

Yo hablo español.

Language, of course, is the way people communicate with one another. Knowing how to speak one language well is very important, but being able to communicate in other languages is also valuable. In fact, as the world becomes more like one large global neighborhood, people who know how to speak more than one language will be at an advantage.

In most countries, foreign language instruction is required for all children at some point in their schooling. Because of its growing importance as a world language, English is the most common second language taught. French, Spanish, and German are also popular — and useful — second languages.

What languages do you speak, and where did you learn them? Is there a particular language you would like to be able to speak? A sampling of languages can be found in the box below, including some that you may know.

I SAY!

Do you know what all these children are saying? They are saying, "Hello!"

30 Say something in Esperanto.

Imagine what it would be like if everyone on earth spoke the same language, and had a truly global means of communicating. It's something many people have tried to create. Perhaps you've heard of Esperanto — the best known of these artificial languages, as they're known.

Esperanto was developed by L.L. Zamenhof, a Polish physician, in 1887. He modeled his language after several European languages (making it more useful for those who speak European languages, and less so for those who don't). Esperanto has a limited following; still a number of books have been translated into the language, and there are even radio stations that broadcast in Esperanto.

Here's a handy phrase you may want to learn in case you ever meet someone who speaks Esperanto:

Keil vi fartas? **(KEE-el vee FARR-tahs)**

This means "How are you?"

31

Learn sign language.

Deaf people all over the world communicate with sign language. Using hand gestures and facial expressions, they are able to indicate whole words and ideas — sometimes faster than can be spoken! While many of the gestures are the same, the meanings vary from one language to the next. A Russian child can not understand the signs made by a French child, for example.

Each sign language also has a manual alphabet for spelling out words. The Swedish and English manual alphabets use both hands, while the American uses only one hand.

Would you like to learn to sign? Your hearing-impaired friends may be willing to teach you, or you can teach yourself. See the bibliography for some names of books that illustrate the hand and body movements.

Soon you'll be able to sign whole sentences including this:

HAPPY   SEE

It means, "I'm glad to see you."

1

Host a language *Eisteddfod.*

Wales is officially a bilingual country where both English and Welsh are spoken, but the Welsh are partial to their native language. There is a proverb they recite often:

A nation without a language is a nation without a heart.

Each summer a national *eisteddfod* (eye-STED-fahd), or "session," is held in Wales. Its purpose is to promote the Welsh language and to keep many of the old Welsh customs alive.

You and your friends can put on a language *Eisteddfod* of your own, emphasizing the different languages everyone knows. Have participants read poetry in various languages, or sing songs from around the world (for some ideas for songs to include, see May 10–15). You might try to think of the longest words in each language, or some of the words that sound alike but which have different meanings, such as *oui* (wee), which is French for "yes," and wee, used a lot in Scotland to mean "little."

2

Name some words borrowed from other languages.

There are more words in the English language than in any other in the world. The experts say the number is somewhere between 400,000 and 600,000 words! This isn't surprising when you think about how many words are borrowed from other languages.

Because of this, there are often many ways to say the same thing in English. Take the word eat, for example. English-speakers have several different ways to describe this activity. Here are some of these, and the languages they were borrowed from:

Gulp — Dutch
Nibble — German
Devour — French
Masticate (a fancy way to say chew) — Greek

Not to mention feed, dine, and gnaw, which all trace their origins to Old English. What other examples can you think of? Look them up in a dictionary that includes word origins to see where they came from.

English has also borrowed many words from Spanish, such as barbecue and lasso. From Hindi, the most widely spoken language of India, come such words as veranda and pajama. Sofa is derived from an Arabic word; sleuth from a Norse word; pistachio from Italian. Robot, a word that was invented only in 1920, is a Czech contribution. Black Americans have enriched the language with many words including okay, an expression some believe evolved from a West African word *o-ke.*

Pick any word and see if you can guess its origin. Now check the dictionary. Were you right?

Other languages also borrow words from other sources. You can buy aspirin in France at le drugstore; the boy with whom a Japanese girl spends a lot of time may be her boifurendo, or "boyfriend."

Keeping Cool

While it may get hot during the summer months where you live, in many places around the world it is very warm year-round.

How do people in those places keep cool — and keep their cool? As you'll see ahead, there are all sorts of ways to make life a little more bearable when it's hot.

3

Shade your head with a hat.

In hot climates all over the world, people wear hats to help them keep cool. Wearing a broad-brimmed hat is like having a portable tree that offers shade from the hot sun!

In Southeast Asia, most hats are conical-shaped and made from straw. Women in Thailand often wear a type that rests on a frame placed on the head. This allows even more cooling air to circulate around the head.

Palestinian boys and men often wear a cloth headcovering called a *kaffiyeh* (kah-FEE-yah). This is a square cloth folded into a triangle and held in place with an *agal* (ah-GAHL), or cord.

Turbans are popular warm-weather head-coverings among African women, and men and boys in India. Try wrapping your head with a long scarf or wide strip of fabric (tear an old sheet into strips). Center the strip over your head, and cross the ends behind your head. Bring them back up to the front and cross them again. Tuck in the ends at the back.

4

Make a fan.

You've probably noticed how even a gentle breeze can make a hot day bearable. When the air is still, a fan can bring much-needed relief.

You can make your own simplified version of a Japanese folding fan called a *sensu* (sehn-soo). These are often given as gifts to those going on a trip or getting married. The instructions can be found below.

Legend has it the folding fan was invented over 1,200 years ago by a Japanese craftsman who studied the way a bat's wings are jointed.

FAN-TASTIC!

You can make a folding fan from poster board, embroidery thread, a needle, and two small buttons. Decorate the fan, either before or after it's assembled, with paint, crayons, or markers.

Cut 12 fan pieces, each 7″ (18 cm) long, measuring 2″ (5 cm) at one end tapering to ½″ (1.5 cm) at the other end. Poke three holes in each with the needle (1). Sew the fan pieces together at the narrow end, sandwiching them between the buttons. Knot (2).

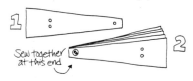

Rethread the needle, knotting the end. Insert the needle into the right-hand hole of the top fan piece from *behind*. Poke the need-le through the other hole, pulling the thread tight.

Now insert the needle into the right-hand hole of the second fan piece, only this time from the front. Bring the needle through the second hole from behind, and once again push through the first hole from the front. Pull the thread just tight enough so the top fan piece overlaps half of the second fan piece.

Pull thread taut after sewing

Continue in this way until all fan pieces are loosely sewn to one another. Knot securely.

5

Go to the beach for Salt Water Day.

If you have ever had a chance to splash in the ocean's water on a hot day, you know how refreshing it can be!

In many countries throughout the world, special days are set aside for going to the beach. Some have religious significance. Puerto Ricans recall *San Juan Bautista* (sahn wahn bow-TEES-tah), or "St. John the Baptist," when they walk backwards into the water each June on the eve of the saint's feast day. In Malaysia, people flock to the seaside during what was once solely a Muslim holiday called *Mandi Safar* (mahn-dee sah-FAHR). Today, people simply enjoy swimming, playing on the beach, and even spending the night there.

Ask your friends from other countries or cultures whether there are any special celebrations that take place near the ocean. Think of these when you're enjoying yourself at the beach!

6

Set up a cold drink stand.

What kinds of drinks really quench your thirst on a hot day? Here are some drinks found around the world you might like to try.

Lassi (LAH-see) is a yogurt drink enjoyed in India. There are both sweet and salty versions. Make your own from equal amounts of plain yogurt and water; sweeten with sugar to taste. Add a small handful of finely chopped pistachios, and whisk, or blend, until frothy.

Fruit drinks are popular all over the world, from citrus drinks to pomegranate juice to the milk of the coconut sipped right from its shell. In Thailand, as in other countries in Southeast Asia, a dash of salt is usually added to fruit juice to help the body restore salt lost through sweating.

You and your friends can set up a cold drink stand in your neighborhood. Various inexpensive drinks can be made from the outer skins of fruits. Experiment by boiling (ask a grown-up for help) pineapple peelings or one sliced orange in 4 cups (1 liter) of water for 10 minutes. Flavor with a few whole cloves. Sweeten with sugar to taste; strain and chill. Delicious!

7

Make frozen fruit pops.

Kids everywhere love frozen treats. In China, hand-held popsicles are known as "ice sticks" and "snow cakes." The Italians are famous for their frozen concoctions, including *gelato* (jeh-LAH-toe), which comes in dozens of flavors from anisette (licorice) to apricot. Russians so love ice cream that it is sold on street corners year-round, even when it's well below freezing outdoors!

Make your own frozen treats from fruit juice, or pureed fruits (such as baby foods) or yogurt mixed with a little fruit juice. Pour into small paper cups; cover with foil. Carefully make a slit in the foil and insert a popsicle stick (the foil will keep the stick upright until it's frozen in place). Freeze until hard. To remove a pop from its cup, dunk quickly in hot water and pull the pop out. Save the cups for your next batch of pops!

8

Eat some spicy food.

Spicy food can be found all over the world, but generally people living in hot climates eat it most often. Why is this? Spicy food causes one to sweat, and sweating, of course, is the body's way to cool off.

The "heat" in spicy food can come from a number of ingredients — *chile* peppers, the spice pepper, ginger, mustard, and horseradish. Do you like spicy food? Here's a recipe for *salsa cruda* (SAHL-sah CREW-thuh), a fresh sauce found on many Mexican tables. Use it as a dip for tortilla chips, or as an international topping for a hot dog!

Salsa Cruda

1 tomato, chopped
1 small onion, finely chopped
3 *chiles* (any fresh, hot green *chiles*), chopped
6 sprigs fresh coriander leaves, minced
½ teaspoon (2.5 ml) salt
¼ cup (60 ml) water

Mix all the ingredients together in a small bowl.

Note: Your market may call fresh coriander by its Spanish name, *cilantro* (see-LAHN-troh). Parsley may be substituted, but with some change in flavor.

Best Buddies

When many adults look back on their childhood, it's often the time spent with friends they recall most fondly.

As you'll discover, you can make friends with the kids next door, or with children halfway across the world! Ahead are some of the special ways you can share your friendship.

Make new friends, but keep the old. One is silver, and the other gold.
Jewish saying

9

Make new friends.

You can never have too many friends! But it's important to always try to be a *good* friend, one who is there when problems arise, not just when it's easy.

This is something to remember when you're making new friends, especially with kids whose backgrounds may be different from your own.

There may be kids in your school, for instance, who come from another country or culture. They may feel left out because they sense they are "different." You can assure them that you see more similarities between you than differences! But you can also acknowledge the cultural differences by showing an interest in their religion, customs, or the language they speak at home. Share things from your heritage in return!

Kids all over the world are faced with having to "fit in" as more and more communities become multicultural. They, too, are hoping to find friends just like you, who will accept them for who they are, just as you would like to be accepted for who *you* are.

10

Write to a pen pal.

Have you ever made friends with someone you've never met? You can when you correspond with a pen pal from another country.

Write to one of the organizations listed on page 143 to learn how you can get in touch with kids who are also looking for international pen pals.

What should you write in your first letter to your new friend? For starters, of course, tell a little about yourself — how old you are, who is in your family, and where you live. Send a recent photograph of yourself, too. Describe some of the things you enjoy doing in school and on your own. Your pen pal can model his or her response after your letter, or you can make it easier by writing such lines as, "I like to collect cards picturing baseball players. What are some of the hobbies you enjoy?"

As you get to know each other your friendship will grow. And who knows, maybe someday you'll even get a chance to meet in person!

11

Start an international club.

Kids all over the world belong to clubs for the very same reasons you probably do — the activities are fun and it's a great way to spend time with friends!

Kids everywhere like to start their own clubs, too, and this is something you might want to do. Why not organize an international club that emphasizes everybody's different cultural heritage? Ask a parent or teacher to "sponsor" your club so that you'll have an adult's help whenever you need it.

You might want to make the focus of your club hands-on fun. You can make international crafts, cook delicious dishes from other countries, and even act out folk tales from around the world in front of an audience.

Invite people from your community who may have moved from other countries to share something of their culture (don't forget your own parents and grandparents who may have immigrated to North America). Schedule activities to coincide with street fairs and festivals that may be celebrated in your community.

12

Call a friend on the telephone.

When you want to talk to one of your friends, you probably just pick up the telephone and dial his or her home number. This isn't the case for kids everywhere.

In many countries, even local phone calls are charged by the call, so the telephone is not used as frequently as it is in North America. Of course, in such places as rural Chile or Laos, few families have access to telephones so they are never used.

In England, people answer the phone and instead of saying "Hello," they usually give the telephone number. That way the caller knows at once if he has reached the right house. In France, however, a child usually picks up the receiver and says *"Allô"* (ah-LOW), and the person on the other end of the line says the number she dialed. If it's the right number the child says *"Oui"* (wee), which is "yes," and then the conversation begins.

13

Send secret messages.

Friends everywhere like to share secrets with each other. It's especially fun to send secret messages! Here's one way you can do this using a simple code.

The Noughts and Crosses Code substitutes symbols for letters. Draw a Tic Tac Toe grid (kids in England call this Noughts and Crosses after the symbols used in the game) and write the 26 letters of the alphabet in the spaces. Follow the order shown here, or scramble the letters however you like.

A B C	D E F	G H I
J K L	M	O P Q
R S T	N U V W	X Y Z

Now see if you can decipher the message below. Note how the letters can be found in the grid.

⌐⌐⌐/ ⌐⊓⊔/
⊓⌐/ ⊔⌐⌐⊔⊓⊔

You got it! It says, "You are my friend." Make copies of the grid to give to your friends. Explain how it works and you're ready to start sending secret messages to one another!

14

Make friendship bracelets.

Show your friends how much you care with special friendship bracelets you make yourself!

There's an interesting story behind these popular tokens of affection. It seems some Americans traveling in Guatemala in the 1970s showed some children there how to knot them. The kids quickly caught on, and before long whole villages were knotting bracelets and exporting them to other countries — including the United States!

Start with a simple four-strand striped bracelet that is about ⅛" (4 mm) wide. Just follow the directions below and you'll be knotting like a pro in no time!

THE TIES THAT BIND

Cut four 24" (60 cm) strands of embroidery floss, each in a different color. Make an overhand knot 8" (20 cm) from one end, and tie to the back of a chair.

Assigning letters to the strands as shown, hold A and B in your two hands. Wrap A over and under B, pulling the end of A through the loop with your right hand (1). Holding B taut in your left hand, pull up on A, tightening it into a knot (2). Repeat, making a second knot with A over B.

Drop B and make two knots with A over C. Drop C and make two knots with A over D. This completes one row (3).

Make the second row by knotting B over C twice, B over D twice, and B over A twice. Continue in this way until the bracelet is the desired length; tie an overhand knot. Leave enough floss at both ends to tie the bracelet into a circle; trim away any extra.

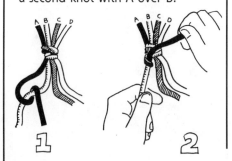

The Dancing Master

Dance is believed to be the oldest of the arts. Long before recorded history — even before our ancestors created the first instruments — people expressed themselves through dance.

Dance continues to be of great importance in many African communities and among many Native Americans. Care to try a few steps? Put on your dancing shoes, and let's dance!

15

Dance for joy for *Homowo.*

The continent of Africa practically shakes from the rhythm of dancing feet! People throughout Africa dance for many reasons — to celebrate birth, cure sickness, and bring rain (for more on this, see April 18).

Dancing can be a way of expressing emotions, too. The Ga people of Ghana dance during a month-long festival called *Homowo* (how-MOH-woh), also known as "Hooting at Hunger." Long ago the Ga suffered from hunger during a famine. The following year when the harvest was in (and this time it was a good one!), they recalled the hard times by mocking them. The relief the people felt is recalled each year by the villagers as they dance.

Who knows, maybe dance can help people get over rough spots! Try dancing to let off steam when you're angry, or to relax before you have something difficult to do. And when the worst is over, you can dance for joy!

16

Learn a folk dance.

Want to learn an easy folk dance? Here's one from Israel called the *hora* (HOR-ah), which is perfect for a whole group of kids.

The *hora* is danced to music that has two beats per measure. See if you can find a recording of Israeli music or dance to a song like *She'll Be Comin' Round the Mountain,* which is in 2/4 time.

Form a circle, and join hands or hold onto each other's elbows or shoulders. Make the following moves while counting out the beats:

one and	Step to the left with left foot.
two and	Cross right foot behind left.
one and	Step to the left with left foot.
two and	Hop on left foot and swing right foot across in front of left.
one and	Step in place with right foot.
two and	Hop on right foot and swing left foot across in front of right.

Repeat these three measures over and over until the end of the song.

17

Tell a story with dance.

Some dances are used to tell stories. Many ballets, for instance, are based on legends and tales, such as the French fairy tale, "The Sleeping Beauty."

Some ritual dances also tell stories. The Maori of New Zealand mimic the paddling of canoes in some of their dances, which tell of their great migration from Polynesia long ago. In front of the paddlers are women who "dance" sitting down. They sway back and forth to suggest the movement of the waves.

Make up your own story and tell it with a dance. Costumes and props can be a help, but use your body expressively, too. Move your hands as traditional Hindu dancers of India do. There are over 4,000 *mudras* (MOO-drahs), or positions of the hands to represent animals and plants, as well as feelings such as love and sorrow. The illustration below shows two traditional *mudras* and their meanings.

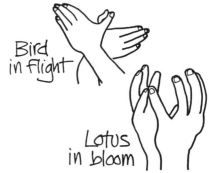

Bird in Flight

Lotus in bloom

18

Learn the ballet positions.

Taking ballet lessons is a part of childhood many children around the world share.

One of the first things you learn in ballet are the five positions. They are pictured below. Did you know these basic positions originated in France in 1661?

Ballet terms are all in French, but the word ballet comes from the Italian *balletti,* or "court dance displays." The extravagant Italian court pageants inspired the French ballet, born in the 1580s. Today, ballet is the pride and joy of Russia, where dozens of dance troupes are kept busy performing year-round.

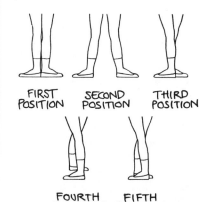

FIRST POSITION   SECOND POSITION   THIRD POSITION

FOURTH POSITION   FIFTH POSITION

Did you know that there once were no ballerinas? Until 1681, men played both the male and female roles in ballets. By 1850, it was male dancers who were rare!

19

Make a hula skirt.

Both male and female dancers in the Pacific Islands wear grass skirts as part of their dancing costumes. You may have heard these called hula skirts, from the Hawaiian word *hula* (HOO-lah), which simply means "dance."

You can make your own hula skirt by adapting materials you have on hand. If you have some cattails growing on your property, you can gather the long leaves from some of the plants and fold them over a belt to make a skirt. Or cut strips from paper grocery bags and attach these to the belt in the same way.

To make your costume complete, string some flower blossoms to make a *lei* (lay-ee), or garland of flowers that is worn around the neck. (Use the tissue paper flowers described in the box on page 58.) Boys can make a grass headdress by tying two short pieces of grass to a stretchy headband.

20

Have your parents teach you a dance.

Some dances are timeless, hardly changing over the years. The ritual dances of Africa, for instance, are much the same as they have been for centuries.

Other dances have shorter lives. So-called social dances — the kind boys and girls (and men and women) dance together — may be all the rage for a year or two and then are replaced by the next dancing fad.

Your parents (and grandparents) may remember some of the steps of the dances that were popular when they were younger. Many of the dance crazes over the years originated in Central and South America. Ask if anyone remembers the *tango* (TAHN-goh) from Argentina, which swept dancers off their feet around 1910. Maybe they recall the Cuban *rumba* (ROOM-bah), popular in the 1930s, or the *bossa nova* (BOHS-ah NOH-vah), which was born in Brazil. Now have your parents teach you how these dances went. Saturday nights will never be the same again!

21

Make up a dance.

You and your friends can make up your own dance! Pick some music you like and work out the steps of a dance you can do together.

Invent a circle dance (like the *hora* on August 16), the most widespread type. The circle has always been a powerful symbol because it has no beginning or end.

Create a line dance. The Swedish weaving dance is a line dance. The movement of the dancers is meant to imitate a weaver at work, as the lead couple skips between the two lines of dancers like a shuttle thrown between the warp threads of a loom.

Mimic everyday activities in your dance (going to school, brushing your teeth!), or represent a flower opening or the flames of a fire. The possibilities are endless!

Wash & Wear

For the most part, people around the world dress the same, at least when they have on their everyday clothing. Western-style dress (such as is worn in the United States, Canada, and Europe) is so widespread that someone from the African country of Angola might be wearing the exact same thing as someone from Argentina in South America.

That isn't to say that some regional styles of clothing are not still worn. Ahead are some of these outfits, as well as some things that you can make yourself!

For more on traditional costumes and clothing worn for special occasions, see November 15–19.

22

Wear your favorite outfit.

Your favorite clothes are probably the ones that are the most comfortable. If you are like a lot of kids all over the world, you couldn't live without T-shirts and shorts, at least when the weather is warm.

A girl in Laos is more likely to wear a *sihn* (seen), or length of cotton fabric wrapped around her waist and held in place with a wide belt, instead of shorts. (She's probably got a T-shirt on top!) A similar garment called a *sarong* (sah-RAWNG) is worn by both boys and girls in Southeast Asian countries, including Malaysia and the Philippines.

Pakistani and Indian children often wear a lightweight, loose shirt called a *kurta* (KOOR-tah) over a pair of drawstring pants. Boys in Iraq often wear a *deshdasha* (desh-DAH-shah), or long robe when they're dressed for comfort at home.

23

Stitch a garment.

Lots of clothes around the world are very simply constructed. You can create several garments from a length of fabric and a needle and thread.

Take a piece of fabric that is twice the measurement from your shoulders to the floor, and fold it in half. Cut an opening for your head, and stitch under the arms and down the sides to make a robe such as boys and men wear throughout the Middle East. A shorter piece of fabric can be turned into a *dashiki* (dah-SHEE-key), a West African garment.

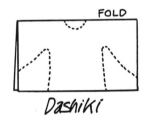

Make a *rebozo* (ray-BOH-soh) or *poncho* (PAWN-cho), both cloak-like outer garments popular in Central and South America, from a square piece of fabric or an old blanket.

24

Slip on your shoes.

Shoes are much the same all over the world, too. From rubber-soled athletic shoes to leather slip-ons, people everywhere have a wide choice of footwear.

Several types of shoes are more popular in certain regions, however. The clog, for instance, is a favorite in Scandinavia. These are worn outside only, and traded for softer-soled shoes or socks when indoors. In Spain and France, lots of children wear rope-soled cotton shoes called *espadrilles* (ess-pah-DRILL).

If you were to name the most popular footwear around the world, it would probably have to be no footwear at all! More children and adults in tropical and temperate zones would rather go barefoot than wear shoes. This is true, at least, in rural areas of Africa, Southeast Asia, and Central and South America. When people do wear shoes, they usually slip on sandals. Craftmen in Mexico make woven leather sandals called *huaraches* (wahr-AH-chase), which often have soles made from old tires. But because they are so inexpensive, plastic sandals are the most prevalent around the world.

25

Weave a belt.

In many places around the world, clothing continues to be made from handwoven textiles. From the narrow bands of *kente* cloth that are sewn together to make garments in Ghana to the fabrics woven from tie-dyed yarn known as *ikat* (ee-caht) in Indonesia, handweaving is an art that is still very much alive.

You can weave something to wear yourself. A belt is a good project to begin with. The box below has instructions for a ¾″ (2 cm) belt, easily made on a heddle loom adapted from an ancient design.

IT'S A CINCH

Narrow woven bands are easy to make with a popsicle stick heddle loom. A single band can be worn as a belt, or several bands can be sewn together along the edges to make placemats or small rugs.

Assemble the heddle from ten popsicle sticks, drilling an ⅛″ (3 mm) hole in the middle of eight of the sticks. Glue these with white glue, as shown. Let dry.

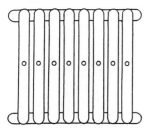

Cut 17 strands of yarn 6 feet (2 m) long. Choose different colors for a striped effect. Tie the yarn at one end, then thread the heddle, with one strand through each hole and on either side of each stick.

Pull the yarn evenly tight; knot the other end. Stretch the yarn between two objects, such as a doorknob and chair, so the strands are taut.

Notice what happens then you lift the heddle, and when you push it down. The 17 strands separate to create two different openings.

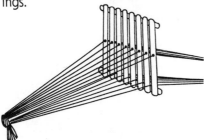

Double a length of yarn and wrap it around a small piece of

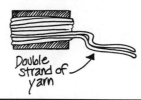
Double strand of yarn

cardboard. Lift the heddle and pass this yarn through the opening. Now push the heddle down and pass the yarn back through the new opening. Pull the doubled yarn as you are weaving to bring the 17 strands together nice and tight.

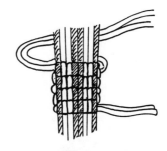

Continue until your belt is the desired length. Cut the strands a few inches (10 cm) beyond the weaving and tie them together in twos. Do the same at the beginning of the belt.

26

Wash your clothes.

When your clothes get dirty what do you do with them? Throw them in the hamper and wait until your mother washes them and puts them back in your drawers?

Perhaps you have a washer and dryer at home (in which case, you can help do the laundry!), or maybe you make weekly trips to a laundromat. In lots of places around the world, these methods of washing clothes are not available.

In many rural areas, from Ethiopia to El Salvador, clothes are washed in rivers, and layed out to dry directly on the ground or draped over low bushes. Many women and young children gather along the river to wash their clothing at the same time.

In Malaysian cities, such as Singapore, people hang their clothes outdoors to dry, even if they live in one of the modern, multistory, apartment buildings. Long bamboo poles stick out horizontally from every window, and the clothes are pinned or draped over these. Singaporeans jokingly point to the laundry and call it their national flag!

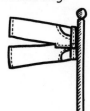

School Days

For many children around the world, it's back to school around this time of year. (For some, as you'll see, school may be just ending!)

Going to school is certainly one of the most important opportunities a child can be given. So it's no wonder that communities do what they can to give their children an education, even where classrooms and teachers are in short supply.

You'll find schools and school days described here. For more on school subjects, see pages 102 and 103.

27

Honor teachers on the first day of school.

The first day of the school year is certainly exciting, for both teachers and students!

In many countries it's customary to bring a little something for the teacher at the beginning of school. Burmese children in Myanmar often bring a coconut or other piece of fruit, just as you might bring an apple.

Perhaps nowhere is it more festive on the first day of school than in Russia. Bands play, decorative banners are hung, and parents and neighbors watch as children stream into schools bearing bouquets of flowers for their teachers. Part of the first morning is spent simply finding room for all of the flowers!

What would you like to bring in for your teacher? Perhaps you have some flowers from your garden, or a choice specimen from a fruit tree. A handmade card would be nice, too.

28

Make a *Schultüte.*

German children entering the first grade are given a gift on the first day of school. A large, decorated paper cone called a *Schultüte* (SHOOL-tur-tuh) is filled with such things as candy, pencils, and small gifts, and presented either in the morning or after school. The excitement—and surprise gifts—make that scary first day of school a little easier!

Do you have any younger brothers or sisters ready to start school? Surprise them with *Schultüten!* In Germany, the cones themselves are usually purchased, but you can make your own.

Cut a large square of poster board as shown below (1). Decorate it with crayons or markers, then roll into a cone shape and glue the overlapping edge.

1. 2.

Glue a wide strip of soft paper, such as tissue paper or crepe paper, to the inside of the cone so that most of it sticks up above the cone (2). Fill the cone with little goodies, then tie the paper closed with a ribbon.

29

Dress for school.

What kinds of clothes do you wear to school each day? Is it up to you to decide what you'll wear, or is there a strict dress code at your school? (Your parents may remember how kids once dressed more formally. Your mother may also recall that wearing trousers was something girls were allowed to do only if it was unusually cold during the winter.)

Perhaps your school has a school uniform. This is the trend in most countries. Uniforms are popular for a number of reasons. They have a way of making everybody "equal," at least in appearance. They also promote school spirit. And kids everywhere like uniforms because they certainly simplify getting ready for school each day!

If you were in charge of deciding what the kids in your school wore each day, what would your recommendations be, and why?

30

Describe a typical school day.

How would you describe a typical day at your school? How much time is spent in class and on the playground, and how many kids are in each class? (For more on school subjects, see September 3-8.)

Laotian children spend their mornings in the classroom, but after lunch they help out in the school gardens for several hours. Japanese kids concentrate on single subjects for up to 45 minutes, then take a break on the playground. They may have five or six recesses each day.

A typical school day for children in the Australian outback includes receiving instruction one-on-one by two-way radio. Radios broadcast lessons in rural parts of Africa and South America, where there are neither enough books nor teachers to go around. In India, a shortage of teachers means classes may be made up of children of many different ages. This is an idea which is gaining acceptance in other countries, too. A child who is good at math can do sums with older students, while he or she may prefer to read with a younger group.

Ask your international pen pal to describe a school day in his or her school. How does it differ from yours?

31

Eat lunch at school.

Kids and teachers alike look forward to lunch time. It's a time to refuel bodies as well as take a break from class work. Do you eat the food your school provides or do you bring a lunch from home?

In some countries, such as France, children are sent home for lunch. As a result, the lunch break is usually long. In Spain, kids have nearly three hours to eat and relax before returning to school. (They stay as late as 6:30 to 7:00 in the evening.)

In Japan, lunch is regularly eaten right in the classroom. A trolley loaded with food is wheeled into the classroom and kids in aprons and protective face masks serve the food to their fellow students. Each child spreads a paper napkin from home on his or her desk as a placemat.

1

Compare school years.

For children in North America, Russia, and Israel, the school year starts sometime in late August or early September. In Chile, however, school traditionally starts in March, and in Australia it begins in late January.

Japanese schoolchildren start their year in April, continuing until September, when they have about a month off. They start up again in October, finishing school the following March. The Japanese school year is among the longest in the world, with over 240 days. Children in Thailand and the Netherlands go to school for 200 days each year. How long is the school year at your school?

In Vietnam, children attend classes six days a week practically year-round. However, they only have four hours of instruction each day. Most children around the world go to school six days a week. Muslims take Friday off, which is the Islamic holy day; Jewish boys and girls in Israel don't go to school on the Sabbath, which is Saturday.

2

Draw a picture of your school.

What does the school you attend look like? Draw a picture of its exterior, or of your classroom. As you can probably guess, some schools around the world may resemble yours, while others are quite different.

Many rural areas have very basic schools, sparsely furnished, if at all. In Cambodia, for instance, children kneel on the floor behind low planks of wood that serve as desks. In parts of Pakistan and India, there aren't enough schools, so classes are held outdoors. Students sit on the ground or stand while listening to the teacher.

Most schools have playgrounds and playing fields if there is room. During recesses around the world, you'll find children playing on playground equipment much the same as you have in your school yard, playing many of the same games you and your friends enjoy. (For more on outdoor games, see March 25 and 26 and September 9-13.)

Reading, Writing & 'Rithmetic

The basics of learning are often referred to as "the three Rs," which stand for reading, writing, and arithmetic. While schools all over the world teach these important skills, many other subjects are also covered.

What are some of these? Read on to find out! You'll also see that other valuable learning experiences often take place at school.

3

List your school subjects.

What are some of the subjects you are studying in school this year? Now here's a harder question — which do you like the best?

Children around the world learn many of the same basic skills in school, but additional subjects of local importance are sometimes taught. Children in Nigeria and Laos learn to garden at school. The kids not only get plenty of fresh vegetables and grains to eat, they also learn a valuable skill they'll use the rest of their lives.

Are there art and music classes at your school? In some communities in Guatemala, children spend time crafting useful articles to sell, while in Ghana, all students learn the basics of drumming.

Schools everywhere also offer foreign languages, usually starting in the elementary grades. Learning widely-used languages such as French and English is especially valuable for children who speak lesser-known languages. It opens doors to higher education and allows even small communities to compete in world markets.

4

Take an examination.

Taking tests and exams is a part of school life everywhere, but in some countries examination results are taken very seriously.

In Japan, for instance, there are exams for gaining entrance to both middle and high schools. Japanese students spend hours studying for these tests, often enrolling in special *juku* (JOO-koo), or "cramming schools," to increase their chances of doing well. (These schools also offer intensive classes in traditional arts such as calligraphy, or decorative writing.)

French children also take entrance exams, while the British are tested near the completion of their schooling. When British students are around 15 years old, they take their O-levels (O stands for ordinary). A second series of exams, known as A-levels (A for advanced) comes later.

Do you dread examinations? You may be like some kids who do well in school but do poorly on tests, in part because taking tests makes them nervous! Some teachers also think examinations are good indicators of how much information a student has memorized, but they don't always show how well that person *thinks*.

5

Add with an abacus.

Children in many Asian countries learn to do simple mathematical calculations using an abacus, a wooden frame that holds rows of counting beads strung on wires. Here is what a Chinese abacus looks like:

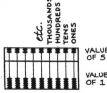

Note how the rows stand for ones, tens, and so on, and how the beads below the horizontal bar are each worth one, while the beads above the bar are worth five.

Let's see how addition is done on the abacus. (If you don't have an abacus, draw a diagram on paper and use pennies for beads.) Let's add 53 and 24. Move the beads as shown to represent 53 (1). Now move the beads for 24 — moving one bead down above the bar in the ones column and removing one bead below the bar to represent the 4. Move two beads up in the tens column to represent the 2 (2).

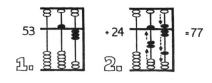

6

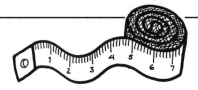

Make a metric conversion chart.

The metric system of measuring distance, weight, volume, and temperature is based on the number ten. Designed to be convenient to use, it's a simple matter of changing the decimal point to go from centimeters to meters to kilometers (as opposed to calculating inches to yards to miles!).

The United States is one of the few places where the metric system is not widely used. Perhaps someday the switch will be made. Until then, the conversion chart below will help you jump from inches to centimeters . . . and beyond!

MEASURE UP

Use this handy chart to help you convert some everyday measurements to their equivalent metric measurements.

TO CHANGE	TO	MULTIPLY BY
Length		
inches (in.)	centimeters (cm)	2.54
feet (ft.)	centimeters (cm)	30
yards (yd.)	meters (m)	0.91
miles (mi.)	kilometers (km)	1.6
Weight		
ounces (oz.)	grams (g)	28
pounds (lb.)	kilograms (kg)	0.45
Volume		
teaspoon (t.)	milliliters (ml)	5
tablespoon (T.)	milliliters (ml)	15
fluid ounces (fl. oz.)	milliliters (ml)	30
cups (c.)	liters (l)	0.24
pints (pt.)	liters (l)	0.47
quarts (qt.)	liters (l)	0.95
gallons (gal.)	liters (l)	3.8
Temperature		
Fahrenheit (°F)	Celsius (°C)	5/9 after subtracting 32

7

Do extracurricular activities.

Does your school offer any extracurricular activities during the school day or after classes? Perhaps you're a member of the school band, or play on one of the sports teams.

In many schools around the world these types of activities are not offered at schools but elsewhere. In China, for instance, children go to Children's Palaces for sports and arts instruction. Japanese kids go to *juku* (see September 4).

Many countries also have schools for children who want to pursue a career in the arts. Iraqi children may attend a school in Baghdad that trains them in traditional Arab music as well as Western classical music and ballet. This is not an afterschool program but a full-time school, that includes classes in basic reading and writing skills so that the students do not miss out on those. For these children, the "three Rs" are extracurricular!

8

Help someone read on International Literacy Day.

If you're an older child and able to read, you probably take reading for granted. But think back what it was like when you were younger and you had no idea what the marks in books, on food packages, and on signs meant!

You can appreciate how important knowing how to read is. But did you know that millions of older children and adults around the world do not know how to read? Illiteracy is something every country is working to eliminate, and in honor of the United Nation's International Literacy Day, you can do your part!

If reading comes easily to you, offer to tutor some of the kids who need some help. If your parents or other relatives were never taught how to read, you can help them. You can also help non-native English-speakers in your community to read, because learning to speak English is very different from learning to read it (with all the irregular spellings!).

Free Time

What do you and your friends like to do together when you have a little free time? Do you enjoy playing games? Then you're a lot like kids everywhere!

Ahead are some of the outdoor games enjoyed around the world. Try them out! When you tire of running around, you can relax and read a book or go to the movies. These are popular pastimes in other countries, too.

For more fun things to do when you have free time, see Games in the index.

9

BELGIUM

Play outdoor games for *Bruegel Feesten.*

Thanks to the detailed paintings of Pieter Bruegel the Elder, we have a visual record of life in Belgium in the 1600s. One of Bruegel's best known works shows children at play, engaged in dozens of activities from blowing bubbles to rolling a hoop with a stick— games kids all over the world still play today!

Every other year in September in the town of Wingene, a festival known as *Bruegel Feesten* (BRUR-guhl FEES-tehn) takes place. People dress in costumes of the period, feast on hearty peasant food, and play many of the games Bruegel depicted in his paintings.

Get together with your friends and play some outdoor games! Which of the international favorites below sound like fun to you?

FUN & GAMES

Kids everywhere play many of the same games—only the names are different. Cops and Robbers, for instance, is known as Cossacks and Robbers in Russia.

Some games that are usually thought of as indoor games are played out-of-doors in other countries. In Java, children have pillow fights while straddling a thick bamboo pole. This is even more fun when the pole spans a shallow body of water!

Not all outdoor games are wild, of course. Marbles is a popular pastime from Tahiti to Togo. In several West African countries, hide and seek games are played in the sand. In Mali, children play *sey*, during which players hide pebbles in the sand, hopefully fooling their opponents with quick hand movements! Beninese children play a game called *godo*. A noose made out of string is covered with sand, and players push sticks into the sand, hoping to land within the noose. A tug on the string proves whether the player has been successful or not.

10

Determine who is It.

In lots of games, one player is chosen to be It. How do you and your friends usually determine who'll be It?

Japanese kids usually use a traditional method called *Jan-Ken-Pon* (john-kehn-pone). You may know this as a game for two players called Scissors, Paper, Stone (or Rock, Scissors, Paper). Players hold one hand behind their backs and at the count of "one, two, three!" bring their hands forward in one of the three positions shown. Scissors can cut paper (and so becomes the winner); paper can wrap around (and beat) stone; stone smashes the scissors (thereby winning).

To adapt this game into a method for determining who shall be It, the winner from the first match challenges a new player. The winner of that match plays against another player, and so on. The final winner is It.

11

Play some street games.

Street games are just that—games meant to be played on paved streets or sidewalks. Not surprisingly, kids who live in the country often don't know some of the games that are so familiar to children who live in towns and cities.

Some international street games can be found elsewhere in this book (see March 25 and 26 for more on jump rope and hopscotch, for instance). Here's a game for ten or more players called Greek Ball.

Draw a large square on the pavement with chalk, at least 15 feet (4.5 m) to each side. Place a large ball in the very middle of the court. Divide the players into two equal teams, each lining up along opposite sides of the square. When the word "Greek!" is called, players at the opposite corners race to the ball, and the one who grabs it first tries to throw it over the opposing team's base line. That team tries to prevent the ball from going over by catching or bumping it. Points are scored for each successful throw. Rotate the players so everyone gets a chance to race for the ball.

12

Play a cooperative game.

Have you ever played a game where there are no winners or losers? These types of games are called non-competitive or cooperative games, and they're fun for everyone!

Children in Papua, New Guinea play cooperative games all the time. In fact, in the Hanahan language, there isn't even a word for "winning." Here's a popular game for four players called *Ver Ver Aras Lama,* or "Taking Coconuts."

Draw a series of circles in the dirt, as shown below.

Place five coconuts (or balls) in the central circle; have each player stand behind one of the smaller circles. The object of the game is to get three coconuts into your circle. You must place them—not roll or throw them—one at a time. Players may take coconuts from the central circle and from each other! No matter how fast the players move, the game becomes a continuous movement of coconuts, and the game ends when you've all had enough!

13

Watch educational television.

Did you know that many American television programs are re-run all over the world? Children from Chile to China learn about American culture by watching television.

You can learn a lot about other countries and cultures by watching T.V. too! Check out the educational channels that broadcast in your area. Public television stations offer all sorts of exciting programs, from geography game shows to animated versions of folk tales. If you get cable, you can tune into programs broadcast in different languages (this is a great way to learn a language), and be treated to international film classics (you have to make your own popcorn!).

Your parents may wisely put a limit to the amount of television (and types of shows) you watch. But even your parents will approve of these shows, and you'll soon be hooked yourself!

14

Go to the movies.

You and your friends may look forward to the latest movies that come out of Hollywood each year, and so do kids around the world. People in other countries may not get a chance to see these films when they're first released, but sooner or later many American films make their way around the world.

That's not to say that other countries don't make movies. India is perhaps the largest producer of films; other countries also have a thriving film industry. Have you ever seen some of the foreign classics, such as *The Red Balloon* from France?

The Chinese are avid film-goers. In some places where there are no auditoriums to show films, screens are put up outdoors. The audience sits on both sides of the screen. This works well with movies that are dubbed, or made with a reworked soundtrack in Chinese. Subtitled movies (those with the translation written on the screen) are less popular, especially with those people sitting behind the screen. For them, the Chinese characters, or letters, show up backward!

Playing Pieces

When you're looking for something quiet to do, board games and card games can't be beat. Some games are meant for two players, others are for larger groups. There are even games you can play by yourself.

You may find some of your favorites here, as well as some games, new to you, that are popular in other parts of the world. Read on; then find yourself a partner and play a game or two!

15

Play a board game.

At this very moment, somewhere in the world, a group of kids is enjoying a board game — possibly one that you and your friends know and love! Many board games have an international following. Some, such as checkers, are played in slightly different ways in different countries. Some games don't even have a board as such, but are played with whatever is at hand.

The box below describes some board games that are played around the world. Which of these are you familiar with?

YOUR MOVE

Checkers is a popular game all over the world. There are several versions of the game, including Polish checkers played on a board marked off into 100 squares. Each player gets 20 play pieces. Chinese checkers is a relatively modern game, dating from the 1880s. Despite its name, it originated in Europe, not China. It eventually made its way to China via Japan!

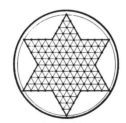

Chess also has a worldwide following. The game traces its origins to India, over 1,000 years ago. Chess is the national game of Russia.

India's national game is *Pachisi* (similar to the game you may know as Parcheesi). The board is made of cloth, which makes it easy to roll up and store.

Not all games have an actual board. *Yoté*, popular throughout West Africa, is played in a series of holes scooped out in the dirt. Pebbles or short sticks serve as play pieces.

See March 27 for another board game.

16

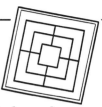

Make a morris board.

Nine Men's Morris is one of the oldest board games in the world. A very early example of the board was found in an Egyptian temple built around 1400 B.C., which is almost 3,400 years ago!

You can make your own morris board by drawing the diagram below on stiff paper. Use a ruler for best results.

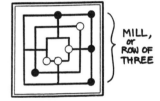

MILL, or ROW OF THREE

Two people play this game, each with nine play pieces (use checkers or other markers). Determine who will go first.

Take turns placing the pieces on the board (wherever lines intersect and on the corners of the squares). Keep in mind that when both placing the pieces and playing the game, the object is to form a "mill," or row of three pieces on a line. When a player makes a mill, he gets to remove one of his opponent's pieces (taking one from a mill only if there are no other pieces to take). Be advised that by moving one piece from a mill and returning it on the next turn, a new mill is made! The game ends when one player has only two pieces remaining.

17

Deal a card game.

Some of the card games you may know originated in various countries around the world. Take War, for example, a game of chance that comes to us from France, where it was played as early as the 14th century.

This is a game for two players. Shuffle a deck of cards and deal them evenly between the two of you, face down. At the same time, turn over the top cards in your piles. The player with the highest card (aces are high), takes both cards and places them at the bottom of his or her pile.

If the players' cards are of equal value (both sixes, for example), each player places three cards face down, while counting, "one, two, three," and a fourth one, face up, declaring "War!" The player with the highest card takes them all. (If the turned-up cards are of equal value, "war" is repeated.)

The object of the game is to win all 52 cards, something that can take a long time! You can set a time limit to the game if you like, and then count the cards to determine the winner.

18

Play Patience.

Here's one of the card games you can play by yourself, known as Solitaire, or in England, Patience.

Shuffle and deal four cards face up in a row. If there are any of the same suit, remove all that are lower than the highest in that suit (aces are high). Deal a new row of four cards on top of the first row. Continue taking away the lowest cards of matched suits. The object of the game is to be left with only four aces.

If removing a card results in an empty spot, fill that spot with a card from another column. Choose carefully! In the example below, both the 3 of clubs and the 7 of clubs may be removed because of the 10 of clubs.

It is best to move the 9 of hearts, enabling you to pick up the 8 of hearts.

Now move the 10 of clubs and pick up the 8 of diamonds.

Now you have a go!

19

Make a set of spillikins.

Some indoor games require a degree of dexterity and coordination. Spillikins (as Pick-up-sticks is called in Great Britain) is one such game. Thought to have originated in China, this game is popular in many countries.

You can make your own spillikins set. You need 50 ⅛" (3 mm) dowels cut in 10" (25.5 cm) lengths, and waterproof paint in yellow, red, blue, and green. Sharpen both ends of each stick using a pencil sharpener. Paint 20 sticks yellow, ten red, five blue, three green, and two striped with red.

To start the game, mix the spillikins randomly and hold them in a bunch upright on a flat surface; then let them fall. Each player in turn tries to pick up one stick at a time without disturbing any others. If another is moved, his or her turn is over and the next player goes. Players picking up the red striped sticks may use them to help retrieve other spillikins.

The final scores are tallied using these figures: yellows are worth 3 points; red, 5; blue, 10; green, 15, and striped, 20.

20

Invent your own game.

You may have thought of ways to improve some of the games you and your friends enjoy. Or maybe you have had some ideas for innovative games of your own. Now's your chance to make your own board game!

Be creative with materials. Sturdy cardboard can be painted or covered with decorative paper for the playing board (hinge two or more pieces together for compact storage). If you like to sew, stitch a game board from felt.

Have fun making the play pieces. You can use found objects such as nuts, shells, pebbles, and bottle caps. Or model tiny figures from bread "clay" (see March 4 for the recipe).

Make a three-dimensional board complete with stairs and ladders. This would certainly add an exciting twist to a "race" game!

Autumn Air

Autumn is a wonderful time of year. Walks through fields and woods offer rewards of ripe nuts and wild mushrooms (happily, many of the pesky insects of summer have disappeared!).

These same treats are appreciated all over the world, and by Native Americans who gather in North Dakota this time each year to celebrate their ancient cultures. Ahead are ways to enjoy some of the gifts that these people and nature have bestowed on us.

21

Decorate gourds for the first day of autumn.

In the Northern Hemisphere, the first day of autumn falls on or around September 21 (in the Southern Hemisphere, it's the first day of spring). The growing season is coming to an end, so this is a good time to honor the harvest of an important plant throughout the Americas and Africa—the calabash gourd.

These shapely, hard-skinned gourds are decorated and made into bowls, scoops, and containers —even musical instruments! They are dried for six months to a year before being dyed and carved. You can decorate gourds using another method. Here's how:

Cure your own homegrown gourds or purchase some that are already dried. Wash each gourd with a scouring pad and water; let dry. Cover the gourd with black crayon, pressing hard to coat it thoroughly. Smooth the coating with your palm or a soft rag.

Scratch designs in the crayon with a nail. The shape of your gourd may suggest certain designs, such as the bird shown here, or you can make overall geometric designs.

22

Make nut brittle.

Autumn is the time when nuts ripen and fall from trees. Celebrate the season—and the harvest!—by making nut brittle, a traditional Mexican confection often made with peanuts. Be sure to have an adult help you at the stove.

Nut Brittle

1 cup (250 ml) light corn syrup
2 cups (500 g) sugar
½ cup (125 ml) water
4 tablespoons (60 g) butter
2½ cups (300 g) raw mixed nuts
1½ teaspoons (7.5 ml) baking soda

Combine first four ingredients in a heavy saucepan. Bring to a boil, stirring occasionally. Continue cooking until a candy thermometer reads 275°F (135°C), or until candy separates into hard but bendable threads when dropped into a glass of ice water.

Add the nuts, and cook until 295°F (146°C), or until candy forms brittle threads when dropped in water. Remove from the stove; stir in baking powder. Pour onto buttered baking sheets, pulling the candy with two forks as it cools. Let cool completely before breaking into pieces.

23

Play Conkers.

British boys look forward to autumn because this is when horse chestnuts ripen. It's time to challenge someone to a game of Conkers!

You and your friends can play this game. You each need to make a conker, which is a chestnut with a hole bored through it, strung on a shoelace or other strong cord. The lace gets wrapped around the hand a couple of times for a secure grip.

Two people play at a time. The player who is first to shout, "First!" makes the initial strike. He tries to break his opponent's conker, which is held still at arm's length, with the impact of his own conker. He gets three tries to crack it, then the players switch roles. The winner is the player whose conker remains unbroken.

There are other rules, such as how to handle tangled strings (the first to yell, "Strings!" gets an extra turn). Lucky is the player who saves a good conker from one year to the next. "Yearsies," as these are known, are tough nuts to crack!

24

Hunt for mushrooms.

Whole families head to the woods throughout Europe at this time of year, looking for wild mushrooms. There they might find such favorites as boletes, oyster mushrooms, and shaggy-manes (the French call these "bottles of ink" because the mature mushrooms disintegrate into an oozy, black "ink").

On your walks in the woods, see if you can spot some of these. Or look for a mushroom growing at the base of hardwood trees that you might mistake for a hen ruffling her feathers! No doubt this is how hen of the woods got its common name.

You may also find puffballs along the edges of meadows and along old roads. One of the largest puffballs is aptly named the giant puffball. Some grow as huge as two feet (60 cm) across and weigh more than 40 pounds (18 kg)! Be sure to take a tape measure with you (and a witness to vouch for you!) if you come across any really big ones.

One last thing—don't eat any of these mushrooms, as many wild mushrooms are poisonous.

25

Bead a band for the United Tribes Powwow.

Each year in September, Native American tribes from all over North America gather in Bismarck, North Dakota for the United Tribes Powwow. During this celebration, there are traditional dance and singing competitions, native foods to eat, and demonstrations of craft techniques.

In recognition of Native American crafts, make a narrow beaded band using tiny seed beads. The box below shows you how!

BEAD BAND

First you need to chart a design on graph paper. Nine beads will make a band about ½″ (13 mm) wide. Use one of the traditional designs shown, or make up your own.

Make a beading loom from a small cardboard box. Make ten evenly-spaced slits on two opposite ends, just slightly wider than your beads. Wrap dental floss around the box to create your warp threads.

Start work in the middle of the loom. To attach a row of beads, thread a beading needle with nylon thread and pick up a full row of beads, in the right colors and in the proper order. Lay these over the warp threads, one bead per space. Push the row of beads down with your finger, and pass the needle through them in the opposite direction, this time going *under* the warp threads.

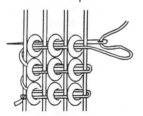

Continue in this way until the band is complete. Cut the warp threads at either end and knot them two by two. Stitch the band to a strip of leather for a bracelet, or sew directly onto an article of clothing.

26

Watch the harvest moonrise.

The full moon at any time of the year is a sight to see, but the full moon in September is especially spectacular. Known as the harvest moon, this full moon rises at a lower angle than usual, so that it lingers close to the horizon, making it appear very large. (For more on the full moons and their names, see July 8.)

The Chinese are partial to the full moon this month. They celebrate with a festival that some say honors the moon's birthday. Moon cakes, round cakes made from dough filled with red bean paste and sesame seeds, or fruits, nuts, and spices, are eaten at this time.

Make your own moon cakes to munch while you're watching the moonrise. Cut rolled-out biscuit dough into circles. Sandwich some bean paste (available at markets selling Asian foods) between two circles; pinch to seal the edges. Brush the tops with beaten eggs, and sprinkle with sugar. Bake according to biscuit recipe instructions.

Good Deeds

You probably lend a helping hand around the house, perhaps following a list of daily chores — including keeping your room neat (read on for one solution to this problem!). Have you ever thought of seeing what else you could do in your community, or for others around the world?

Here are some ideas for doing good that will make you feel good!

27

TO DO TODAY!
1. Finish home-
   work
2. Walk Ms.
   Renee's dog
3. Water garden

Make a chore chart.

Doing good deeds starts at home! Kids everywhere are given chores at home. A child in Tibet might include fetching a five-gallon container of water as one of his or her daily chores. An older child in Namibia might be asked to look after younger siblings everyday. Samoan boys and girls include cooking among their daily chores. Traditionally, children in Samoa take over cooking the family meals when they are ten years old.

What are some of your daily chores? Do you ever have trouble remembering what needs to be done? Make yourself a chore chart and your troubles will be over! See how below.

CHECK!

Here's a chart that can help you keep track of the chores you are asked to do (as well as the ones you voluntarily take over!), one month at a time.

Draw a grid like the one shown on a large sheet of paper. Use a ruler for best results. Number the squares at the top 1 through 31. Cover the paper with a sheet of clear Contact® paper.

Use a water-soluble marker to write the name of the month at the top left-hand corner and to write down all the things you need to do. It helps to list them in approximate order of when they should be done. Include weekly and once-a-month chores, if you like.

As you complete your chores, check them off with the marker. At the end of each month, you can see how well you've done. (Your parents may even reward you for completed chores!) Erase the chart with a soapy sponge, and you're all ready to write down the next month's list.

Write numerals 1-31 in squares

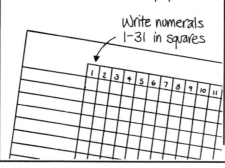

28

Clean your room.

Keeping your room neat is no doubt one of the chores given to you. You probably know from experience that this is easier said than done!

Do other kids around the world have this same problem? For those kids who have a separate room in which to sleep, the answer is yes, but having a room of one's own is a privilege most children around the world do not have.

You and any siblings who share your bedroom may not be able to break old habits completely, but you can make tidying up easier if you have sufficient storage space. You can create this by making storage boxes for toys and other items.

Check your local grocery store for tomato boxes, sturdy cardboard boxes that have hand-holds and separate lids. These can be stacked on top of one another to save space. Paint the boxes (leftover latex housepaint is perfect) and label them, so that you can find your toys, your favorite collections, and anything else!

29

Help out in your community.

Extend your helping hands to your community. After all, a community is made up of people working together. People from different cultural backgrounds can be drawn together by sharing activities. Here are some ideas your community might consider:

Establish a community garden by planting trees, tending flowers, or growing vegetables to eat. The choice of plants and the method of cultivation can reflect your community's cultural diversity.

Have a community center or school host recreational events that will bring different cultures together. Skilled people from other cultural backgrounds may be able to lead or teach some of the activities.

Start a program to teach English to non-native speakers. A similar program offering instruction in reading skills is also valuable.

How can *you* get involved in these programs? Volunteer to help spread the word about these offerings, and help weed gardens and tutor kids in English whenever you have the chance!

30

JEWISH HOLIDAY

Do good deeds during the Days of Awe.

The ten days between the Jewish New Year, *Rosh Hashanah*, and *Yom Kippur*, or "Day of Atonement," are commonly known as the Days of Awe. During this time, Jewish people believe they are being judged by God.

It is said that God has three books—the Book of Life, the Book of Death, and the Book of Judgement. Names of very good people are entered in the first book and names of wicked persons written in the second one. The names of everyone else are entered in the third book.

Throughout the Days of Awe, each person's name is brought up for review. By admitting any wrongdoings and righting any wrongs during this time, a person ensures his or her name will be included in the Book of Life when the final judgement comes on *Yom Kippur*.

No matter what your religion, this is a good time to think about —and do!—good deeds. As is said in Hebrew, *"Hatimah Tovah!"* (hah-tee-MAH toe-VAH), or "May you be inscribed and sealed in the Book of Life!"

1

Write a fable.

You are probably familiar with Aesop's fables, the name given to a collection of stories told by a Greek slave named Aesop around 600 B.C. You know, like the story about the race between the hare and the tortoise that ends with the moral: *Slow and steady wins the race.*

Fables are brief stories that teach moral lessons and how to behave properly. Many suggest ways in which good deeds are rewarded. They exist in every culture.

Write your own fable! Put animals in human roles, as tales from Greece and India usually do, or create characters from plants or everyday objects. What kind of fable might you write about the rewards of kindness, and the acceptance of others as they are?

2

Work for peace.

Imagine a world where wars and other conflicts didn't exist. One in which different countries respected one another, and communities within countries were at peace.

Will this ever happen? It certainly can, especially if people with different points of view take the time to talk and listen to one another. This is something you can see work for yourself.

Bring a lunch someday for someone who comes from a different cultural or religious background than your own. Over lunch, talk about what makes that person feel included—and excluded—in everyday activities at school. Share some of your feelings, too.

You will have made a new friend, but more importantly, you will have given someone a sense of belonging. A sense of belonging is something we all crave, and one that brings peace of mind.

The Story Hour

Meet some amazing characters and go on awesome adventures without ever leaving your seat! How? By reading a book!

As you'll discover, many books have a truly international following. Kids in countries all over the world grow up listening to and reading stories about some of the same characters. Ahead, you'll also find some interesting ways to make stories come alive!

3

Find books written in other countries.

Some of your favorite books may have originally been written for children in other countries. How can you find out if this is so? Look for the name of the person who translated the book from the language in which it was written. Or check the copyright page for information about a book's country of origin.

You'll discover that Pippi Longstocking was written by a Swedish author, but millions of children outside of Scandinavia know of this plucky heroine's exploits. British children, of course, aren't the only ones who love Winnie the Pooh, a very British bear if there ever was one! The story of Pinocchio is well-known from India to Italy, the country of the puppet's birth.

This proves that good stories appeal to kids no matter where they live!

4

Read some world folk tales.

Every culture has its own folk tales. Some are meant to explain natural happenings; others, moral lessons. And some are just for fun!

Amazingly, many stories around the world closely resemble one another. The story of Cinderella, for example, has similar versions in many different cultures. The version you probably know is the one written by Charles Perrault, a Frenchman who collected tales in the late 17th century. But there's a Chinese version that dates from around 850, in which the girl at the story's center is called *Yeh-hsien*. An even older retelling was recorded by a Roman historian in the first century B.C. In that story, Cinderella is a Greek slave named *Rhodopis* (roe-DOH-pes), which is Greek for "rosy-cheeked."

You'll find lots of folk tales in your local library (for the names of some to ask for, see the bibliography of this book). While some of the stories may resemble others you've read or heard, each has a special flavor that reflects the country of its origin.

5

MUSLIM HOLIDAY

Read from a holy book for *Lailat al-Qadr.*

Lailat al-Qadr (LAY-laht ahl KA-dur), or "Night of Power," commemorates the first revelations Muhammad is said to have received from Allah. These revelations are contained in the Quran, Islam's holy book, considered to be one of the most beautifully written religious texts. Muslim children start reading the Quran when they are quite young, and on this night many read aloud some of the verses they've learned.

You may know of some other sacred texts. Christians study a holy book called the Bible. The section known as the New Testament describes the life of Jesus. Parts of the Old Testament are familiar to both Christians and Jews, followers of Judaism. Jewish people have two holy scriptures. There's the Torah, which is part of the Hebrew Bible, and the Talmud, which gives directions for numerous details of Jewish life.

Ask one of your friends whose religion is different from yours to share his or her holy book with you. Do the same for your friend. How do the two texts compare?

6

Record a story.

Storytelling is a tradition in many cultures. In fact, many African and Native American tales are handed down from one generation to the next, without ever being written down.

You know from listening to stories that reading aloud can really make a difference. Giving characters different voices and matching the mood of the story by speaking softly or very quickly just seems to happen naturally! You can capture this special quality by making an audio tape of one of your favorite stories, or one you make up.

This would make a perfect gift for younger brothers and sisters who don't read yet. Record one of their favorite books, perhaps even adding signals (such as a bell ringing or the sound of a page turning) to allow them to "read" along while they're listening.

7

Fold a book.

Turn a favorite story into a book! Here's a simple way to fold a single sheet of paper to make a six-page booklet (plus front and back covers).

To make a booklet measuring 6″ × 9″ (15 cm × 23 cm), you'll need an 18″ × 24″ (45 cm × 61 cm) sheet of paper. Use a sheet of art paper that size, or cut your own from newsprint.

Fold the paper in half crosswise, then in half crosswise again. Unfold, and fold in half lengthwise. Unfold completely, and cut a slit in the paper as shown, using scissors or an X-acto knife.

Fold the paper in half lengthwise, and holding the paper at both ends, push your hands together to form pages.

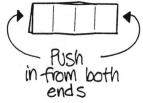

Fold in half to complete the booklet.

8

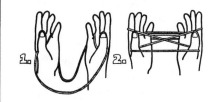

Tell a story with string.

String figures, such as the familiar cat's cradle, are found in many cultures. In some places, they are used to "tell" stories.

The Batwa people of Africa make a figure called "the mouse" which is a series of loops over each of the fingers on the left hand. As the string is pulled, the loops come undone to show the mouse "running away."

Make up your own stories to go with some of the string figures you know. Or invent one for the figure illustrated below!

THE INS & OUTS

Many string figures start out with the following basic position. Place a 5-foot (1.5 m) piece of string tied in a circle behind your thumbs and little fingers (1). Slip your right index finger under the string that crosses your left palm, then slip your left index finger under the string on your right palm. Draw your hands apart (2).

To make the outrigger canoe, a figure made by native peoples in British Columbia, start with the basic position. Place your thumbs between the two strings on either side of your index fingers, hook the far string with your thumbs, and pull your thumbs back.

VIEW FROM ABOVE

INSERT THUMBS HERE

With your teeth, lift the string closest to your body up and over your thumbs. Then release your little fingers from their loops, and pull your hands apart. Do you see the canoe with its balancing outrigger beam joined by two poles?

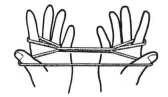

Rhyme Scheme

Poetry is the oldest form of literature, and one that is found throughout the world.

If you think all poems are like the familiar nursery rhymes you heard when you were younger, you're in for a surprise! Poetry comes in as many shapes and sizes as . . . well, people!

TOGETHER...
WHATEVER THE
WEATHER!

9

Recite some of your favorite poems.

Children and poetry are made for each other! Why? Because many poems are short and to the point, and easy to remember because of their carefully chosen words and rhyme scheme.

What are some of your favorite poems? Do you know any that describe the different seasons, or that are about brothers and sisters? You probably like funny poems, like this favorite from an unknown British author:

**Algy met a bear,
A bear met Algy.
The bear was bulgy,
The bulge was Algy.**

Poetry is held in high regard in Russia, where it's celebrated on Poetry Day each December. Poems are also an important part of Vietnam's heritage. Children in that country are familiar with many classic poems, including the 18th century epic poem entitled *Kim Van Kieu*, or "The Tale of Kieu." It is loved by many, including some adults who can recite the entire lengthy poem from memory!

10

Compose a limerick.

Some of the funny poems you enjoy may be limericks. These are humorous poems made up of five lines. The first, second, and fifth lines rhyme with one another, as do the third and fourth lines, which are slightly shorter in length. Here's an example of a limerick that's also a bit of a tongue twister:

**A fly and a flea in a flue
Were imprisoned, so what
could they do?
Said the fly, "Let us flee!"
"Let us fly!" said the flea,
And they flew through a flaw
in the flue.**

Limericks are named for Limerick, Ireland, but they were popularized by the English author and illustrator, Edward Lear, who wrote many in the mid-1800s.

Many limericks are about people. They often start like this:

There once was a girl (or boy) named . . .

Now you write one about yourself!

...boy named Joe

11

Write a *haiku*.

Haiku (HIGH-koo) are short poems in a particular style that developed in Japan in the late 1600s. A poet named Matsuo Basho was interested in capturing the essence of nature in as few words as possible. He restricted himself to writing just three lines, with a total of 17 syllables. The first line was made up of five syllables; the second line, seven syllables; the third line, five.

Here is an example of another Japanese poet's work, translated so that the poem in English conforms to the style:

**Look at that rascal
crow in the cornfield . . . acting
like he was farmer!**

Write your own *haiku*. Although the lines don't rhyme, you'll have to choose your words carefully to add up to the required number of syllables.

12

THE AMERICAS

Write a cultural poem for *Día de la Raza.*

Ever heard this short poem?

> **In fourteen hundred ninety-two,**
> **Columbus sailed the ocean blue**
> **And found this land, land of the Free,**
> **Beloved by you, beloved by me.**

These are actually the first lines of a long poem entitled *History of the United States,* written by Winifred Sackville Stoner.

Columbus, of course, did not discover the Americas. How could he have when there were people here to greet him? The mariner is remembered on this day, however, which in Central and South America is known as *Día de la Raza* (DEE-ah day lah RAH-sah), or "Race Day." This refers to the new race of people that came about as a result of the Spaniards having children with the native peoples.

Write a poem about your own culture, and how it has blended with others to make it what it is today. Or write about how you and others maintain your ethnicity. Make yours a personal poem, or write about how you think different cultures can coexist no matter where they are in the world.

13

UMBER
CRIMSON PUCE CORAL
EBONY MAHOGANY
ULTRAMARINE

Write a poem about a color.

Colors make good topics for poems because they are rich with symbolism. We think of some colors as representative of happiness, others symbolizing sadness. What is your favorite color, and why?

Here's an anonymous poem in which colors are important:

> **I'm glad the sky is painted blue**
> **And the earth is painted green.**
> **With such a lot of nice fresh air**
> **All sandwiched in between.**

Your poem might use colors in a descriptive way like this, or to create a mood.

Children in other countries might not choose some of the same colors that you would to describe happiness and other emotions. That's because some colors have different meanings in other cultures. Some of these are mentioned in the box below.

COLOR CODED

Yellow is considered a happy or lucky color in many countries, including India. For Bulgarians, however, yellow symbolizes hatred.

Red is a good luck color in China. Not surprisingly, many festival decorations in that country are red. Red flowers are never sent to someone in the hospital, however, because the color also symbolizes blood and may bring bad luck.

White is associated with purity in many European countries. But in India, it is thought of as an unlucky color. The Chinese associate both white and blue with mourning.

You've probably heard jealous people described as being "green with envy." Green is the beloved color of Ireland, sometimes referred to as the Emerald Isle. In recent years all over the world, green has come to symbolize sound environmental policies and practices.

14

Illustrate a favorite poem.

Some poems are so skillfully written that it's easy to conjure up images when reading them. You can imagine the look of twilight when a poet writes that the night came "leaking out of the sky." Or how mouse tracks in snow resemble a message "written in mouse."

The above examples show how many poems "say" a lot in very few words. So it's natural to team up a poem with an illustration.

Pick a favorite poem and draw a picture to illustrate its meaning or its mood. Choose a poem from another culture (check an anthology of poetry for examples), and use colors as viewed by other cultures in a symbolic way. (For more on colors, see the box on this page.)

Food, Glorious Food

Want to sample some of the world's cuisines? You're in luck, because most libraries have a good selection of international cookbooks, which include many dishes made from everyday ingredients available in markets everywhere.

Read on for a taste — pun intended! — of what it's like to sit down to a meal in a few places around the world. Limber up your fingers, because you're going to be eating with chopsticks, too!

For more on food, see February 24, April 5, and Cooking in the index for the listing of international recipes included in this book.

15

Eat something filling.

For many people around the world, meals are comprised of one main, filling food that is eaten with vegetables and small amounts of meat in a seasoned sauce.

Rice is by far the most important filler, eaten by over half the world's population. It's a main part of most Asian diets, although in parts of China and India wheat is eaten in the form of steamed buns and flat griddle breads.

Corn is the main filler in Central America, where it is made into *tortillas* (tor-TEE-yahs). Potatoes are eaten in great quantities in many European countries, along with breads made from wheat, rye, and other grains.

Ethiopians rely on several filling foods, including millet. A unique bread called *injera* (in-JEER-ah) is an important part of Ethiopian meals. Somewhat like a huge spongy pancake, *injera* is sometimes referred to as an "edible tablecloth." Small amounts of spicy stew and vegetables are placed on the *injera*, which is eaten bit by bit along with the rest of the meal.

16

Share food with others on World Food Day.

Did you know that nearly half of all the people in the world do not have enough to eat? Sadder still, millions die of starvation each year.

The United Nations hopes to make people aware of this each year on World Food Day. Is there anything you can do about this tragic situation? There certainly is!

You can start by helping people in your community who may be hungry. Offer to help out at a soup kitchen, or drop a few nonperishable items in a community collection bin every time you go to the market. Remember others on traditional feast days, such as Thanksgiving. In Iraq, families customarily prepare twice as much food as is needed during certain festivities. What isn't eaten is delivered to a mosque where it is given to the needy.

17

Plan a vegetarian meal.

Many people around the world eat little or no meat, either for religious reasons, because they do not want to kill animals, or because meat is scarce or expensive.

The protein needs of vegetarians are easily met with other foods, including legumes, such as peas and beans. In Israel, spicy chick pea patties called *felafel* (feh-LAH-full) are fried and put into pita pockets. Make your own and serve with a tossed salad and cheese and fruit for a meatless meal!

Felafel

1 16-ounce (450 g) can chick peas, drained and rinsed
3 tablespoons (25 g) unsweetened wheat germ
2 cloves garlic, minced
1 teaspoon (5 ml) ground cumin
1 teaspoon (5 ml) salt
½ teaspoon (2.5 ml) cayenne pepper
½ teaspoon (2.5 ml) black pepper
1 egg
Oil

Mash the chick peas in a bowl with a potato masher. Add the next six ingredients; mix well. Form into 12 small patties.

Heat about ½" (2 cm) oil in a skillet. Fry the *felafel* on both sides until brown and crispy. Drain on paper towels. Enjoy!

18

Save room for dessert.

Do your parents tease you about always having room for dessert even when you say you're full? In some places, such as China and Japan, it isn't customary to serve dessert at the end of a meal. Instead, sweets are snacked on between meals.

In lots of countries, fresh fruit is offered for dessert. In Malaysia, there are all sorts of fruits to choose from, including 15 varieties of bananas! One fruit, called the durian, is a particular delicacy. It has a wonderful taste and custard-like texture, but it smells strongly of garlic when it is cut open. In many public places in Malaysia, signs are hung that read, "NO DURIAN EATING ALLOWED!"

19

Set the table.

One of the ways you may help out at home is by setting the table. At your house, what usually goes on the table at each meal?

Many peoples around the world have little use for table utensils. Instead, they scoop up food with bits of bread, or use their fingers. The right hand is used almost universally for eating, as the left hand is considered unhygienic (it is used for cleaning the body).

The Koreans, Chinese, and Japanese eat with chopsticks. (For more on these, see October 20.) Soups may be eaten with a large porcelain spoon, although people commonly sip directly from the small hand-held bowls. Korean children are not asked to help set the table because most homes have no fixed dining area, and food is carried to wherever the family members choose to eat.

Most Europeans use cloth napkins (throwaway paper is considered very wasteful). Family members have their own napkin rings to distinguish their napkins. In Asia, napkins aren't used. Instead, water bowls and towels are provided for washing the hands before and after a meal.

20

Use a pair of chopsticks.

Did you know that the three cultures that use chopsticks each have their own unique type? Chinese chopsticks are thick and have a blunt end; Japanese chopsticks are slender and slightly pointed. Korean chopsticks are thin and are the only kind made from metal.

Have you ever eaten with chopsticks? It's really not hard once you get the hang of it. Practice with two unsharpened pencils if you don't have a pair of chopsticks in the house.

Place one chopstick in your hand as shown below. This chopstick doesn't move and is kept steady by putting pressure on it with the tip of your ring finger.

Hold the other chopstick between your first two fingers and thumb. Hold it so the tip extends slightly beyond the other chopstick. Move this chopstick up and down to pick up morsels from your plate.

21

Have a snack.

Can't wait until the next meal? Then what you need is a snack!

Kids everywhere snack between meals. The Chinese and Japanese who don't usually eat dessert often snack on sweets. Healthier snacks are popular, too, such as sunflower seeds, a favorite in China.

In most countries, street vendors peddle snack foods. In Belgium, *frites* (freet), or fried potatoes, are a favorite. These are sold in little paper cones, topped with a dollop of mayonnaise. In Mexico and other Central American countries, cornmeal concoctions filled with cheese, beans, or pork are cooked on the spot on many street corners.

In Russia, thirsty shoppers and children buy juice from coin-operated dispensers that have a communal glass that is washed out by the user before it's filled with juice. In Malaysia, the evening meal is often eaten "on the street." For this snack-like meal, people bring their own dishes from home.

Sweet Tooth

It's that time of year when stores are filled with Halloween treats. Not surprisingly, kids everywhere love candy and other sweets!

Ahead, you'll find some simple candies you can make yourself, including some that are even good for you! Share these with your friends at Halloween or during the Turkish Candy Festival, or whenever you need to satisfy your sweet tooth.

22

Sample some sweets for *Seker Bayrami.*

Even though children are not expected to go without food from sunup to sundown during *Ramadan,* the Muslim month-long fast, they do look forward to its end. At that time there is a 3-day celebration when children are given gifts, money, and candy. In fact, the Turks call this time *Seker Bayrami* (SAY-kur bye-RUM-ah), or the "Candy Holiday."

Perhaps the best known Turkish confection is Turkish Delight, a jellied candy containing bits of pistachios and other nuts. As with other foods, there are regional differences in the types of sweets that are popular. The box below describes some of the mouth-watering treats enjoyed around the world.

SUGAR CANDY

Ever heard this British nursery rhyme?

**Handy Pandy, Jack-a-dandy,
Went to buy some sugar
   candy.
He went into a sugar shop,
And out he came, with a hop,
   hop, hop!**

What do you suppose he bought?

If Handy Pandy were Swiss or Belgian, he might have bought some chocolates, as these two countries produce some of the best chocolates in the world. Carob is sometimes used as a substitute for chocolate. Children in countries around the Mediterranean eat dried carob pods just like candy bars!

In Mexico, many candies contain ground *chile* pepper, which gives the candy a red tint as well as a bit of a bite! Similarly, many sweets in Japan are made from the same red beans used in many condiments and dishes.

Nougat, a chewy candy made from sugar syrup, egg whites, and almonds, is a specialty of both Italy and Spain. Halvah is a sweet confection made from sesame flour and honey, and is enjoyed throughout the Middle East.

The word candy comes from the Arabic word for sugar. Confections in the Middle East tend to be very sweet.

23

Chew some gum.

Children all over the world chew gum. You might not, however, recognize some of the flavors it comes in. The Japanese, for instance, select from dozens of different flavors, including pickled plum gum.

There's no telling who was the first to think of chewing the sap from trees. For that's what the main ingredient in gum is — chicle, which comes from the latex of the sapodilla tree, a tropical evergreen found in Central America. Native Americans in North America invented their own gum, chewing the resin of the black spruce (a habit they passed on to the early English settlers).

Now you know where Chiclets® gets its name!

24

Make marzipan figures.

Have you ever eaten miniature fruits and vegetables made from almond-flavored paste? Then you've had marzipan, a delicious confection that originated in the Middle East.

Look for ready-made Danish marzipan in the international food section of your market (if it's not there, check the aisle where baking ingredients are shelved). It's available in tube-shaped packages in its natural color, as well as pre-colored in kit form.

You can easily tint your own marzipan before modeling it, adding a few drops of food coloring to a small piece. Work the food coloring into the marzipan with your fingers, adding a little powdered sugar if it's too sticky.

You can also paint finished pieces with food coloring. The colors are usually stronger when added in this way. The illustration below shows just some of the many things you can make from marzipan.

25

Make chocolate truffles.

Have you ever heard of truffles, an edible fungus that grows underground beneath oak trees? Much loved in France, truffles are unearthed with the help of trained dogs and pigs who excitedly sniff out the location of the dark delicacies.

Equally well known are French chocolate truffles, rich candies rolled in powdered cocoa. Watch the chocolate lovers in your family sniff these out!

Chocolate Truffles

3 ounces (85 g) unsweetened chocolate
1 stick butter or margarine
2 tablespoons (30 ml) heavy cream
½ cup (75 g) confectioners' sugar
2 tablespoons (15 g) nuts, finely chopped
Powdered cocoa

Melt the chocolate and butter in a heavy saucepan over low heat. Stir in the cream. Gradually add the sugar and nuts, stirring until lump-free.

Cover and refrigerate until firm; then form into small balls with your hands. Roll in cocoa to coat. Store in the refrigerator.

26

Munch on natural sweets.

Everybody knows sugar-laden sweets should be eaten in moderation. Thank goodness for dried fruits, which can satisfy even the sweetest tooth!

Kids everywhere love dried fruit. Brazilians make something they call "Mother-in-law's Eyes," which are pitted prunes stuffed with marzipan and rolled in finely chopped Brazil nuts. Dates are popular throughout the Middle East, and raisins are eaten wherever grapes are grown.

You can turn dried fruit into a candy that has no added sugar. Here's how:

Fruit Nuggets

1 pound (.5 kg) assorted dried fruits
Rind of one orange
Orange juice
Finely chopped nuts

Grind the dried fruit and orange rind in a food processor, using the finest blade. Add just enough orange juice to hold the mixture together. Form into bite-sized balls, and roll in the chopped nuts.

27

Fold a candy box.

Make a gift of candy even more special by packaging the sweets in an origami-style box you've made yourself.

You need two square sheets of paper, at least 9″ × 9″ (23 cm × 23 cm), one about ¼″ (.5 cm) larger than the other.

Fold one sheet diagonally in half, first one way and then the other; unfold. One by one, fold the corners so they all meet the center point; unfold. Now fold them to the crease lines made in the previous step; unfold. Lastly, fold the corners to the crease lines on the opposite side; unfold. Your square should look like this:

Cut the paper along the thick lines shown in the diagram. Fold two opposite sides in, bending in the ends to form a box. Fold the other flaps over these to anchor the box.

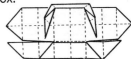

Repeat with the remaining sheet to make the lid. Decorate the box (either before or after assembly) anyway you like.

All Saints & Souls

People pay special tribute to those who have died in different ways around the world. In some countries, these are solemn days, while in others they are more festive, resembling Halloween as we know it.

Speaking of Halloween, you'll also find some memorable ways to celebrate this holiday. Make your own mask from a culture of interest to you, and share some grinning skull cookies with your friends!

28

Compare ways people honor the dead.

In many cultures, it is customary to remember those who have died on the anniversary of their death. Vietnamese families, for instance, create shrines in their homes in honor of deceased loved ones, offering food and flowers each year at that time.

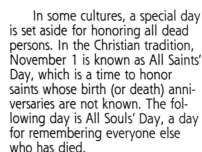

In some cultures, a special day is set aside for honoring all dead persons. In the Christian tradition, November 1 is known as All Saints' Day, which is a time to honor saints whose birth (or death) anniversaries are not known. The following day is All Souls' Day, a day for remembering everyone else who has died.

Some other customs are described below.

DEARLY DEPARTED

Japanese Buddhists clean their homes and prepare special foods for *Obon* (OH-bawn), a three-day festival dedicated to the dead that takes place in July. The spirits of the dead are believed to return home at this time. Cemeteries and streets are ablaze with the light from lanterns and bonfires, which are meant to show the spirits the way.

In Mexico, the dead are honored on November 1 and 2, collectively known as *Día de los Muertos* (DEE-ah day lohs MWAIR-

tohs), or "Day of the Dead." This is a very festive holiday that is a blend of Christian traditions brought to the New World by the Spaniards and the far older native peoples' beliefs (dating back thousands of years). Families take picnics to the cemeteries where their relatives are buried and make merry. The annual event celebrates life, while shrugging at the inevitability of death, making it less fearsome.

Funerals in Ghana are also happy occasions. It is believed that the deceased look after the living, which is cause for rejoicing.

29

Stamp *adinkra* designs.

A special decorated fabric called *adinkra* (ah-DINK-rah) cloth is traditionally worn at funerals in Ghana. Brown or black fabric strips are stamped with designs carved from pieces of calabash gourds, using a black ink made from tree bark. The strips are then sewn together to make a full-size cloth.

You can stamp your own *adinkra* designs on fabric or paper using carved potatoes. Cut a potato in half; make a simple raised design on the flat surface of one half, by carefully cutting away what you don't want to print with a slender knife.

Acrylic paint works well as "ink." Divide the fabric into squares, and create a repeat pattern in each using different stamps. Use the traditional designs shown here or make up your own.

30

Make a mask.

Wearing masks and other disguises at Halloween is a custom borrowed from the ancient Celtic festival called *Samhain*. Supposedly during this time, the spirits of those who had died the previous year returned to earth. The living sought protection from the spirits by hiding behind masks.

Disguise yourself this Halloween with a mask from one of the world's cultures. Papier mâchè masks are especially effective. Staple a cardboard ring into a circle to fit around your face; stuff with crumpled-up newspaper. Paste several layers of torn newspaper strips over this, using a paste made from equal amounts of flour and water. Build up features, such as horns, eyes, and nostrils.

side view

Let the mask dry for a day; then remove the stuffing and allow to dry completely (this may take several days). Make holes for your eyes and for elastic braid to hold the mask on your face. Paint the mask, adding hair and other decorative elements as desired.

31

Trick or treat for UNICEF!

When you're trick-or-treating this year, make it a point to collect money for UNICEF. Helping the United Nations Children's Fund each year at Halloween began in 1950, and remains a tradition in North America. For more information on how you can aid UNICEF in this way, write to one of the committee addresses found on page 143.

Collecting money at this time of year to help those in need is not a new idea. It was once customary in Great Britain to give food and money to the poor when they came asking for it on All Souls' Day. (At one time, "soul cakes" were distributed.) The tradition of asking for food led to children begging for treats, which is rarely done in England any longer. If kids where you live attend school and community parties instead of trick-or-treating, include a collection box for donations among the goodies.

Scottish children blacken their faces with soot at Halloween, and are known as "guisers."

1

Make gravestone rubbings.

Graves in many countries are marked with carved stones, some of which are beautiful. If you have an older cemetery near where you live, you've probably seen the plaintive angel faces and other designs atop some of the gravestones.

You can capture the haunting quality of the gravestone art by making rubbings. This is a popular hobby in England and other European countries where centuries-old brass markers are found inlaid in the floors of churches. All you need are some thin paper and a black crayon (remove the wrapper so that you can hold it flat). Holding the paper over the surface of the stone (or brass) with one hand, lightly color with the crayon. The writing and any decorations on the gravestone will appear in reverse —that is showing up white against a black background.

2

Decorate skull cookies.

Among the playful images found throughout Mexico during *Dia de los Muertos* (for more information on this holiday, see the box on the preceding page) are sugar candy skulls, which are personalized for the children who eagerly purchase them this time of year.

In keeping with this tradition, make your own decorated skull cookies. Roll out your favorite rolled cookie dough and cut out basic skull shapes. Bake according to recipe instructions; let cool. Decorate with royal icing (the kind that is piped out of a pastry bag and allowed to harden), using a store-bought icing or following a recipe in a general cookbook. Mexican sugar candy skulls are decorated in pastel colors, so tint your icing if you like.

Let There Be Light

Imagine how our ancestors felt when they first learned how to make fire. At last, they were able to light their way in the dark and cook food whenever they wanted to. What a magical moment this must have been!

Fire continues to have a magical effect on people. From flickering candles to roaring bonfires, fire is an important part of many customs around the world to this day.

3

Light your home for *Diwali.*

Each year in late October or early November, Indian villages and cities are ablaze with light. Tiny earthenware lamps (and in some cases, electric bulbs) line walkways, courtyards, and outer walls and roofs of homes and businesses. It's *Diwali* (dee-WAH-lee), the Festival of Lights.

For some Indians, this festive occasion commemorates the return of Rama, the legendary prince who was exiled for 14 years.

Others view it as a tribute to Lakshmi, the goddess of luck and prosperity. In each case, the lights are lit as a welcome for these important visitors.

You can make your own oil-burning lamp, called a *dipa* (DEE-pah). Use self-hardening clay to sculpt the basic shape shown here.

Let the clay dry completely. Coil a length of wick in the bowl of the lamp, and pour in just enough vegetable oil to cover the wick. Be sure to light with adult supervision only.

GOLDEN GLOW

Fire is an important element in many different celebrations around the world. Here are just a few occasions when candles or bonfires are lit.

Candles figure in the Thai celebration known as *Loy Krathong.* The meaning of this popular festival has been obscured by time. Floating vessels called *krathong,* made from banana leaves and each containing a lit candle, are launched on water. It is said that if the candle stays lit until your *krathong* is out of sight, any wish you've made will come true.

It is traditional to burn candles on many religious holidays, including the birthday of Buddha, *Hanukkah* (see December 9), *Luciadagen* (December 13), and Christmas (December 25). Candles also figure prominently on that important lifelong event — the birthday! (See May 27 through 31 for more on birthdays.)

Small bonfires are lit on the last day of the Iranian year (for more on the celebration surrounding this event, see March 21). Everyone leaps over the fire, which symbolizes leaving old sorrows behind.

Bonfires are also lit in England to commemorate the foiled plot to blow up Parliament in 1605. Stuffed figures representing Guy Fawkes, one of the conspirators, are thrown into the flames.

4

Make dipped tapers.

There was a time when every family made its own candles. Today in Sweden, families often make their own candles for *Luciadagen* (see December 13) and Christmas festivities.

You can make your own dipped candles *with the help of an adult,* as working with hot wax is very dangerous. You'll need a box of paraffin, some wicking or braided cotton string, a tall metal juice can, and a saucepan.

Place broken chunks of wax in the juice can, and stand the can in the saucepan filled with water. Bring the water to a simmer on the stove and heat the wax until it melts. Lower the flame enough to keep the melted paraffin hot.

Cut one or two 20″ (51 cm) lengths of string. Fold a single string in half and dangle both ends in the wax for 60 seconds. Lift, let cool slightly, and straighten by pulling the wicks.

Dip this double wick into the wax for 3 seconds. Hang over a chair or from a nail to cool. Continue dipping and cooling in this way until the layers have built up and the candles are as thick as you want. Let cool completely before using.

Paraffin

Simmering water

Candles

5

Make a candelabrum.

A candelabrum is a candleholder designed to hold more than one candle. Make one to show off your dipped tapers!

You can make a candelabrum from a number of fire-proof materials, including self-hardening clay or synthetic sculpting clay that is baked in a regular oven (ask for this at an art store). Design your own holder, or create a traditional candelabrum for one of the holidays mentioned in this book.

Make a Jewish *menorah*, either the 7-branched type that is used throughout the year, or the 9-branched *menorah* used during *Hanukkah* (see December 9). Make a *kinara*, the candelabrum that holds the seven candles of *Kwanzaa* (December 26). Or make a circular holder for four candles to add to your Advent observance. Light one (then two, and so on) on the four Sundays preceding Christmas.

6

Make a pierced lantern.

Pierced metal lanterns make appealing holders for squat candles. The light shining through the holes makes patterns on tables and walls. Lanterns such as these are made from tin in Mexico, but you can make your own from empty food cans.

Choose a food can with a removable paper label. A plain-sided can with no ridges works best. Chip any remaining glue off the *chilled* can with a knife.

Fill the can with water and freeze for at least 48 hours, or until frozen solid. Meanwhile, plan your design on a piece of paper to be taped around the outside of the can.

The actual piercing is done with a hammer and an assortment of nails, awls, and chisels (or use a screwdriver). Place the can on its side on a folded towel, and hammer the holes. When you're done, let the ice melt.

Stand a stub from one of your tapers or a votive candle in the lantern. Light, under adult supervision. Be aware that the sides of the lantern are hot to the touch when there's a candle burning in it.

7

Cook over an open fire.

Cooking over an open fire may be a special treat in your family, something that you do during the summer months, for instance. Roasting a piece of meat over coals is a weekend ritual many South American families look forward to, also.

In many parts of the world, however, the only way food can be cooked is over an open fire. From India to the West Indies, fires are lit inside and outside of homes each day to cook the family meals.

This not only requires a lot of time—starting, tending, and extinguishing fires—but is quickly depleting the trees in many countries. We think of wood as a renewable resource, but this is only true if trees are replaced as they are cut. In some countries, such as India, energy-efficient wood stoves are being made available to families. But other measures, such as reforestation, must also be taken.

Art for Art's Sake

Everyday objects all over the world, from eating utensils to clothing, are made more beautiful with decoration. But people everywhere enjoy creating a type of art that's made for no other reason than to please the creator!

That's not to say others don't enjoy this kind of art. You'll find several types of fine art here, equally satisfying to make as to view.

8

Make handprint art.

The earliest examples of art we know of were created around 25,000 years ago. Much of this art depicts animals, designed perhaps to cast spells on the real animals these people hunted for food. Another common motif was the human handprint.

We'll probably never know why our ancestors left their prints on cave walls. Did you know the practice is still alive in Australia? The Aborigines commonly leave an outline of their hands on rock surfaces. A mixture of white clay and water is sprayed around the hand which is held flat against the rock. This is what it looks like when the hand is removed.

Make some handprint art of your own. Splatter poster paint around your hand held on a sheet of paper (this is a messy project, so plan on doing it outdoors!). Dip your hand in paint and press it on paper for a different type of print. What other ways can you think of to use your hands to make art?

9

Paint a self-portrait.

Once our superstitious ancestors realized that painting a portrait of someone didn't necessarily cast a spell on that person, they began to draw likenesses of humans. Various styles of portraiture developed around the world.

You can have fun drawing a self-portrait in one of these historical styles. Draw yourself as the Egyptians once drew people, with the head, arms, and legs as they look from the side, but the body and eyes facing forward.

Japanese artists in the 18th and 19th centuries made prints from carved wood blocks. Make a self-portrait in that Japanese style.

Draw yourself as a Russian *matroyska*, or wooden nesting doll, or as the Hindu god, Krishna, was often depicted—with blue skin!

10

Paint a landscape.

What do you see when you look out your bedroom window? If you have a nice view, or have a favorite spot in a nearby park, create a landscape painting of this view.

Do as a group of French painters in the late 1800s did, and try to capture the atmosphere of your landscape, rather than faithfully representing trees and grass. One painter, Georges Seurat, was especially interested in how small dots of different colors next to each other were "mixed" by the eye. His method of painting was called *pointillism* (PWAHN-teel-iz-um), and is one you can experiment with.

Practice painting blue and yellow dots near each other. Up close, you'll be able to distinguish the two colors easily, but stand back and see how they create the color green! Experiment creating shadows without using any black paint (look closely and you'll see real shadows are made up of many colors). When you're ready, use what you've learned to capture your landscape in paint!

11

Make cut-paper designs.

Paper is used to make decorative art in many countries, including China and Poland.

The Polish cut-paper designs are called *wycinanki* (vee-chee-NON-key). One type is made from brightly colored paper cut out and glued in layers, each successive layer slightly smaller.

Make your own layered *wycinanki* from thin colored paper such as origami paper. Fold a sheet in half and draw half a design on it, placing it along the folded edge. Copy the traditional rooster shown here, or make up your own design. Note how the central design is attached to the outer circle. Cut out all the shaded areas, using nail scissors or an X-acto knife for the inner cuts.

Unfold the paper and glue onto a poster board square. Build up your design by gluing shapes cut from different colored paper onto the basic design.

12

Create hammered metalwork.

The Nigerians are skilled metalworkers. They cast bronze sculptures, as well as smaller pieces designed to be worn as jewelry. They also make decorative panels from hammered sheet metal.

You can make your own hammered designs using this technique. You need a small piece of sheet aluminum (ask for .020 gauge at a hardware store), a hammer, and tools such as a screwdriver and blunt nail (or nail set). Tape the edges of the metal with masking tape to protect your fingers.

Draw a simple design on the metal, such as the lion shown here. Gently hammer straight lines and small circles to indicate the lion's mane and facial features. Take care not to break through the metal at any time.

Now hammer the background, packing the marks close together to make an even pattern. You'll notice that this causes the lion's shape to be slightly raised.

Remove the tape before hanging your artwork.

13

Make an *ikebana* arrangement.

Arranging flowers in pleasing compositions is considered an art, perhaps no more so than in Japan, home of *ikebana* (ee-kay-BAH-nah), the centuries-old art of symbolic arrangements.

The art of *ikebana* traces its origins to Buddhist temples, where it was customary to leave flowers in front of the statue of Buddha. Gradually, certain rules were adopted, such as using a minimum of blooms and paying especial attention to line rather than color (drooping branches symbolize sadness; uplifting lines are "happy").

Arrange a choice bloom from a flowering houseplant along with some bare branches from a tree in your yard to make your own *ikebana* arrangement. The illustration below may inspire you, as might your mood!

14

Organize an art show.

You and your friends can showcase your artwork with a show, complete with an opening reception! You can even sell your work to raise money for a special cause.

Put on an international art show, using some of the art and craft projects in this book to inspire you. Invite working artists in your community to serve as advisors, or as judges, should you choose to award prizes to the best pieces in the show.

Hold the show in a public place, such as the library of your school or in a room at your community center. Advertise the event, or send out invitations. This is a great way to get people together, celebrating the artist in all of us!

The artist is not a special kind of man (woman), but every man (woman) is a special kind of artist.

Eric Gill

Best Dressed

Today, the costumes associated with different countries are rarely worn as everyday clothing. Few Dutch wear wooden clogs and white starched caps; most Japanese women and girls wear Western-style clothing instead of *kimono* (kee-MOH-noh), or "robes."

These special garments are brought out for special occasions, however, providing an important link with the past for people all over the world.

For more on everyday clothing, see August 22-26.

15

Dress up for *Shichi-Go-San*.

In Japan, November 15 is a special day for seven-year-old girls, five-year-old boys, and both boys and girls who are three years old. All of these children are honored with a celebration called *Shichi-Go-San* (SHE-chee goh sahn), or "Seven-Five-Three."

On this day, the children dress in their very finest, often traditional, clothing. For girls this means a *kimono* held shut with a stiff *obi* (OH-bee), or "sash." Boys wear a garment called a *hakama* (hah-KAH-mah), which is a shortened version of a *kimono*. Both wear raised wooden thong-like clogs called *geta* (GAY-tah) with socks that have a separate place for the big toe.

The children visit Shinto shrines with their parents where they give thanks. Usually this is followed by a party where one of the treats is a foot-long candy stick called *chitoseame* (CHEE-toh-say-ah-may), which symbolizes long life.

What types of clothes do you traditionally wear on special occasions?

16

Compare traditional costumes.

Traditional costume varies considerably around the world. The native dress from the country you or your ancestors came from is probably quite different from garments found on other continents.

Dig through your closets and books to come up with examples of traditional dress. For all their differences, you'll begin to note some similarities. You can even categorize the clothing in certain ways, such as was done in the box below.

COSTUME BALL

There are dozens of ways of comparing traditional clothing from around the world. Here are just a few ideas to get you started:

Compare examples of printed fabrics used to make clothing, from the *batik* of Indonesia to the stamped *adinkra* cloth of Ghana.

Name some different headdresses, such as the turbans worn by Sihks in India and the *kaffiyeh*, popular among Palestinians.

List some of the long robes worn around the world. The Arabic burnoose is worn more often than the Swedish gown that girls wear only once a year on *Luciadagen*.

Think of all the clothing made from a simple length of fabric, including the Indian *sari* and Southeast Asian *sarong*.

Compare traditional wedding garments worn by men and women around the world.

17

Cut out paper dolls.

Make some paper dolls, complete with international wardrobes!

You might want to make several female and male figures, coloring each a different skin tone. Make the figures quite basic, such as they are here, drawing them on thin cardboard. Color and cut them out.

Place one figure at a time on white paper and lightly trace around it with a pencil. Remove the figure and sketch some clothing on the doll's outline. When you're happy with your clothing sketch, draw the outline of the garments with a black felt-tipped pen. Don't forget to include tabs for holding the clothing on the dolls. Let the ink dry com-

pletely before erasing any pencil lines. Color the clothing, cut it out, and try it on for size!

Ghana

Israel Pakistan

18

String a necklace.

Do you ever wear jewelry when you dress up? In many cultures, jewelry is an important part of traditional clothing.

In some cases, jewelry offers a link to nature. Native peoples in the Amazonian jungle string seeds and monkey's teeth and wear them around their necks. The Pueblo Indians of New Mexico wear corn necklaces, honoring the food plant that has been grown in that region for thousands of years.

String your own necklace from melon and squash seeds (washed and dried), and multi-colored corn and whole coffee beans (soaked in water to soften them up). Use a needle with a large eye and buttonhole or carpet thread, making a necklace large enough to slip over your head.

19

Put on some make-up.

You probably think of make-up as coloring worn on the face. In many countries around the world, not only the face but other parts of the body are decorated.

Women in Saudi Arabia, for instance, paint designs on their hands with henna, a reddish dye derived from a plant. Here's an example of how hands are sometimes decorated:

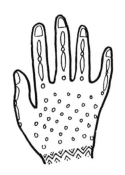

In the West, make-up is worn mostly by women, but many African men decorate their bodies with dyes obtained from plants as well as colored clays.

Children don't generally wear make-up as much as adults. In parts of India and Pakistan, however, boys and girls often decorate their foreheads with a red mark called a *bindie* (BIN-dee). A *bindie* may be used as a sign of beauty, or to show what class or religious group a person belongs to.

Harvest Home

In those countries where people raise much of their own food, the harvest is celebrated with great fanfare. It's just as important for those of us who purchase what we eat to be reminded of its origins and give thanks for it.

Here are some ideas for honoring nature's bounty at your annual Thanksgiving gathering or any time of year!

In the United States, Thanksgiving is celebrated on the fourth Thursday of November. In Canada, the holiday falls on the second Monday of October. The harvest in Canada is earlier due to the shorter growing season.

20

Learn about harvest celebrations.

Sukkot (SOO-koht) is the Jewish harvest festival that takes place in early October. All over the world, Jewish families decorate wooden frames representing *sukkot*, or "huts," with fresh fruits and vegetables. Meals are often eaten inside the *sukkot* during the five-day celebration.

The Ga of Ghana celebrate the harvest during the month of August with a festival called *Homowo*. (For more on this festival, see August 15.) The Ga grow corn, and each year they serve specially-prepared corn from the previous year, before sampling the new harvest. In this way, they honor the harvesting cycle.

In parts of Switzerland where cheese is made, the harvest is a time to divide up wheels of cheese among those who own the herds and the mountain pastures where the herds graze.

What other harvest festivals do you know about? Are any of them celebrated in your community?

21

Cook a Native American Thanksgiving dinner.

Each year as American families sit down to enjoy the Thanksgiving dinner, they recall the first Pilgrim thanksgiving that supposedly took place in 1622. Many people don't realize that the Native Americans had long been honoring the harvest and successful hunting with celebrations of their own. Many Native Americans still do, including the Seminole of Florida and the Iroquois in Canada, both of whom celebrate the Green Corn harvest.

This year, plan a Thanksgiving dinner that honors Native Americans and the foods they were gathering and cultivating long before Europeans set foot on these shores. You'll find a sample menu in the box below.

NATIVE NIBBLES

Use the following menu as inspiration for creating your own, or plan on serving some of these dishes from different tribes at your Thanksgiving meal. You'll find the recipes for these and more in the Native American cookbook listed in the bibliography.

Soup
Hazelnut Soup
(Algonquin)

Appetizer
Roasted Peanuts
(Choctaw)

Main Course
Roast Saddle of Venison
(Wampanoag)

Bread
Piñon Cakes
(Taos)

Vegetable
Succotash
(Powhatan)

Dessert
Steamed Cranberry Pudding
(Mahican)

Vegetable
Wild Rice
(Chippewa)

Dessert
Oranges Marinated in Honey
(Seminole)

22

Fold napkins.

Make a harvest meal even more memorable by including specially folded napkins on the table.

Here's a fold that resembles an ear of corn, a meaningful harvest symbol for a Native American, Mexican, or West African meal. Use square napkins, made from either cloth or paper.

Fold the napkin in half to make a triangle. Fold the upper point down (1). Then fold those points in half (2).

Fold the lower point so that it reaches the midline (3). Fold this bottom portion in half, and in half once again, so that it covers the midline (4).

Pick up the napkin and insert the right corner into the left (5). Stand the napkin upright (6).

23

Make a harvest figure.

Harvest figures, which represent the spirit said to be living within plants, are made all over the world. The figure is traditionally made from the last sheaf of wheat or stalk of corn in the field, and is kept until the following spring when planting takes place, or until the next harvest.

Make your own harvest figure from bundles of grass, as is done in the country called Ivory Coast in West Africa, or from corn husks, used in Mexico and Czechoslovakia. Here's one way to make a husk figure. Use fresh husks, or soak dried ones in water to soften them. You'll also need string and cotton.

Make the head and body by placing some cotton in a piece of husk; tie at the neck and waist. Slide a rolled husk (tied at the ends for the hands) above the waist for arms (1). Arrange some husks around the figure's waist; tie in place (2). Fold these down, and trim straight across for a women's skirt (3), or divide in two and tie at the ankles for a man.

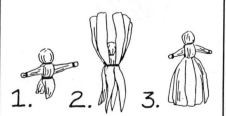

24

Make a wreath.

The circle, a shape with no beginning or end, has long been regarded as a magical symbol in many cultures. Among the many things it symbolizes is the cycle of the seasons. This is why many harvest wreaths are round.

Have you ever made your own wreath? If you have access to grape or bittersweet vines, you can make a sturdy wreath from these natural materials. Form a circle with lengths of vine, twisting and tucking in the ends.

You can also make wreaths by attaching different items to a wire or cardboard wreath form. Hold herb sprigs, cones, and nuts in place with thin wire. (This same technique can also be used to make evergreen wreaths.)

Here's another idea for a wreath, one you and your family or classmates can make together. Have everyone trace and cut out a pair of hands from construction paper. Glue them into a circle, overlapping them slightly.

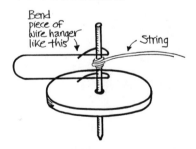

25

Spin a top.

In some parts of the world, including Malaysia and New Guinea, tops are charms used to ensure a good harvest. Just like circular wreaths, the spinning tops symbolize the seasonal cycles. In many communities, there are even top-spinning competitions. Serious stuff!

You can make your own tops from a variety of materials. Stick a sharpened pencil through the center of a plastic coffee can lid (or through a hole drilled in a large plastic screw top from a jar). Do you notice how the larger and heavier the top, the longer it will spin? You can put some extra "spin" on your tops by wrapping string around the stick and steadying the top with a device such as the one shown below.

Bend piece of wire hanger like this ↓   — String

You and your friends can have spinning contests, or try this: Set a top spinning and see if you can run around the room, or outside and back, before the top comes to a stop!

Year After Year

As the last month of the year draws near, it's time to start thinking about replacing the calendars in your home. This year, why not make your own?

Ahead, you'll discover how the number of months in a year and days in a week differ in some cultures, as well as learn what kids in Asia are doing while you're asleep each night!

26

Compare world calendars.

The calendars you have hanging in your home and in your classroom in school are just like calendars found all over the world. The Gregorian calendar, as it's called, isn't the only one in use, however. Some countries use several calendars, all of which are older than the Gregorian calendar.

You'll find more information about the Chinese calendar (which is based on the phases of the moon) as well as the Jewish calendar (which calculates its year by the sun and its months by the moon) on pages 11 and 12 in the introduction of this book. You'll also find the World Calendar, one that was proposed in 1930 but never adopted.

Your friends from other cultures may also be able to tell you something about the calendars used by their native countries or religions.

Which calendars do you think work best? How might you change any of them to better track the passage of time?

27

Make up some month names.

Most calendars have twelve months, varying in length just as the Gregorian calendar's months do. The Jewish calendar has 13 months, however, the last being a leap month. It is called Adar II and follows the month of Adar seven times during a 19-year cycle.

Many calendars have names for the months, but some are simply numbered. This is the case with the Chinese calendar, although it does have 24 15-day periods with descriptive names such as The Waking of Insects and Clear and Bright period.

What kinds of names can you come up with for the months of the year? What changes in nature might you honor? The Finns call February "the pearl month" because of the frosty whiteness; October is referred to as "the mud month"! Invent your own names with special meaning for you!

For more on the full moons for which Native American months are named, see July 8.

28

Count the number of days in a week.

Did you know that the week is a human invention, not related to the day, the months, or the year —all of which are based on nature's cycles?

The ancient Babylonians were the first to divide a month into weeks of seven days. But not all cultures had a seven-day week. In fact in Nigeria and Ghana today, three-, five-, six-, nine-, and ten-day market cycles are more important to various tribes than the seven-day week.

Some countries have also experimented with changing the number of days in a week. In the 1790s, French calendars were made up of ten-day weeks. The former Soviet Union instituted a five-day week, which existed from 1929–1931 and was then replaced with a six-day cycle. In 1940, the seven-day week was restored.

How many days do you wish a week had? How many of those would be for going to school, and how many for doing other things?

I LIKE IT THE WAY IT IS!

29

Find the International Date Line.

If you live on the East Coast of the United States and have relatives on the West Coast, you may know something about time zones. Even if your Uncle Mark is an early riser, you would never call him on the telephone as early as 7:00 in the morning. That's because it would only be 4:00 a.m. where he is!

Because the earth is constantly turning, day and night occur at different times around the world. When you're getting ready for bed, children in Afghanistan are just getting up!

In 1884, 24 global time zones were created. Take a look at a map or globe and see if you can spot the 180° longitudinal line (longitudinal lines are the ones running up and down). It is along this line (making a few detours around land masses) that one day becomes the next. This is called the International Date Line, and if it's November 29 where you live, it's already November 30 west of that line!

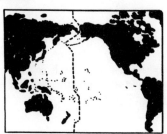

30

Construct an Advent calendar.

The four Sundays leading up to Christmas are known as Advent (from the Latin word for "arrival"). Christians mark this passage of time in a number of ways, including a favorite among German children — the Advent calendar.

Most Advent calendars are made up of 24 numbered windows, one of which is opened each day starting December 1. Behind each window is a picture, bit of Scripture, or even a candy or little gift.

You can make your own Advent calendar, designed to hold treats, such as candy or tiny ornaments. Everything you need to know is in the box below!

FOR OPENERS

This Advent calendar takes a little time to make, but it can be used year after year. All you need to do is replace the front picture and any edible treats!

Find a cardboard gift box with a separate top and bottom, a sheet of paper the same size, an X-acto knife, tape, and crayons or markers. You'll also need 24 candies or ornaments hanging from short pieces of thread.

Cut 24 openings in the top of the box with the X-acto knife. Place the box face down on the paper and trace around all the openings with a pencil. Cut three sides of every drawn opening; turn the paper over and decorate the front. Number the windows 1 through 24.

To assemble the calendar, tape each ornament or candy piece so it dangles in the cut openings of the box top. Fit the box top and bottom together; tape shut. Finally, tape the decorated paper in place.

Adapt this calendar to help you count the final days to other important events in your life, such as your birthday!

1

Design next year's calendar.

This is a good time to make next year's calendars for you and your family to use or give as gifts.

Design a conventional monthly calendar with a grid in which appointments and other information can be written. You can make your calendar with just one illustration that shows all year, or draw 12 different pictures, one for each month.

You may want to put together a week-at-a-glance calendar for a working parent or teacher. Make a desk version using a three-ring binder (these come in all sizes). This is a chance to recycle, too, by making your calendar from paper that's been printed on just one side.

Don't forget to include some of the cultural holidays you would like to remember next year. Check your library for a copy of *Chase's Annual Events* for the dates on which any movable (variable in date) holidays will fall next year.

Gifted & Talented

Children all over the world exchange gifts with family and friends on special occasions, including the three holidays that fall in December, *Hanukkah,* Christmas, and *Kwanzaa.*

Ahead are some ideas for putting a little something extra in your gift-giving! You'll also find other ways to put your talents to use.

2

Make greeting cards.

Many people keep in touch with family and friends in distant places by sending cards, especially around this time of year. Greetings are doubly appreciated when the cards are homemade.

Use some of the ideas in this book to create cards with an international flavor. Stamp *adinkra* patterns (see October 29) on folded note cards. Make simple *wycinanki* paper cutouts (November 11) and glue them to cards. Write out the recipe for a favorite bread or cookie traditionally baked for the holidays. Design a card that says "peace" in different languages.

3

Design wrapping paper.

No need to buy wrapping paper for the gifts you give others when you can design your own! Here are some ideas for making wrapping paper that reflects cultural traditions around the world.

For the paper itself, use newsprint, which comes in rolls (in several widths), and is available for a nominal fee wherever newspapers are printed. You can decorate the paper using any number of methods, but paint is fastest.

How about designing some gift wrap that resembles a Navajo blanket? Using black, grey, and red paint, you can make some striking paper that looks like this:

Other over-all designs can be taken from African art. Make a pattern by repeating one of these motifs:

Or you might want to paint a group of children from around the world, holding hands. Feel free to copy the design on the front of this book!

4

Knot a *mizuhiki* design.

Traditional Japanese gifts are wrapped and tied with a bow made from thin colored cords. The cords are called *mizuhiki* (mee-zoo-HEE-key), and can be found at many art and craft supply stores.

Here's a simple *mizuhiki* knot that can be used to dress up a gift box or card. Select eight cords, four of one color and four of another (four silver and four gold, for example). Make a loop about 6″ (15 cm) from one end with four of the cords, making sure they lay flat.

Weave the cords of the other color in and out of the first loop as shown. Trim the ends near the knot evenly.

Center the knot on the front of the box; flip the entire box over, holding the *mizuhiki* in place. Tape the cords to the box where they overlap, then trim any excess with your scissors.

5

Hunt for presents on *Sinterklaas Avond.*

Dutch children look forward to December 5, the day they call *Sinterklaas Avond* (SIN-ter-clahs AH-font), or "Saint Nicholas Eve." This is the night St. Nick and *Zwarte Piet* (ZWAHR-tuh peet), or "Black Pete," make the rounds, delivering gifts for all. Children leave wooden shoes filled with straw and carrots for *Sinterklaas'* snow-white horse, in the hopes something will be left behind in return for them.

Before going to bed, families exchange small gifts among themselves. This is a truly silly time! Gift tags are written in rhyme, full of clues meant to disguise the identities of those giving the presents. And the gifts themselves are cleverly wrapped to create confusion and a laugh. Small items may be hidden in a loaf of bread, or there may be a trail of clues that take children all over the house before finally finding the gifts!

This is a tradition you might adopt in your family. Can you think of any good hiding places?

CLUE #5
Look on
your bed,
where you
rest your
head!

6

Put on a craft sale.

Put your talents to work, while providing a valuable service for your school or community, by holding a craft sale. This can be similar to an art show (for more on this, see November 14), but the items sold might be generally more "useful." This is the perfect place to sell cards and gift wrap, in time for the holiday season!

You and your friends can sell small items you've made, such as friendship bracelets (see August 14) and *migajón* miniatures (March 4). Make some items that would be meaningful to people who celebrate *Hanukkah,* such as blue and white gift wrap with a pattern made from the Star of David, or sturdy *dreidels* (see the box on page 134 for how to make these). Remember your potential customers may be other children who are looking for unusual, but inexpensive, gifts to buy for family and friends. A portion of the proceeds from your sale could be used to benefit your school or community in some way.

7

Stage a talent show.

If you like to perform in front of an audience, now's the chance to strut your stuff! You and your friends can get together and put on a talent show.

Make the theme of your show an "international showcase," and invite all sorts of different performing artists. Perhaps some kids have a *salsa* band; others might perform a traditional dance from another culture. Encourage kids who speak other languages to put on skits in their native language.

Talent shows are great ways to make a cultural exchange happen. Everybody wants to see his or her friends and classmates perform on stage, so even people who might not be inclined to learn something about other cultures will get a chance to do so without even realizing it!

8

Act in a play.

Not everyone wants to sing in front of others (some prefer to save this activity for the shower!). But lots of people do enjoy acting. If you're looking for some good roles, why not see what kinds of plays have been written about other cultures?

Look in your school or local library for a copy of *Dramatized Folk Tales of the World.* You and your friends could act out one of the many versions of *Cinderella* (for more on this tale, see October 4), or some tales written by Denmark's famous storyteller, Hans Christian Andersen. Or write your own play, based on one of your favorite stories from another culture.

Putting on a play requires group effort, with people willing to act, round up costumes and props, and direct the play (an adult may be happy to take on this role). But few experiences are more rewarding, and you're sure to want to do it again!

Actors in Japan's Noh plays, based on religious and folk myths, wear expressive masks over their faces.

Keeping Traditions Alive

Traditions enrich people's lives everywhere. Be they religious, cultural, or individual family customs, traditions are like a glue that holds a lifetime's experiences together.

Many traditions are ancient — so old no one remembers when or why they began. Others are newer, just taking shape. You'll discover some of each here, as well as get a chance to start your own traditions!

9

JEWISH HOLIDAY

Make a *dreidel* for *Hanukkah*.

Hanukkah is a Jewish celebration with a long history. Continually observed for over 2,000 years, it commemorates an event that took place in Jerusalem when that city was freed from foreign rule. The Holy Temple needed to be rededicated but there was only enough sacred oil to keep the temple's *menorah,* or "candelabrum," lit for one night. Miraculously, the flame continued to burn for eight nights, which everyone felt was a clear sign of the strength of their faith.

Lighting a special nine-branched *menorah* is a part of the eight-day celebration. So is playing with a *dreidel* (DRAY-dull), a square-sided top. See how to make your own in the box below.

10

Read about traditions.

This book has touched on many of the traditions and customs observed around the world, but as you can imagine, there are lots more!

People from other countries and cultures can provide you with answers to many of your questions about particular traditions, but books are a good source of information, too. You'll find a number of helpful books listed in the bibliography starting on page 147. Check both your local library and school library for these and others.

LUCKY SPIN

To make this simple *dreidel,* you need stiff paper (such as oak tag), a ruler, tape, white glue, and a short pencil.

Draw a grid of 1" (2.5 cm) squares on the paper. Sketch and cut out the body and cover shapes.

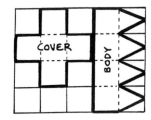

Draw one of the following Hebrew letters on each of the cover flaps.

נ ג ה שׁ

NUN GIMEL HAY SHIN

Fold the paper along the dotted lines and assemble the *dreidel* by taping the body together and gluing the cover over it. Insert the pencil in the very center of the top. Secure with glue.

HOLE FOR PENCIL

Nun, gimel, hay, and *shin* are the first letters of *Nes gadol haya*

sham, which means "A great miracle happened here," referring to the sacred oil. For those playing a game of chance with the dreidel, they stand for *nikhts* (Yiddish for "nothing"), *gantz* ("everything"), *halb* ("half"), and *shtell-arein* ("put in"). Players start out with an equal number of nuts or candies, part of which is placed in a pile between them. Each player spins the *dreidel* and takes nothing, all, or half the pile, depending on how the *dreidel* lands. When *shin* shows face up, players add two pieces from their own stash to the pile. The winner is the player who ends up with everything!

11

Visit a museum.

Museums are fabulous places to search for clues about traditions, too. Do you have any historical or cultural museums near where you live? Pay a visit to them soon!

Museums can explain everything from why the streets in your town are named what they are (some may be named after prominent people from other cultures who once lived in your area) to the meaning of important traditions halfway across the globe. Museums are also great places to see costumes, art, and other artifacts from all over the world.

You can also get some ideas for setting up your own cultural displays at home and at school (for more on this, see January 6).

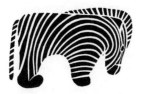

Among the great museums around the world are the Prado in Madrid, Spain; the Egyptian Museum in Cairo, Egypt; the Shanghai Museum in Shanghai, China; the Louvre in Paris, France; and the British Museum, in London, England.

12

Walk through historic districts.

Are there any old buildings of historical interest where you live? Perhaps your town has an entire district that has been preserved. Spend some time learning about some of the architectural traditions in your area.

Children all over the world can proudly point to buildings of historical importance, some of which are very old. Just think of the pyramids in Egypt (dating from as early as 2613 B.C.), and Stonehenge in southern England, which was started around 2750 B.C. and completed, 1,200 years later.

The Great Wall of China is a tremendous landmark, some 1,500 miles (2,400 km) long! Started around 210 B.C., it was intended as a defensive wall, but it also served as a means of communication, since for most of its length, it is wide enough for five horses to travel side by side. Now here's something even more astounding: the Great Wall is so large that it can be seen from the moon!

13

Serve your parents breakfast on *Luciadagen*.

Luciadagen (loo-SEE-ah-dah-gen), or "Lucia Day," is an example of a tradition in the making. The day honoring the Italian Saint Lucia has long been observed in one part of Sweden, but only in the late 1800s did it become a widespread custom.

The eldest girl in the family dresses up as Saint Lucia, in a long, white robe and crown of greenery adorned with glowing candles. She serves her parents coffee and *lussekatter*, special Lucia Day buns, in bed. Younger siblings also dress up, including boys, who wear tall, conical hats decorated with stars. These "star boys" were once associated with another traditional observance, but have become a part of *Luciadagen*.

You might want to make a batch of Swedish buns (use any sweet yeast dough, shaping the buns as shown). Or serve your parents their favorite breakfast food instead. You can do this with or without the costume!

Raisin

14

Start your own traditions.

Some traditions are so old no one can say with certainty when they began. Others, as you've seen, are still being shaped. "Star boys" didn't always figure in *Luciadagen*, but happily they do today, allowing boys to take part in the festivities.

You and your family may have certain traditions you cherish, such as making homemade jam each summer or doing something special on the first day of school. You may also look forward to making special things for certain holidays, perhaps baking your own cookies to give as Halloween treats.

As you read this book, you may discover traditions from different countries and cultures that you would like to adopt. Choose from those that reflect your heritage, or from cultures that are very different from your own. Or start some brand-new traditions, ones you make up! Your life will be richer for it!

Winter Watch

The arrival of winter is cause for celebration. You may not be able to really tell at this point, but the days will gradually get longer from now until June. Hurray!

While you're counting the days until winter's arrival, take a look at some other "counts." These, and the other suggestions ahead, will certainly brighten your days!

15

Make a "winter count."

Many of the Plains Indians, including the Crow and Blackfoot, once made robes from whole buffalo hides. Many were decorated with paint, either with geometric designs or with pictures of events, such as tribal wars. Some hides, known as "winter counts," recorded annual events of importance. A single symbol representing the event, such as a solar eclipse or the coming of the white man, would be added each year, usually starting in the center of the robe and spiralling outward.

Make your own "winter count" to record events in your life (or in your family's history). Tear a paper grocery bag in the shape of a buffalo skin. Draw pictures on it with crayons, applying heavy pressure. When you're done with the drawing, crumple up the paper and dunk it into a pail of water stained brown with paint. Remove the paper and spread it out to dry on newspapers. When it's dry, it will have a leatherlike appearance.

16

Identify birds.

Each year at this time, thousands of people in North, Central, and South America are busy counting birds. Small groups are assigned a circular area 15 miles (24 km) in diameter. On a single day during the 16-day Christmas Count, the groups identify and count as many birds as they can within their area. The tally is reported to the National Audubon Society to aid its bird research.

Just think, the birds you have nesting on your property during the summer months may be winter residents of some South American child's home now! And the birds that frequent your feeder, spend their summers even farther north. How many can you identify?

17

Hang paper banners for *Las Posadas.*

In Mexico, Christmas begins on December 16, with the first of nine nights of festivities known as *Las Posadas* (lahs poh-SAH-thahs). Each evening, groups proceed by candlelight through neighborhoods, reenacting the journey Mary and Joseph made to Bethlehem, searching for a *posada*, or "inn."

Arranged beforehand, the groups knock at doors, only to be refused entry. Finally, they are let into the host's home, designated for that evening, where a party takes place.

Decorate your home with the same *papel picado* (pah-PELL pee-CAH-thoh), or "pierced paper," banners found throughout Mexico. See how to make your own below!

PAPEL PICADO

Fold one long edge of a rectangle of tissue paper 1" (2.5 cm) from the top. Fold the paper in half, flap to the outside (1). Fold the paper at an angle, just up to the flap. Fold up two more times (2).

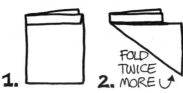

Scallop or pink the uneven edge. Cut shapes along the folded edge (unfold partially to cut additional shapes). Unfold completely and hang by gluing the flap over a length of string. String many banners next to each other; hang.

18

Learn some legends about winter.

When the temperature drops and lawns and car windshields are covered with a fine coating of white, children in Germany say Father Frost has paid a visit. In Russia, they say Mother Frost has been there.

If this sounds familiar, it's because children in North America usually refer to Jack Frost. Why is "he" called Jack? The name Jack Frost is thought to have originated in Scandinavia (where it can get mighty cold!). There's a Norse legend about a god who was the son of Kari, god of the winds. He was sometimes called *Jokul* (YUR-kul) or *Frosti* (FRAWS-tee). The two names were eventually joined, and in English became Jack Frost!

What other legends do you know about winter? Sit near the fire where it's nice and warm, and tell them!

19

Decorate with greenery.

Decorating with greenery at Christmastime is a tradition in many countries, but it's an ancient custom that predates Christianity. Long ago, plants that remained green in the dead of winter were greatly valued, in part because they held the promise of spring.

Decorate your home with evergreen wreaths and boughs. Other plants are special this time of year, too. Did you know the poinsettia is a native of Mexico, where it's called *la flor de Nochebuena* (lah floor day NOH-che-BWAY-nah), or "the flower of the Good Night," referring to Christmas Eve?

In some parts of Europe, it is customary to cut a branch from a fruit tree and put it in water. If the branch blossoms by Christmas, it is said good luck will follow.

20

Hang a kissing ball.

You are probably familiar with mistletoe, an evergreen plant with white berries that is hung in doorways and rooms this time of year. You probably also know that you're likely to get kissed if you are caught standing under the plant!

Kissing under the mistletoe is an English tradition with a long history. The ancient Druids considered the plant sacred, and hung it year-round to protect against witchcraft, and as an expression of goodwill. Long ago, enemies meeting beneath a sprig of mistletoe cast aside their weapons and declared a one-day truce. Wouldn't it be wonderful if mistletoe could aid world peace today?

You can make your own kissing ball using mistletoe or other evergreens. Stick small branches of greens into a potato or apple (the moisture will help keep the greens fresh). Hang where it can be seen . . . and appreciated!

21

Light a fire on the first day of winter.

The first day of winter falls on or about December 21. (In the Southern Hemisphere, it's the first day of summer.) Also known as the winter solstice, this is the shortest day of the year.

Today, we know the days will gradually get longer from this day on, but our ancestors weren't certain of this. The Scandinavians, living where winters are especially dark, sought to encourage the sun to return to its full glory by burning a Yule log. Originally, this was an entire tree, fed into the fire little by little over the course of many days. Today, the Yule log is associated more with Christmas, both in Scandinavia and other countries. In France, where few families burn an actual log, every table at Christmas is graced with a *bûche de Noël* (bush duh noh-ELL), or "Christmas Log" cake, cleverly frosted to resemble a log!

With your parents' supervision, light a fire (or a few candles) in honor of the winter solstice. Winter has arrived!

Joy To The World

Christmas is a joyous time in households all over the world. Delicious aromas waft through homes; the sounds of familiar carols fill the air. Children anxiously await that moment when presents are exchanged!

Ahead are some ideas for ways to share the joys of the season and the warm feelings you have for your family and friends . . . and all humankind!

22

Bake holiday cookies.

Baking cookies this time of year is a tradition in many families all over the world. This year, include some international favorites to eat and share with others.

Look for recipes for German "pepper nuts," spicy cookies enjoyed in Sweden and Denmark, too. Make some *leckerli* (LEH-kerr-lee), a Swiss specialty sweetened with honey, and *speculaas* (speh-coo-LAHS), a Dutch treat.

Mexican families enjoy round, fried fritters called *buñuelos* (boon-you-EH-lohs), which are traditionally served on cheap pottery plates. The plates are smashed to the ground afterward to bring good luck!

Greek cooks also make a fried pastry eaten at Christmas. These triangular-shaped morsels are called *diples* (DEE-place), which means "folds," in reference to the Christ Child's diapers or swaddling clothes. You can make your own version of *diples* from left-over bits of pie dough cut and folded and then baked.

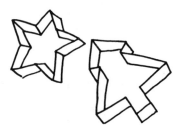

23

Make ornaments.

The Christmas tree, laden with decorations, is thought to have originated in Germany, itself a descendant of the paradise trees featured in medieval religious plays. But the ancient Romans also hung treats from trees, especially during *Saturnalia*, the pagan festival which took place each December.

The nicest ornaments you can hang on Christmas trees and throughout the house are the ones you make yourself! Make your tree truly international by using some of the ideas below.

HANG UPS

Thread *wycinanki* to hang from the tree. (see November 11 for how to make these Polish cut-paper designs.)

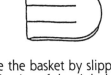

Hang origami models, such as the frog on March 23, for a Japanese look.

Make bread "clay" ornaments, using the recipe on March 4. Sculpt a llama laden with presents in honor of South America where *migajón* originated.

Weave Danish heart baskets from two different colored pieces of paper, three times as long as they are wide. Fold each in half, and make two evenly-spaced cuts nearly to the end. Round off the ends.

Weave the basket by slipping the folded strips of the right-hand section *around* and *through* the strips of the left-hand section, one at a time. (The middle strip will be just the opposite of the two outer strips.) Attach a handle to either side of the basket.

24

Go caroling.

Take part in one of the nicest holiday traditions — caroling! Gather family and friends together and go from house to house in your neighborhood, or pay a visit to those who cannot get outdoors, such as hospital patients and residents of nursing homes.

What are some of your favorite carols? The popular carols sung in English trace their origins to many countries. *Bring a Torch, Jeanette, Isabella*, is a French carol; *Deck the Hall*, a Welsh one. *Silent Night* is a German carol written in 1818. On Christmas Eve that year, the parish priest in Obendorf discovered that the organ could not be used at the Midnight Mass. Quickly he penned some words, asked the organist to compose a melody, and that night the choir sang the song *a cappella*, or unaccompanied, for the first time.

Ask your friends who speak other languages to sing these and other carols as they know them. They can also teach you some of their favorite carols. Add these to your repertoire!

25

Include international customs at Christmas.

North Americans already include a number of customs from around the world when they celebrate Christmas. After all, the Christmas tree originated in Germany; the *crèche*, or manger scene, got its start in Italy. Many of the familiar carols we sing today represent several different countries.

Some of the people in your community may honor the season in other ways. Perhaps there are special decorations and foods that reflect different ethnic backgrounds. Some of your friends may traditionally receive gifts on a day other than December 25, such as December 6, January 1 or 6.

Below are just a few of the different customs surrounding Christmas. Include some of these in your holiday observances!

IN THE SPIRIT

In Poland, the most important gathering is the family feast known as *Wigilia* (vee-GEE-lee-ah), which takes place on Christmas Eve. The dining table is covered with a white cloth laid over a bed of straw, in memory of the stable in Bethlehem where Jesus Christ was born. The meal begins with everyone sharing the *oplatek* (oh-PLAH-tehk), a large wafer that has been blessed by the parish priest. Family members who are not present are sent a piece of the wafer.

For many people in various countries, the period before Christmas is a time of meatless fasting. Fish is served the night before Christmas from Sweden to Sicily. Roast goose is the main attraction on French tables that night, in honor of the geese that were said to have greeted the Wise Men when they arrived in Bethlehem.

Animals themselves are given special recognition in many parts of the world. Seed and suet are put out for wild birds, and domestic animals are given extra rations. This ancient practice predates Christianity, but was strengthened by the belief that animals are given the power of speech at the stroke of midnight on Christmas Eve.

And children? They delight in helping with everything from baking holiday foods to decorating the tree (although parents do this in secret in Austria, Germany, and England). Naturally, kids eagerly await opening presents, on whichever day is customary. Who brings the presents? Read on!

Pere Noël **(pair noh-ELL)** — France

Jultomten **(YOOL-tome-tehn)** — Sweden

La Befana **(lah bay-FAH-nah)** — Italy

Svaty Mikalas **(SVAH-tee may-coh-LAHSH)** — Czechoslovakia

Christkindel **(KRIST-kin-dell)** — Germany

It was once customary to give Jewish children small amounts of money (gelt) each night of Hanukkah (for more on this holiday, see December 9). Today the gifts include toys and other items.

26

27

28

Looking Ahead

The last week in December is a good time to reflect on the past year and look ahead to the coming months. Take some time to enjoy your family's company, as many African-Americans do at *Kwanzaa*.

Take a moment, too, to think how you might play a more active role as a world citizen. If we all did what we could to make this world a better place, we might be looking ahead to happier times for everyone.

Share family memories at *Kwanzaa.*

December 26 marks the first day of *Kwanzaa* (KWAHN-zah), a seven-day celebration many African-Americans observe. Borrowing many of its symbols from harvest festivals, *Kwanzaa* is a relatively new holiday (first observed in 1966) that focuses on African heritage and pride.

Each night families light one of the red, green, and black candles in the *kinara* (key-NAR-ah), or candleholder, which symbolize seven ideals to live by. Other items are placed on a woven mat, including a bowl of fruit, vegetables, and nuts, and the *kikombe* (key-COMB-bay), or unity cup.

Families drink from the *kikombe* each night, sharing a special drink and family memories. Those members of the family who have been an inspiration to the others are given special recognition.

This is a custom you might want to adopt in your home. Family bonds are like no other, and it's nice to be reminded of this now and again.

Make a *mkeka.*

The woven mat on which items are placed during *Kwanzaa* is called a *mkeka* (mm-KAY-kah). You can easily make your own from newspaper, a stapler, and acrylic paints. Cut full-size newspaper sheets in half along the vertical fold.

Make a frame by folding three sheets every 2" (5 cm) from either short end, so the folds meet at a "v" in the middle (1). Place the ends of two of these strips within the folds of the third, as shown (2).

Fold other sheets into 2" (5 cm) strips and insert them into the frame's end; staple (3). Now weave horizontal strips over and under these, tucking the ends into the side sections of the frame, and stapling them. Complete the mat by adding and stapling the final section of the frame (4).

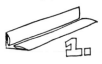

Paint the mat with red, green, and black paint, the traditional colors of *Kwanzaa.*

Predict the future.

What do you suppose the future has in store for all of us? There's no telling, or is there?

Fortune tellers, or seers, claim to be able to "see" into the future. Some read tea leaves. They interpret the patterns left in the bottoms of teacups (the tea must be made with loose tea, not a tea bag). It is said that a design like a star means you will have good luck; a cat-like shape indicates a quarrel is on its way.

Other seers prefer to read palms. The lines on your hands supposedly tell something about your health, your destined profession, and your love life! Still others rely on astrology (for more on this, see July 10).

These and other methods of predicting the future are found in many cultures throughout the world. Who's to say whether or not some people actually have the ability to sense future events? It's hard to argue with those who "know" something will occur, only to have it really happen just like they said.

29

Bury a time capsule.

The future is likely to bring lots of changes to everyday life as we know it. Everything from hair and clothing styles to the food put on our tables will probably be very different someday from what you're accustomed to. School and work schedules may also be different, affecting how people spend their leisure time.

Wouldn't it be great if you could look back, say in 20 or 30 years, and compare popular styles and customs? You can with a time capsule! All you need to do is gather up some mementos—a few photos of family and friends, a list of your favorite books, a page from your diary, some ads torn out of current magazines and newspapers—and enclose them in a sturdy plastic container with a tightly fitted lid. Be sure to mark the date you create the capsule.

Find a good place to bury your time capsule, preferably one that's likely to remain dry and undisturbed. Don't forget to make a detailed map showing where the capsule is located (and put this in a safe place!) Now all you have to do is wait!

30

Make a New Year's resolution.

This year make, and keep, a special New Year's resolution. Resolve to be a world-class citizen!

What does this mean? Simply to think of yourself as a very important member of the global family—the family of man. Even though the world is too large for you to be a part of everything that is happening, you still can make environmental issues, cultural acceptance, and world peace your business.

Use this book to help you come up with ideas for getting involved. Check to see what your school, religious center, and community are doing to help solve problems, not only where you live but throughout the world.

You may be only one person with two hands, but just imagine what can be accomplished if everyone joins hands and works together!

31

Bid the year farewell on New Year's Eve.

For those nations using the Gregorian calendar, today is the last day of the year. It's your last chance to do all those things you promised yourself you would do at this time *last* year!

All over the world, people prepare to bid farewell to the old year. For most, it means staying up until midnight, when the new year officially begins (see January 1). But there are lots of little ways these last moments are made extra special. The box below describes some of these.

OUT WITH THE OLD

In Ecuador, families stuff old clothing with straw to make a figure known as *Año Viejo* (AHN-yo bee-EH-hoe), or "Old Year." Some children even dress in black, impersonating the *Año's* widow, and beg for money for his funeral. At midnight, each family reads a last will and testament, which is actually a list of the family's shortcomings. Then both the *Año* and the will are set on fire in hopes that the family's faults will disappear with the smoke.

The Japanese eat a special food on New Year's Eve. *Toshikoshi soba* (toe-she-koh-she SOH-bah), or "sending out the old year noodles," are extra long buckwheat noodles. Whoever can swallow at least one strand without chewing it will surely have good luck in the coming year!

In Spain and many Latin American countries, people eat a dozen grapes while the clocks chime twelve. In Japan, Buddhist temples resound with the tolling of their bells, which are rung 108 times. This number represents the 108 human weaknesses described by Buddha in his teachings.

Would you like to make friends with children in other countries? Perhaps you'd like to start a tradition of giving to others on those occasions when you traditionally receive gifts yourself, such as your birthday or Christmas. Want to know more about what you can do to help save the earth? Write to some of the organizations below for information on how you can get involved. With their help, you can extend your hands around the world!

PEN PALS

International Friendship League
55 Mount Vernon Street
Boston, MA 02108

World Pen Pals
1694 Como Avenue
St. Paul, MN 55108

ORGANIZATIONS PROMOTING PEACE AND OFFERING SELF-HELP ASSISTANCE

Alternative Gift Markets
9656 Palomar Trail
Lucerne Valley, CA 92356

Canadian UNICEF Committee
443 Mount Pleasant Road
Toronto, Ontario M4S 2L8

Children As the Peacemakers
950 Battery Street, Second Floor
San Francisco, CA 94111

Heifer Project International
1015 South Louisiana
Little Rock, AR 72202

Oxfam America
115 Broadway
Boston, MA 02116

Save the Children
50 Wilton Road
Westport, CT 06880

United States Committee for UNICEF
333 East 38th Street
New York, NY 10016

ENVIRONMENTAL ORGANIZATIONS

The Children's Rainforest
P.O. Box 936
Lewiston, ME 04240

Friends of the Earth
530 7th Street SE
Washington, DC 20003

World Wildlife Fund
1250 24th Street, NW
Washington, DC 20037

As your interest in people from other countries and cultures grows, you may find you would like to purchase certain multicultural materials. Shops in your area that sell books, audio and video tapes, toys, and imported clothing and gifts, will likely have many items of interest. If there's something you can't find, ask. Most shop owners are more than happy to place special orders for their customers, if they are able.

Otherwise, look into purchasing goods from one of the mail-order companies listed here. Some of these companies specialize in multicultural materials, selling everything from books about what it's like to be born in another country and adopted by an American family to international craft kits and games that promote peace and understanding. Other companies offer just a few choice items of multicultural interest.

Write and ask for a catalogue (most are free of charge), and bring the world to your mailbox!

Animal Town
P.O. Box 485
Healdsburg, CA 95448
(games, toys, and books)

Aristoplay, Ltd.
P.O. Box 7529
Ann Arbor, MI 48107
(board games)

Audio-Forum
96 Broad Street
Guilford, CT 06437
(language instruction and music audio and video tapes)

Bits & Pieces
1 Puzzle Place
B8016
Stevens Point, WI 54481-7199
(puzzles and games)

Claudia's Caravan
P.O. Box 1582
Alameda, CA 94501
(full range of multicultural materials)

HearthSong
P.O. Box B
Sebastopol, CA 95473-0601
(craft kits, toys, and books)

The Heritage Key, Inc.
6102 E. Mescal
Scottsdale, AZ 85254
(full range of multicultural materials)

Multicultural Publishers Exchange
Praxis Publications, Inc.
P.O. Box 9869
Madison, WI 53715
(books)

Music for Little People
Box 1460
Redway, CA 95560
(audio and video tapes, instruments, and books)

Pacific Puzzle Company
378 Guemes Island Road
Anacortes, WA 98221
(map puzzles)

Shepherd's Garden Seeds
30 Irene Street
Torrington, CT 06790
(seeds from around the world)

Shibumi Trading Ltd.
P.O. Box 1-F
Eugene, OR 97440
(items from Japan and other Asian countries)

World Around Songs, Inc.
5790 Highway 80 South
Burnsville, NC 28714
(song books)

World Wide Games
Colchester, CT 06415
(games)

While this book is packed with information about kids from other countries and cultures, no doubt your appetite is whetted and you're hungry for more!

Happily, there are lots of books that explore in greater detail many of the aspects touched on in *Hands Around the World.* Where can you find these books? They're as close as your local library or bookstore!

The following list is by no means complete. For the most part, only those books that cover many different countries and cultures are included here. Ask your librarian to help you locate these, as well as cookbooks and folktales from specific countries (check both the children's and adult's sections).

Because the books in this bibliography cover so many topics, they have been arranged into eight categories (plus an additional one labeled *Periodicals*) to make it easier for you to find what you're looking for. Here are the categories and the types of books listed in each:

PLACE & TIME
Atlases and other geography books; books on calendars

BEGINNINGS
Books on world history and on family history

THE BARE NECESSITIES
Books on food, clothing, and housing

CUSTOM-MADE
Books about the customs of holidays and festivals; books on religions

SAY THE WORD
Books on alphabets and language; world folk tale and poetry anthologies

ARTIST-IN-RESIDENCE
Books on folk arts and crafts, music, dance, and drama

FAIR PLAY
Books on games and sports

EVEN MORE BOOKS
Books that don't fit neatly into other categories

PERIODICALS
Magazines of interest

You'll notice each book is labeled "juvenile" or "adult." This is simply an aid to help you in locating the books. Juvenile books can generally be found in the children's departments of libraries and bookstores; the adult books on the adult shelves. Books marked "juvenile/adult" are just as likely to be found in one place as the other.

PLACE & TIME

Atlases & Geography

The Book of Where or How to Be Naturally Geographic by Neill Bell, (Little, Brown and Co., 1982), *juvenile*

The Doubleday Children's Atlas edited by Jane Olliver, (Doubleday, 1987), *juvenile*

The Facts on File Children's Atlas by David and Jill Wright, (Facts on File, 1991), *juvenile*

The People Atlas by Philip Steele, (Oxford University Press, 1991), *juvenile*

Rand McNally Children's World Atlas (Rand McNally and Co., 1991), *juvenile*

Calendars

Blue Monday and Friday the Thirteenth: The Stories Behind the Days of the Week by Lila Perl, (Clarion Books, 1986), *juvenile*

Calendar Art: Thirteen Days, Weeks, Months, and Years from Around the World by Leonard Everett Fisher, (Four Winds Press, 1987), *juvenile*

Calendars by Necia H. Apfel, (Franklin Watts, 1985), *juvenile*

This Book is About Time By Marilyn Burns, (Little, Brown and Co., 1978), *juvenile*

BEGINNINGS

World History

Illustrated Atlas of World History by Simon Adams, John Briquebec, and Ann Kramer, (Random House, 1992), *juvenile*

Rand McNally Children's Atlas of World History, (Rand McNally and Co., 1988), *juvenile*

The Usborne Book of World History by Dr. Anne Millard, (Usborne Publishing Ltd., 1985), *juvenile*

Family History

Do People Grow on Family Trees? by Ira Wolfman, (Workman Publishing, 1991), *juvenile*

The Great Ancestor Hunt: The Fun of Finding Out Who You Are by Lila Perl, (Clarion Books, 1989), *juvenile*

My Backyard History Book by David Weitzman, (Little, Brown and Co., 1975), *juvenile*

Only Human: Why We Are the Way We Are by Neill Bell, (Little, Brown and Co., 1983), *juvenile*

Recording Your Family History by William Fletcher, (Dodd, Mead & Co., 1986), *adult*

THE BARE NECESSITIES

Food

The Art of American Indian Cooking by Yeffe Kimball and Jean Anderson, (Avon Books, 1965), *adult*

Betty Crocker's New International Cookbook (Prentice Hall, 1989), *adult*

The International Cookie Cookbook by Nancy Baggett, (Stewart, Tabori & Chang, 1988), *adult*

The Jewish Holiday Cookbook: An International Collection of Recipes and Customs by Gloria Kaufer Greene, (Times Books, 1985), *adult*

Kwanzaa: An African-American Celebration of Culture and Cooking by Eric V. Copage, (William Morrow, 1991), *adult*

Many Friends Cooking: An International Cookbook for Boys and Girls by Terry Touff Cooper and Marilyn Ratner, (Philomel Books, 1980), *juvenile*

Many Hands Cooking: An International Cookbook for Girls and Boys by Terry Touff Cooper and Marilyn Ratner, (Thomas Y. Crowell Co., 1974), *juvenile*

Clothing & Costumes

Costumes & Clothes by Jean Cooke, (Bookwright Press, 1987), *juvenile*

Costumes to Make by Peggy Parish, (Macmillan Publishing, 1970), *juvenile*

Folk Costumes of the World by Robert Harrold, (Blandford Press, 1978), *juvenile/adult*

Maskmaking by Carole Sivin, (Davis, 1987), *adult*

Masks by Lyndie Wright, (Franklin Watts, 1990), *juvenile*

Shelter

The Children's Book of Houses and Homes by Carol Bowyer, (Usborn Publishing Ltd., 1978), *juvenile*

The Igloo by Charlotte and David Yue, (Houghton Mifflin Co., 1988), *juvenile*

Secret Spaces, Imaginary Places by Erin McCoy, (Macmillan Publishing Co., 1986), *juvenile*

Shelters: From Tepee to Igloo by Harvey Weiss, (Thomas Y. Crowell, 1988), *juvenile*

The Tipi: A Center of Native American Life by David and Charlotte Yue, (Alfred A. Knopf, 1984), *juvenile*

CUSTOM-MADE

General World Holidays and Festivals

The Book of Festivals by Dorothy Gladys Spicer, (Gales Research Co., 1969), *adult*

The Book of Holidays Around the World by Alice Van Straalen, (E.P. Dutton, 1986), *juvenile/adult*

Customs and Holidays Around the World by Lavinia Dobler, (Fleet Publishing, 1962), *juvenile*

Festivals by Jeanne McFarland, (Silver Burdett Co., 1981), *juvenile*

Festivals for You to Celebrate by Susan Purdy, (J.B. Lippincott Co., 1969), *juvenile*

The Whole Earth Holiday Book by Linda Polon and Aileen Cantwell, (Scott, Foresman and Co., 1983), *juvenile/adult*

Birthdays

Birthday Parties Around the World by Barbara Rinkoff, (M. Barrows and Co., 1967), *juvenile/adult*

Candles, Cakes, and Donkey Tails: Birthday Symbols and Celebrations by Lila Perl, (Clarion Books, 1984), *juvenile*

Happy Days by Christine Price, (United States Committee for UNICEF, 1969), *juvenile*

Christian Holidays

A Christmas Companion: Recipes, Traditions, and Customs from Around the World by Maria Robbins and Jim Charlton, (Perigee Books, 1989), *adult*

Holly, Reindeer, and Colored Lights by Edna Barth, (The Seabury Press, 1971), *juvenile*

Joy Through the World (Allen D. Bragdon Publishers, 1985), *adult*

Pancakes & Painted Eggs by Jean Chapman, (Childrens Press International, 1981), *juvenile*

Jewish Holidays

Jewish Holidays: Facts, Activities, and Crafts by Susan Gold Purdy, (J. B. Lippincott Co., 1969), *juvenile*

Make Noise, Make Merry: The Story and Meaning of Purim by Miriam Chaikin, (Clarion Books, 1983), *juvenile*

Shake a Palm Branch: The Story and Meaning of Sukkot by Miriam Chaikin, (Clarion Books, 1984), *juvenile*

Sound the Shofar: The Story and Meaning of Rosh Hashana and Yom Kippur by Miriam Chaikin, (Clarion Books, 1986), *juvenile*

Other Celebrations

Hearts, Cupids, and Red Roses: The Story of Valentine Symbols by Edna Barth, (Clarion Books, 1974), *juvenile*

How People Get Married by Caroline Arnold, (Franklin Watts, 1987), *juvenile*

Kwanzaa by Deborah M. Newton Chocolate, (Childrens Press, 1990), *juvenile*

Turkeys, Pilgrims, and Indian Corn by Edna Barth, (The Seabury Press, 1975), *juvenile*

We Celebrate Family Days by Bobbie Kalman, Susan Hughes, and Karen Harrison, (Crabtree Publishing Co., 1986), *juvenile*

We Celebrate New Year by Bobbie Kalman and Tina Holdcroft, (Crabtree Publishing Co., 1985), *juvenile*

Witches, Pumpkins, and Grinning Ghosts by Edna Barth, (The Seabury Press, 1972), *juvenile*

The World of Weddings by Brian Murphy, (Paddington Press, Ltd., 1978), *adult*

Religions

My Friends' Beliefs by Hiley H. Ward, (Walker and Co., 1988), *juvenile*

The Sacred Path: Spells, Prayers & Power Songs of the American Indians edited by John Bierhorst, (William Morrow and Co., 1983), *juvenile*

Thanks Be to God: Prayers from Around the World selected by Pauline Baybes, (Macmillan Publishing Co., 1990), *juvenile*

SAY THE WORD

Alphabets & Languages

Alphabet Art: Thirteen ABCs from Around the World by Leonard Everett Fisher, (Four Winds Press, 1978), *juvenile*

The American Sign Language Phrase Book by Lou Fant, (Contemporary Books, 1983), *adult*

The Handmade Alphabet by Laura Rankin, (Dial Books, 1991), *juvenile*

Handtalk by Remy Charlip, Mary Beth, and George Ancona, (Parents' Magazine Press, 1974), *juvenile*

The Joy of Signing by Lottie L. Riekehof, (Gospel Publishing House, 1989), *adult*

Signing for Kids by Mickey Flodin, (Perigee Books, 1991), *juvenile*

Folktales

Best-Loved Folktales of the World selected by Joanna Cole, (Doubleday & Co., 1982), *juvenile*

The Dark Way: Stories from the Spirit World told by Virginia Hamilton, (Harcourt Brace Jovanovich, 1990), *juvenile*

Favorite Fairy Tales Told Around the World retold by Virginia Haviland, (Little, Brown and Co., 1985), *juvenile*

Favorite Folktales from Around the World edited by Jane Yolen, (Pantheon Books, 1986), *adult*

Favorite Tales from Many Lands retold by Walter Retan, (Grosset & Dunlap, 1989), *juvenile*

Full Moons: Indian Legends of the Seasons by Lillian Budd, (Rand McNally & Co., 1971), *juvenile*

An Illustrated Treasury of Myths and Legends by James Riodan and Brenda Ralph Lewis, (Peter Bedrick Books, 1991), *juvenile*

In the Beginning: Creation Stories from Around the World told by Virginia Hamilton, (Harcourt Brace Jovanovich, 1988), *juvenile*

The Man in the Moon: Sky Tales from Many Lands by Alta Jablow and Carl Withers, (Holt, Rinehart and Winston, 1969), *juvenile*

The People Could Fly: American Black Folktales told by Virginia Hamilton, (Alfred A. Knopf, 1985), *juvenile*

Short & Shivery retold by Robert D. San Souci, (Doubleday & Co., 1987), *juvenile*

They Dance in the Sky: Native American Star Myths by Jean Guard Monroe and Ray A. Williamson, (Houghton Mifflin Co., 1987), *juvenile*

The Whole World Storybook by Marcus Crouch, (Oxford University Press, 1983), *juvenile*

Poetry & Proverbs

Cricket Songs: Japanese Haiku translated by Harry Behn, (Harcourt Brace Jovanovich, (1984), *juvenile*

Street Rhymes Around the World edited by Jane Yolen, (Wordsong, 1992), *juvenile*

A World Treasury of Proverbs from Twenty-five Languages collected by Henry Davidoff, (Random House, 1946), *adult*

ARTIST-IN-RESIDENCE

Folk art and Crafts

Adventures in Art: Art & Craft Experiences for 7– to 14–year Olds by Susan Milord, (Williamson Publishing, 1990), *juvenile*

African Crafts by Jane Kerina (Sayre Publishing, 1970), *juvenile*

Art From Many Hands: Multi-cultural Art Projects by Jo Miles Schuman, (Davis Publications, 1981), *adult*

Decorations for Holidays & Celebrations by Barbara B. Stephan, (Crown Publishers, 1978), *adult*

Folk Arts Around the World by Virginie Fowler, (Prentice-Hall, 1981), *juvenile*

Folk Crafts for World Friendship by Florence Temko, (Doubleday & Co., 1976), *juvenile*

Folk Toys Around the World by Virginie Fowler, (Prentice-Hall, 1984), *juvenile*

Folk Toys Around the World and How to Make Them by Joan Joseph, (Parents' Magazine Press, 1972), *juvenile*

Hand Puppets: How to Make Them and Use Them by Laura Ross, (Lothrop, Lee & Shepard Co., 1969), *juvenile*

The How-to Book of International Dolls by Loretta Holz, (Crown Publishers, 1980), *adult*

Kites and Other Wind Machines by Andre Thiebault (Sterling Publishing, Co., 1982), *juvenile/adult*

100 Craft Projects from Around the World by William Reid, Jr., (J. Weston Walch, 1982), *juvenile/adult*

Fine Art

Creatures of Paradise: Pictures to Grow Up With by Bryan Holme, (Oxford University Press, 1980), *juvenile*

Enchanted World: Pictures to Grow Up With by Bryan Holme, (Oxford University Press, 1979), *juvenile*

Music

A Cry from the Earth: Music of the North American Indians by John Bierhorst, (Four Winds Press, 1979), *juvenile*

All Night, All Day: A Child's First Book of African-American Spirituals selected by Ashley Bryan, (Atheneum, 1991), *juvenile*

East-West Songs (Cooperative Recreation Services, Inc., 1960), *juvenile/adult*

***El Toro Pinto* and Other Songs in Spanish** selected by Anne Rockwell, (Macmillan, 1971), *juvenile*

The Great Rounds Songbook by Esther L. Nelson, (Sterling Publishing Co., 1985), *juvenile*

The International Book of Christmas Carols by Walter Ehret and George K. Evans, (The Stephen Greene Press, 1980), *adult*

Make Your Own Musical Instruments by Margaret McLean, (Lerner Publications Co., 1988), *juvenile*

Music by Neil Ardley, (Alfred A. Knopf, 1989), *juvenile*

Musical Instruments of the World by The Diagram Group, (Paddington Press, Ltd., 1976), *adult*

***Savez-vous Planter les Choux?* and Other French Songs** selected by Anne Rockwell, (The World Publishing Co., 1969), *juvenile*

Sing Around the World (Cooperative Recreation Service), *juvenile/adult*

Sing It Yourself: Folk Songs of All Nations edited by Dorothy Gordon, (E.P. Dutton, 1928), *juvenile*

Walk Together Children: Black American Spirituals selected by Ashley Bryan, (Atheneum, 1977), *juvenile*

Dance

Ballet by Annabel Thomas, (Usborne Publishing Ltd., 1986), *juvenile*

Dance by Lucy Smith, (Usborne Publishing Ltd., 1987), *juvenile*

Dance on the Dusty Earth by Christine Price, (Charles Scribner's Sons, 1979), *juvenile*

Holiday Singing and Dancing Games by Esther L. Nelson, (Sterling Publishing Co., 1980), *juvenile*

Of Swans, Sugarplums, and Satin Slippers: Ballet Stories for Children by Violette Verdy, (Scholastic, 1991), *juvenile*

Drama

Dramatized Folk Tales of the World edited by Sylvia E. Kamerman, (Plays, 1971), *juvenile*

Plays from African Folktales by Carol Korty, (Charles Scribner's Sons, 1975), *juvenile*

Plays from Famous Stories and Fairy Tales by Adele Thane, (Plays, 1967), *juvenile*

Small Plays for Special Days by Sue Alexander, (Clarion Books, 1977), *juvenile*

FAIR PLAY

Games

The Book of Card Games by Peter Arnold, (Christopher Helm, 1988), *adult*

Cat's Cradle, Owl's Eyes: A Book of String Games by Camilla Gryski, (William Morrow and Co., 1983), *juvenile*

Children's Games from Many Lands by Nina Millen, (Friendship Press, 1965), *juvenile*

Play It! Great Games for Groups by Wayne Rice and Mike Yaconelli, (Zondervan Publishing House, 1986), *juvenile*

Street Games by Alan Milberg, (McGraw-Hill Book Co., 1976), *juvenile/adult*

Tops by Bernie Zubrowski, (Morrow Junior Books, 1989), *juvenile*

The World of Games by Jack Botermans, Tony Burrett, Pieter van Delft, and Carla van Splunteren, (Facts on File, 1987), *adult*

The World's Best String Games by Joanmarie Kalter, (Sterling Publishing Co., 1989), *juvenile*

Sports

The Cooperative Sports & Games Book by Terry Orlick, (Pantheon Books, 1978), *adult*

The Second Cooperative Sports & Games Book by Terry Orlick, (Pantheon Books, 1982), *adult*

Sports by Tim Hammond, (Alfred A. Knopf, 1988), *juvenile*

EVEN MORE BOOKS

Nations

Flag by William Crampton, (Alfred A. Knopf, 1989), *juvenile*

Money by Joe Cribb, (Alfred A. Knopf, 1990), *juvenile*

The United Nations from A to Z by Nancy Winslow Parker, (Dodd, Mead & Co., 1985), *juvenile*

Social Issues

The Kid's Guide to Social Action by Barbara A. Lewis, (Free Spirit Publishing, 1991), *juvenile*

Peace Begins With You by Katherine Scholes, (Little, Brown and Co., 1989), *juvenile*

Young Peacemakers Project Book by Kathleen Fry-Miller and Judith Myers-Walls, (Brethren Press, 1988), *juvenile*

Environment

Earth Prayers from Around the World edited by Elizabeth Roberts and Elias Amidon, (Harper San Francisco, 1991), *adult*

Fifty Simple Things Kids Can Do to Save the Earth by The Earth Works Group, (Andrews & McMeel, 1990), *juvenile*

Going Green by John Elkington, Julie Hailes, Douglas Hill, and Joel Makower, (Puffin Books, 1990), *juvenile*

Miscellaneous

Explorer by Rupert Matthews (Alfred A. Knopf, 1991), *juvenile*

The Guinness Book of Names by Leslie Dunkling, (Guinness Publishing, 1991), *adult*

How Did We Find Out About Numbers by Isaac Asimov, (Walker and Co., 1973), *juvenile*

Let's Do Yoga by Ruth Richards and Joy Abrams, (Holt, Rinehart and Winston, 1975), *juvenile*

The New Illustrated Dinosaur Dictionary by Helen Roney Sattler, (Lothrop, Lee & Shepard, 1990), *juvenile*

The Night Sky Book by Jamie Cobb, (Little, Brown and Co., 1977), *juvenile*

Stamps! A Young Collector's Guide by Brenda Ralph Lewis, (Lodestar Books, 1991), *juvenile*

PERIODICALS

The following monthly magazines for children feature people and places around the world. They can be found at most libraries. Current issues must be read in the library, but past issues circulate and may be checked out.

If you would like to receive your very own copies at home, consider subscribing to one of these magazines. Write to the addresses below for more information.

FACES: The Magazine About People
7 School Street
Peterborough, NH 03458

National Geographic WORLD
Department 00592
17th and M Streets, NW
Washington, DC 20036

SKIPPING STONES
P.O. Box 3939
Eugene, OR 97403–0939

MORE GOOD BOOKS FROM
WILLIAMSON PUBLISHING

To order additional copies of *Hands Around the World*, please enclose $12.95 per copy plus $2.50 shipping and handling. Follow "To Order" instructions on the last page. Thank you.

THE KIDS' NATURE BOOK: 365 Indoor/Outdoor Activities and Experiences
by Susan Milord

Winner of the Parents' Choice Gold Award for learning and doing books, *The Kids' Nature Book* is loved by children, grandparents, and friends alike. Simple projects and activities emphasize fun while quitely reinforcing the wonder of the world we all share. Packed with facts and fun! A much-loved book.

160 pages, 11 × 8½, 425 illustrations
Quality paperback, $12.95

ADVENTURES IN ART: Art & Craft Experiences for 7- to 14-year-olds
by Susan Milord

Another winner by acclaimed author Susan Milord! Imagine an art book that encourages children to explore, to experience, to touch and to see, to learn and to create . . . imagine a true adventure in art. Here's a book that teaches artisans' skills without stifling creativity. Covers making handmade papers, puppets, masks, paper seascapes, seed art, tin can lantern, berry ink, still life, silk screen, batiking, carving, and so much more. Perfect for the older child. Let the adventure begin!

160 pages, 11 × 8½, 500 illustrations
Quality paperback, $12.95

KIDS CREATE! Art & Craft Experiences for 3- to 9-year-olds
by Laurie Carlson

What's the most important experience for children ages 3 to 9? Why, to create something by themselves. Carlson provides over 150 creative experiences ranging from making dinosaur sculptures to clay cactus gardens, from butterfly puppets to windsocks. Plenty of help for the parents working with the kids, too! A delightfully innovative book.

160 pages, 11 × 8½, over 400 illustrations
Quality paperback, $12.95

KIDS & WEEKENDS! Creative Ways to Make Special Days
by Avery Hart and Paul Mantell

Packed with truly creative ways to play, have fun, learn, grow, and build self-esteem and positive relationships, this book is a must for every parent, grandparent, baby-sitter, and teacher. Hart and Mantell will inspire us all to transform some part of every weekend — even if it is only 30 minutes — into a special experience. Everything from backyard nature to putting on a magic show to creating a bird sanctuary to writing a book about yourself to environmentally sound activities indoors and out. Whatever your interests, no matter how busy you are, kids and their families will savor special weekend moments.

176 pages, 11 × 8½, over 400 illustrations
Quality paperback, $12.95

KIDS COOK! Fabulous Food For the Whole Family
by Sarah Williamson and Zachary Williamson

Kids Cook! is filled with over 150 recipes for great tasting foods that kids ages 6 and up can cook for themselves and for their families and friends, too. Written by two kids who learned to cook by necessity, their selection includes recipes from sections like "It's the Berries!" "Pasta Perfect," "Home Alone," "Side Orders," "Babysitter's Bonanza," and "Best Bets for Brunch" — real, healthy foods, not cutesy recipes that are no fun to eat. Plus Nutri Notes, Safety First, and plenty of special menus for Father's Day, Grandma's Teatime, picnics, and parties. One terrific book!

176 pages, 11 × 8½, over 150 recipes, 300 illustrations
Quality paperback, $12.95

KIDS LEARN AMERICA! Bringing Geography to Life with People, Places, & History
by Patricia Gordon and Reed C. Snow

Designed to help increase "geo-literacy," *Kids Learn America!* is not about memorizing. This creative and exciting new book is about making every region of our country come alive from within, about being connected to the earth and the people across this great expanse callled America • Activities and games targeted to the 50 states plus D.C. and Puerto Rico • The environment and natural resources • Geographic comparisons • Fascinating facts, famous people and places of each region. Let us all join together — kids, parents, friends, teachers, grandparents — and put America, its geography, its history, and its heritage back on the map!

176 pages, 11 × 8½, state and regional maps, 400 illustrations
Trade paper, $12.95

DOING CHILDREN'S MUSEUMS: A Guide to 265 Hands-On Museums Expanded and Updated
by Joanne Cleaver

Turn an ordinary day into a spontaneous "vacation" by taking a child to some of the 265 participatory children's museums, discovery rooms, and nature centers covered in this highly acclaimed, one-of-a-kind book. Filled with museum specifics to help you pick and plan the perfect place for the perfect day, Cleaver has created a most valuable resource for anyone who loves kids!

272 pages, 6 × 9
Quality paperback, $13.95

PARENTS ARE TEACHERS, TOO: Enriching Your Child's First Six Years
by Claudia Jones

Winner of the Parents' Choice Seal of Approval! Be the best teacher your child ever has. Jones shares hundreds of ways to help any child learn in playful home situations. Lots on developing reading, writing, math skills. Plenty on creative and critical thinking, too. A book you'll love using!

192 pages, 6 × 9, illustrations
Quality paperback, $9.95

MORE PARENTS ARE TEACHERS, TOO: Encouraging Your 6- to 12-Year-Old
by Claudia Jones

Winner of the Parents' Choice Seal of Approval! Help your children be the best they can be! When parents are involved, kids do better. When kids do better, they feel better, too. Here's a wonderfully creative book of ideas, activities, teaching methods and more to help you help your children over the rough spots and share in their growing joy in achieving. Plenty on reading, writing, math, problem-solving, creative thinking. Everything for parents who want to help but not push their children.

224 pages, 6 × 9, illustrations
Quality paperback, $10.95